NEGOTIATING IDENTITY IN CONTEMPORARY JAPAN

THE CASE OF KIKOKUSHIJO

Ching Lin Pang

Routledge
Taylor & Francis Group

LONDON AND NEW YORK

First published in 2000 by
Kegan Paul International

This edition first published in 2009 by
Routledge
2 Park Square, Milton Park, Abingdon, Oxfordshire OX14 4RN

Simultaneously published in the USA and Canada
by Routledge
711 Third Avenue, New York, NY 10017

First issued in paperback 2016

Routledge is an imprint of the Taylor & Francis Group, an informa business

British Library Cataloguing in Publication Data
A catalogue record for this book is available from the British Library

Publisher's Note
The publisher has gone to great lengths to ensure the quality of this reprint
but points out that some imperfections in the original copies may be
apparent. The publisher has made every effort to contact original copyright
holders and would welcome correspondence from those they have been
unable to trace.

ISBN 13: 978-1-138-97688-7 (pbk)
ISBN 13: 978-0-7103-0651-7 (hbk)

For my late mother and grandmother

NEGOTIATING IDENTITY
IN CONTEMPORARY JAPAN

The problem of Japanese identity has been the core object of study in the discourse of Japanese culture (*Nihonbunkaron*). This work investigates changes in the Japanese ethnonational identity, as an outcome of the interplay among different processes in the transnational cultural flow, through a case study of the *kikokushijo* or 'returnees' – Japanese youngsters, the children of expatriate parents, who spend a significant part of their life abroad, and are socialized in a different way to their Japanese counterparts. When abroad, *kikokushijo* mediate between their own and the host society: on returning to Japan, they enter into a negotiation process with other Japanese students in the reintegration process into the school environment in particular, and into Japanese society in general.

While previous studies have seen 'returnees' as disrupted from Japanese society and culture, which is characterized as homogenous and monolithic, this study reflects recent developments in the field, in which a more relational view of Japanese culture is emerging, in which difference is acknowledged and juxtaposed with uniformity and homogeneity as paradigmatic alternatives. Central to the study is the role of education in Japan, in order to understand why Japanese youngsters have to pass through a Japanese education establishment in order to 'reimmerse' and 'reintegrate' into mainstream Japanese society. This work describes how returnees, live, think, express themselves and construct their identity in the context of the tension between Japanese ethnonational identity and the overseas sojourn. Different discourses, including the historical dimension of Japanese ethnonational identity, culture as flow and postmodernism, carried out at the macro, median and micro levels, have been analyzed in order to gain a greater understanding of changing Japanese ethnonational identity in general, and the identity of returnees in particular, in the face of increasing mobility in a globalized world. By challenging many commonly held views concerning Japanese cultural uniqueness and by using dynamic new techniques of analysis, the author shows contemporary Japanese identity to be a discourse in which differences may exist in a complementary way, and supports the merging idea of a new type of cosmopolitan Japanese.

THE AUTHOR

Ching Lin Pang holds a BA in Oriental Philology and a PhD in Social and Cultural Anthropology from the Catholic University of Leuven and an MA in Asian Studies from the University of California, Berkeley. She has written on multicultural society, international migration and identity formation, and is currently FWO postdoctoral researcher at the Catholic University of Leuven.

Contents

Acknowledgements

This book would not have been completed without the support and guidance of many people and institutions. First, I would like to express my gratitude to Eugeen Roosens, my principal advisor. His thoughtful guidance, constructive criticism, valuable comments and persistent encouragement are highly appreciated.

I have been more than lucky to encounter many mentors, fellow graduate students, colleagues and friends, who care for me and my work: Willy Vande Walle, Ulrich Libbrecht, Kazuhito Kuraoka, Toshinao Yoneyama, Kazuhiro Ebuchi, Takamichi Kajita, Johan Leman, Charles Weathers, Thomas Bickford, Naomi Takasu, Atsuko Nenuno, Shizuka Watanabe, Patricia De Witte, Sarah Van Camp, Mei-Yee Chan and Beatrice Van Eeghem.

My research has been made possible by different institutions. I would like to thank the University of Leuven for granting me a research position in the Department of Social and Cultural Anthropology. My two fieldtrips have been supported by the National Fund for Scientific Research (NFWO) and by a generous research fellowship of Japan Foundation. Furthermore, Japan Foundation has also granted a publication grant to this book. I owe a special thank to the University of Nagoya and the University of Kyoto for allowing me to use their facilities and the Nanzan School of Nagoya for allowing me to interview their students. I also owe a great deal to the International School of Brussels for letting me conduct participant observation. It goes without saying that I am especially indebted to the numerous returnees and their family for their time and cooperation. My research would have been impossible without their help and trust.

I am also very grateful to Yoshio Sugimoto, the general editor of this series, for his belief in my manuscript.

I would like to thank my family for their unfailing support and unconditional love. In particular I am greatly indebted to my late mother and grandmother for their support, strength and persistence. These two women, both illiterate by circumstance but wise and empowered by life experience, remain a constant source of strength and comfort in difficult times. To my father, a man of deeds rather than words, who always silently but willingly financed my study, I am of course very grateful. I also would like to mention Yin Yin and Ting Wai, who continue this family tradition of unfailing support and unconditional love.

Last, I would like to thank two men, who have given me the best of themselves at certain crucial periods of my life: Hsueh-Ling Huynh, who with patience and love nurtured my intellectual development and personal growth and Joan Ramakers, who has taught me a lot about the practical side of life.

1 Introduction

This book aims to study the shifting identity of Japanese returnees (*kikokushijo*) within a migrational context. The core findings, based on literature and fieldwork in Brussels and Japan, are drawn from my Ph.D. dissertation. In this book I adopt the terminology and the research paradigm of the anthropology of ethnicity. Particular attention is devoted to the level of interaction of returnees with the different actors and institutions in the host society. In addition their negotiation process with 'ordinary' Japanese students (*ippansei*) in the reintegration process in the school environment in particular and the society in general are discussed. As an anthropologist I firmly believe that findings derived from fieldwork are meaningful because of their richness and immediacy. Of course these data are to a certain degree 'messy' since life at the micro level is informal and at times inconsistent. In order to transcend beyond mere anecdotes, these data are embedded in processes, which take place at the median level such as the school life. At the macro level I explore the discourse on Japanese ethnonational identity, international migration and the emergent discourse on ethnic minorities and multiculturalism in Japan.

The book is divided in three intertwined parts consisting of the micro, median and macro levels, following the recommendation of Barth (1994: 31) concerning the study of ethnicity and culture:

1

> We can facilitate this by heuristically separating three levels of analysis – the micro, median, macro – and by describing some focal arenas within which crucial processes unfold. In these ways – and others, which others will identify – there is much work to be done and much insight to be gained.

The order of presentation – macro, median and micro – will be the reverse from Barth's useful framework. First, there exists an extensive literature on *kikokushijo*. Moreover, because of my undergraduate background as a Japanologist, I was in many ways different from other anthropologists. Instead of going into the field with a pristine mind, void of almost any prior knowledge about the target group of study, I had already mastered the language. Furthermore, I had some basic knowledge about the Japanese cultureand the issue of Japanese ethnonational identity. Yet I hasten to add that I do not regard the findings originating from the field as mere accessory details to back up what I already knew and to embellish and decorate a fixed and pre-existing framework and theory. On the contrary, fieldwork findings are crucial since they constitute the palpitating heart of this book.

Chapter 2, following this introduction, discusses theoretical and methodological issues. They include the discourse on ethnographic authority, the notion of culturein flux, the influence of postmodernism in social sciences, ethnicity, the link between anthropology and Japanese studies and finally the relationship between anthropology and international migration. These topics in conjunction with the postmodernist critique might seem very remote and perhaps disjointed from the realities and experiences of a Japanese returnee. Yet they are necessary tools to contextualize ethnography.

Part One covers major issues at stake at the macro level. The discourse of the *Nihonbunkaron* (the theory of Japanese culture) and the emergence of migrant workers in Japanese society are assessed. Chapter 3 traces the development of the

Japanese ethnonational identity. The discourse on Japanese culture and the Japanese people has been variably called *Nihonbunkaron* (the theory of Japanese culture), *Nihonjinron* (the theory of the Japanese) or *Nihonron* (the theory of Japan). Chapter 4 analyzes this discourse in the postwar period. As a holistic theory, underlining the homogeneity and the uniqueness of Japan and the Japanese people, it has already been subject to incisive critique (Miller 1982; Dale 1988; Mouer and Sugimoto 1990) and restructuring (Yoshino 1992; Aoki 1990). Although the fervor of stressing the uniqueness of Japan, at times humorously called 'the national pastime' (Befu 1993: 107) of self-reflection seems to have past its peak in the 1990s, it is a view, still shared by numerous Japanese and Westerners alike. It is this primordial view of a monolithic and distinctive Japanese ethnonational identity, which has created the 'issue' of *kikokushijo*. In this context, s/he is seen as a Japanese of a lesser degree or even worse as a non-Japanese as the result of having lived abroad and therefore disrupted from Japanese society and culture.

Yet to be fair it should be noted that in recent literature, dichotomous thinking in the representation of Japanese culture has given way to a more relational one, in which difference has emerged and juxtaposed with uniformity and homogeneity as paradigmatic issues of Japanese culture and society. In line with Aoki's analysis of Japan's search for identity, I propose to divide the current period of 'universalism' (1984–present) in terms of conscientization into two periods: 1) internationalization or the outward migratory movement of the Japanese (1984–90) and 2) migrant workers in Japan: the inward migratory movement towards Japan (1990–now). Chapter 5, covering the first period, tackles the semantics of 'internationalization' (*kokusaika*) in the Japanese context. Since the late 1970s, the internal cultural debate of Japan has shifted from the modernization paradigm (*kindaika*) to that of internationalization (*kokusaika*) (Goodman 1990a: 221–6). The expansion of Japanese industry and business has generated the new and rapid-growing group of Japanese expatriates. They are officially labeled 'the long-term residents abroad' (*chookitaizaisha*) and their children, the 'overseas youth' (*kaigaishijo*) and after return to Japan, returnee children (*kikokushijo*). Chapter 6 deals with the second period of 'universalism', in which migrant workers emerge gradually but visibly in Japanese society. The internationalization of people (*hito no kokusaika*) has ignited a heated debate on the 'desirability' of foreign workers. In this polemic, opponents propagate a seclusionist (*sakoku*) policy, whereas supporters point to the humane aspect of migration and migrant workers. A third group aspires to analyze the issue by looking at the practical implications for public policy purposes of migrant workers in Japan and the long-term consequences of migration for Japanese society and culture.

At the median level, Part Two in chapter 6, I assess the centrality of education in Japanese society in the past and now. Given the importance of education for Japanese youngsters, it becomes clear why temporary overseas experiences of returnees might possibly jeopardize their chances to compete on an equal basis with 'ordinary students.' In other words, the international migratory movements of Japanese expatriates have generated problems concerning the education of their children in the host as well as in Japanese society. As explained in chapter 7, a system of tailored educational facilities has been set up for returnees including 'overseas education' (*kaigaikyooiku*) in the host society during their sojourn abroad and a 'reception' (*ukeire*) policy in returnee schools in Japan after return. Both are officially recognized and in part financed by the Ministry of Education (*Monbusho*). The main objective is to gain an insight why Japanese youngsters need to undergo this *rite de passage* through a Japanese edu-

4

cation establishment for the reintegration into mainstream Japanese society. Chapter 8 gives a critical overview of the literature on *kikokushijo*. A multitude of publications exists on the subject, mostly produced by Japanese educational experts and anthropologists. Particularly the classification of Ebuchi is discussed in detail. The view that the issue of returnees is a construction has been posited (Goodman 1990a). It is argued that returnees, instead of being victimized by their overseas experiences, constitute in fact the elite group in Japanese society. My analysis attempts to embed Ebuchi's classification of the 'non-, half and new Japanese' in the discourses of the Japanese ethnonational identity, the Japanese educational system and ideology. Chapter 9 describes the general environment of the host society.

Part Three forms the *kokoro* (heart) of the book. It is the part in which the findings – both fieldnotes and filed notes – are integrated in a three-tier-ethnographic account. Chapter 10 contains the specific experiences of one returnee family. In chapter 11 I explore the field findings of 60 returnees who had lived in Belgium. Chapter 12 contains the voices and views of 20 returnees, studying at the International School of Nanzan, an exclusive returnee school. Some actors emerge in the three accounts and the three sites. This interconnectedness reflects the 'messy' and at the same time 'dense' – in the sense of rich – nature of the study of culture, ethnicity and human behavior.

I am fully aware of the postmodernist critique on (mis) representation and the power relation between the observer and the observed (Goodman 1990b). Generally I applaud and partially subscribe to postmodernist sensitivities. Still the final assessment drawing upon fieldwork – 'fieldnotes' and 'filed notes' – and literature remains my own interpretation from a person-specific point of view, nonetheless based on the findings obtained in the field projected against larger frameworks.

2 Theoretical and Methodological Issues

Postmodernism

Postmodernism and social sciences

The methodology is in first instance ethnographic, drawing the core of the research from fieldwork. These field findings are then contextualized in the complex contemporary world through consulting the literature on Japanese modern history, returnees, ethnicity, internationalization, multiculturalism and the 'postmodernist' stance in social sciences and their insistence on the importance of the textual processes. From the postmodernist perspective, fieldnotes are categorized, interpreted and finally transformed into a neat ethnographic narrative during the writing process. Ethnicity is no longer seen as a purely scientific object in the positivistic sense. It is not a phenomenon, out there to be discovered and defined. On the contrary, there is now a consensus that it encompasses a highly elastic and negotiable dimension. Strictly speaking, the research began in 1990. Yet I started to study the Japanese language and culture some eighteen years ago mainly in Belgium and in Japan at the International Christian University of Tokyo during the summer of 1984. At that time, I also had the occasion to join a home stay program, allowing me to live with a Japanese family with two daughters, who in retrospect would now qualify for returnees. At that time we were not explicitly conscious of their status as returnee and all the implications of being one. In addition, although not a Japanese returnee myself, in my personal life, due to a combination of circumstances and conscious choices, I have made more than one site my 'home.' Therefore I am not completely unfamiliar with the dilemmas and contradictions, confronting the modern 'footloose' in terms of identity, belonging and marginality. I feel compelled to make this point in the current times of self-reflexivity in the field of anthropology, urging for a fine-tuned sensitivity towards the power-relationship between the anthropologist and the 'anthropologized' and for methodological transparency and candor.

The sites of fieldwork in Belgium include the International School of Brussels and the private homes of Japanese families in Brussels; in Japan the International High School of Nanzan, the private homes of returnees in Tokyo and Nagoya and finally numerous coffee shops in Tokyo. The ethnographic data seek to reveal how these youngsters see themselves and how they are viewed by others. These findings are discussed in detail and at different levels in the chapters 10, 11 and 12. At the present one cannot – whether one likes it or not – completely avoid the debate of postmodernism and the multitude of postmodernist expressions and forms of life. Although I do not unconditionally subscribe to all postmodernist ideas and particularly the resulting effect of conducting 'meta' anthropology rather than studying actual cultures – which is the very essence and the whole point of anthropology – I do acknowledge that some points of critique deserve credit. They make us rethink and reassess old practices. Consequently we are urged to think about innovative and perhaps more adequate ways of grasping the contemporary complex reality instead of just adopting the existing models for convenience sake. Generally their critique is widely accepted but not their solution they offer to overcome the problems. For instance Wolf (1992: 1) voices the following opinion:

> I do not intend by this comment to suggest disdain for the work of postmodernists like James Clifford, Michael M. J. Fisher, George E. Marcus and Stephen Tyler. On the contrary, I find their analyses of ethnographic frailties and failings useful on the whole...But, like most anthropologists, I remain more interested in...getting the news out. I see much in the postmodernist ruminations that helps me towards that goal but much also that does not seem to me in the best interests of anthropology at all.

One principal problem of postmodernism or the postmodernist mood is the 'constellation of terms lacking in specificity' (Featherstone in Smart 1992: 142). Before analyzing the idea of postmodernity/postmodernism, it might be useful to differentiate the related but not identical terms of postmodernity and postmodernism. Let us take a closer look at the preceding era, namely the era of modernity/modernism in terms of historical periodization, conceptualization and analysis. Although both terms are frequently used interchangeably in literature, they do not indicate the same phenomena. (Post) modernity in most instances refers to the political, economic and social structures of society, whereas (post) modernism represents the cultural realm of the same historical moment in human history.

There has been a general tendency to mark the turn of the eighteenth century, usually identified as the era of Enlightenment (Bell 1975) as the beginning of the modern age. Others, however, pinpointed the discovery of the New World, the Renaissance and the Reformation (Habermas 1987: 5 in Smart 1992: 145) as the onset of modernity. Kroker and Cook (1988) trace the first manifestations of modernity back to as early as the fourth century. Berman (1983), who distinguishes three distinctive historical stages in the development of modernity, offers a more comprehensive approach. The first stage covers the period from the beginning of the sixteenth to the end of the eighteenth century coinciding with the discoveries of the New World. The second period begins with the French Revolution and the disruption of previous forms of political, social, economic and private life as a result of the different waves of revolutions at the closing of the eighteenth century. The third phase sets off with the modernization of the production processes and the proliferation of commodities. Modernization had a profound impact on the social life as it has transformed a large part of traditional and rural areas into modern cities in the West. Thus, Berman argues that the idea of a distinct modern age emerged around the sixteenth century and came to maturity during the eighteenth century.

Modernism can be best conceptualized as a state of mind or an artistic/cultural and intellectual mood, which emerged at a specific historical moment in Western history. As a state of mind, it penetrated all levels of life – material, mental and spiritual – and consequently manifested itself in a variety of forms. Modernism has been identified by Smart (1992: 148) as 'a rebellion against normative standards, a radically different consciousness of time' and by Bell (1979: 49) as 'the glorification of the self as the self-infinitizing creature.' Given these three characteristics, one can easily understand why the above-mentioned historical moments were singled out as starting points of modernity/modernism. The Age of Enlightenment in conjunction with the Industrial Revolution brought about a new consciousness of the self as a rational being. Moreover, significant transformations at the macro, median and micro level had taken place including patterns of organization at the state level, interaction at the social, economic and cultural realms, and values, beliefs and daily practices at the personal level. In a similar vein, the era of the great sea voyages and major discoveries of new lands broadened the world and the worldview of the Westerner. In addition, increased communication and interaction with non-Western people launched the West into a novel and irreversible stage in history. In the last case, Kroker and Cook (1988) contend that Augustine introduced modernity in the fourth century by departing from the classical conception of reason as it was propagated by the philosophers of the Antiquity and thereby creating a new discourse of Western metaphysics. He established the philosophy that man is constituted of the three dimensions of being, will and intelligence. He furthermore founded an ethical system based on 'the will to truth' as a historical and moral necessity.

Zygmunt Bauman (1992) offers a lucid and judicious analysis of modernity and postmodernity/postmodernism. He identifies the Renaissance as the onset of modernity. This movement celebrated the liberation of man from a preordained order. Man basically usurped the former divine attribute of freedom of creation and self-creation. This newly gained freedom simultaneously prompted a crisis in the human spirit, the fear of nothingness. Henceforth, man had to realize his divine-like capacities for perfection or 'to confess his kinship with worms' (Bell 1979: 49). Perfection was interpreted as the harmony of all parts fitted together in a perfect whole in such a way that nothing could be added, diminished or altered. This brief interlude of openness, diversity, skepticism and tolerance or 'the sweet fruits of the sudden collapse of power-assisted certainties' (Bauman 1992: xiii) was very short-lived, due to the scarcity of intellectual and material means. Not everyone is graced with the same intellectual vigor and shrewdness to transcend human constraints.

Moreover, society proved incapable of providing a viable sys-

11

tem to support a large population of economically non-productive thinkers and artists. This period was followed by the epoch of the 'cosmopolis' (Toulmin in Bauman 1992: xiv), which lasted approximately three centuries until the age of the Industrial Revolution. In this system, the ruler embraced, institutionalized and reserved himself the exclusive right to the idea and execution of freedom of creation and self-creation. He thus busily engaged himself in legislating, defining, structuring, segregating and classifying his nation and subjects. In this cosmopolis, every element was in perfect harmony and balance. As a result, critique – in any form or shape – is seen and judged at best irrelevant and at worst noxious, deviant and cancerous to the established order.

Postmodernism emerged in the 1960s as a reaction against modernism in all its manifestations such as the great modernist poetry of Pound or Eliot in literature, the International Style of Le Corbusier or Bauhaus modernism in architecture, etc. These works, once shockingly modern, have over time become mainstream in society and academic circles. The generation of the 1960s (Jameson in Rabinow 1986: 248) thought the modernist works to be 'the establishment and the enemy-dead, stifling, canonical, the reified monuments one has to destroy to do anything new.' Ironically, this postmodernist movement, born in the 1960s, rejecting the canonization of modernist works in the academia, has entered numerous faculties in major universities during the decade of the 1980s. The postmodernist temper or state of mind seems to be preoccupied by processes of 'deconstruction', 'decentering', 'disappearance', 'dissemination', 'demystification', 'discontinuity', 'dispersion', etc. Postmodernists attack reason and its subject as preservers of 'unity' and 'wholes' or the *cogito*, the totalizing rationality. Instead, they display an epistemological penchant for fragments, fractures or pastiche in the sense of the jumbling of elements devoid of approving and disapproving norms. Postmodernism, as the term manifestly indicates, is a further development of modernism. Modernists cathexically recreate structures and order at the social and personal level in their attempt to fill the void after the demolition of the old worldview. In contrast, postmodernists, who inherited the emptiness, abandon the effort to structure the world and the belief in an objective and normative man-made order. To paraphrase their message would be like the following: The world is empty and there is simply no officially approving agencies and sanction-supported norms to show one's way out of the void.

In a way, this stance is a leap forward towards a more humane society because the collectivized struggle against emptiness has often degenerated into repressive dictatorships and missions of classes, nations or races to promote their own 'superior' cause in recent and more distant times. In the new context, the personal and social worlds become a market-place, which offers the individual a variety of 'value-free' choices to select from. One of the principal agencies of generating signals or messages is the mass media. This is not surprising given the fact that postmodernism is a product of the post-industrial information Western society. In this new age, one absorbs a multiplicity of perspectives and voices, which induces skepticism and irony rather than commitment and piety. Hannerz (1992: 34–5) gives the following description of the postmodern condition:

> Juxtaposition becomes the prevalent experience as you zap your way around the television dial, or wander aimlessly through the shopping mall...In the media, everywhere is here, and transnational capitalism thrives on uprootedness, importing workers, exporting work, being simultaneously present in the time zones of New York, London, Frankfurt, Hong Kong and Tokyo.

Or as Clifford (1988: 46–7) comments on Bakhtin's novel:

13

> The polyphonic novel is not a *tour de force* of cultural and historical totalization...but rather a carnivalesque arena of diversity. Bakhtin discovers a utopian textual space when discursive complexity, the dialogical interplay of voices, can be accommodated.

Postmodernism and culture

The main point of critique on the concept of culture in classic anthropology centers on the perception and representation of a particular culture. To start with, postmodernists find the notion of culture as a monolithic, unchanging and essentialist phenomenon hard to accept. Reality is not simply a caged entity, out there to be discovered, described and analyzed by the ethnographer. In an increasingly interdependent world, it becomes difficult to perceive the world as a totality of autonomous and isolated communities or mono-ethnic nation states with a distinctive cultural inventory. Postmodernists seem to disagree with the essentialist representation of culture in classic anthropology. This aversion for the reification of culture results in the advocacy for discourse. The foremost spokesman of postmodernism in the field of anthropology is undoubtedly James Clifford. Embracing postmodernist ideals, he challenges anthropologists and the very *raison d' être* of the discipline of anthropology by 'unmaking' and deconstructing the notion of culture. He rejects the idea of culture as a consistent entity, which can be represented in a rational whole with a set of distinctive characteristics. It is now widely accepted that cultures are not mere static holistic systems but rather discursive processes (Hannerz 1992; Rosaldo 1993; Werbner and Modood 1998). Clifford also questions the representation of cultures in visual terms. Instead of describing certain visualist rituals or customs, he sets forth the proposal to direct one's attention and energy towards the writing process and especially the textual approach of heteroglossia. In this approach, he rea-

14

sons that voices – similar, dissimilar, and identical or contra-dictory – should be regarded as equally significant and there-fore incorporated in the ethnographic account.

The essentialist approach of culture has – among other things – generated convergence theories, which in the current context of polyvocality and diversity seems more like wishful thinking than a likely outcome of history. The concept of convergence, introduced by Jan Tinbergen in his article *On the Theory of the Optimum Regime* (Tinbergen 1969 in Kerr 1983) was elaborated by Clark Kerr, John T. Dunlop, Freder-ick H. Harbison and Charles A. Myers in *Industrialism and Industrial Man: The Problems of Labor and Management in Economic Growth* (1960). They forecasted a convergence to-wards industrialism on a global basis. Kerr (1983: 3) defined convergence 'as the tendency of societies to grow more alike, to develop similarities in structures, processes, and perfor-mances.' In explicit terms, the current convergence forces in-clude the pursuit of modernization, military and economic competition, education and communication, common human needs and expectations. In his line of thinking, it is universal for each man and woman to strive for a higher standard of liv-ing, better working conditions, personal choice in private life and at work, production and a wide range of sales and service products.

Postmodernism and ethnography

In recent years, the debate between the scientific and human-istic school of ethnography has reached 'a period of *détente*' (Hammersley 1992:1). Ethnography, clearly belonging to the camp of qualitative research, is seen even by the staunchest quantitative researcher as a method having its own logic and research validity. Empirically, the number of social researchers including anthropologists, political scientists, philosophical scholars and opinion makers such as investigative journalists using the qualitative method including fieldwork and taking wide-ranging fieldnotes has increased. This is the view of Van Maanen (1988: 125).

> There is, in fact, some reason to believe that fieldworkers are the leading edge of a movement to reorient and redirect theoretical, methodological, and empirical aims and practices in all the social sciences except, perhaps, the dismal one.

Yet the current criticism in anthropology appears to be an internal affair as the discourse on methodology is mainly generated from within the anthropological community. Criticism concerns the issue of representation or the postmodernist conditions of knowledge (Clifford and Marcus 1986; Clifford 1988) and the blurring relationship between theory and practice. It aims to transform anthropology into a valid form of cultural critique, which may be used as policy guidelines for government and non-governmental organizations.

Certain postmodernist anthropologists such as James Clifford and George Marcus have raised the issue of representation. The main points of their critique center on the source of agency in classic ethnography. Indeed, the self of the ethnographer was usually that of a transcending and universal individual studying other cultures, mostly a Westerner studying non-Westerners. At the present this view seems no longer valid since the anthropologist him- or herself is being decentered and therefore has become part of the reflection along with the 'anthropologized.' Clifford vehemently opposes the existence of one objective truth. Consequently, the narrative created by the ethnographer is not the truth of a given culture. Nor should one see that culture as a fixed phenomenon. Instead of one truth, there are many truths since an ethnographic narrative implies a contingent (yet meaningful) dimension. His/her task is not to paint a coherent picture of a culture and to produce **the** authoritative account of that culture. S/he rather needs to allow the different voices solicited and overheard in the field to speak, including and especially the concerns, opinions, ruminations of the subjects of study into the final narrative. What one needs to disclose in the postmodernist era, among other things, is the multi-phased process from fieldnotes to the final monograph. In other words, the way in which ethnographic accounts come into being has been until now consciously or unconsciously obfuscated and thus the demand for candor and transparency of the painstaking writing process seems urgent. Clifford (1988: 25) thus alerts us to the following points.

> If ethnography produces cultural interpretations through intense research experiences, how is unruly experience transformed into an authoritative written account? How, precisely, is a garrulous, overdetermined cross-cultural encounter shot through with power relations and personal cross-purposes circumscribed as an adequate version of a more or less discrete 'other world' composed by an individual author?

In his book *The Predicament of Culture* and especially the article *On Ethnographic Authority* he discusses the link between the subjective and the objective dimensions of anthropology. He reminds us of the indiscrepancy between the field and the desk by demonstrating how this link is fraught with problems. On the one hand, the 'I was there' element transforms the ethnographer into the unique authority on a group of natives. Ironically these tangible experiences, difficulties, constraints, 'noises' encountered in the field are usually excluded into the final draft in order to render the ethnographic account objective and scientific. The situational and interactional aspects – between the researcher and the people s/he studies – of fieldwork are generally not incorporated in the final account. These details are pushed to the realm of 'corridor talk/gossip in faculty clubs' (Rabinow 1990). To overcome this shortcoming, he sug-

17

gests a dialogical and even better a polyphonic mode. These modes have in common that they do away with the singular voice and interpretation of the author/ethnographer. The dialogical mode is in first instance a discourse between two parties, *in casu* the researcher and the subjects of study. The representation of the interactive dealings, both verbal and non-verbal, between the researcher and the researched is definitely closer to reality than the cold and rational ethnographic narrative. Yet limitations can also be detected in this approach. The major shortcoming in this approach is that individuals albeit autonomous beings are living in a specific physical and human environment. The polyphonic mode or heteroglossia appears to offer the all-encompassing solution because it includes all members and forces in society including inconsistent and contradicting elements.

The rationale for a polyphonous discourse, which he advocates, is important in the process of the increasing interconnectedness of different cultures. In the era of overt imperialism, Western man studied the 'Other', 'the savage' from the Western viewpoint, and painted either a denigrating or a utopian view of foreign cultures. This practice of the Westerner studying and objectifying the other is in the postmodernist context seen and sensed as outdated and ethically non-justifiable in the post-colonial era.

Concerning the relationship between theory and practice, most ethnographers, influenced by social and cultural anthropology and Chicago sociology, see their work as a form of pure rather than applied research. Firth (1981 in Wright 1995) advances the idea that the strength of anthropology is mostly situated in description and analysis, through which it can unmask contradictions, paradoxes and vested interests. In order to guarantee this primary goal, the anthropologist has to be an outsider, keeping a great distance from policy-making organizations. The following (Firth in Wright

1995: 65) is his stance:

> We need to focus our work more on social problems and on communication with those already engaged in such problems, as well as with the general public. But the very nature of anthropology as an inquisitive, challenging, uncomfortable discipline, questioning established positions and proclaimed values, peering into underlying interests, and if not destroying fictions and empty phrases...at least exposing them all this poses difficulty for its application to practical problems.

In the United States there has always existed a minority of ethnographers, who advocated more applied forms of research such as the well-established tradition of applied anthropology (Eddy and Partridge 1978; Van Willigen 1986 in Hammersley 1992: 132). In recent years, the call for a close link between ethnographic research and policy issues has increased because fieldwork is believed to be a more reliable and solid tool than the quantitative method to assess and direct policy issues. Anthropology as cultural critique, suggested by Marcus and Fisher (1986), is the direct outcome of the blurring between anthropological findings and the applied results of these findings in public policy issues. An extreme version of this penchant towards applied anthropology is the so-called 'practitioner ethnography.' In this respect, research is not only conducted to provide concrete guidelines for policy issues but practitioners also actively participate in the research process. A prominent example of this practitioner ethnography occurs in the form of the teacher-as-researcher movement (Stenhouse in Hammersley 1992: 135). In this project, teachers study their own practice and the results obtained prove to be more relevant and transformative *vis-à-vis* the own teaching methods. This kind of research has been referred to as case studies but *de facto* it is one kind of ethnography. Advocates of the practitioner ethnography refute conventional ethnography because of the irrelevance to practice, lack of insider's perspective and exploitative character.

In Europe and more specifically in Great Britain, Wright (1995) in her article *Anthropology: Still the Uncomfortable Discipline* introduces Foucault's concept of 'governmentality' in order to disprove the idea of the anthropologist as a non-political observer, functioning at the edge of society with no real impact on the policy decision-making process and thereby safeguarding objectivity. She discusses in detail the ideas and ideologies underlying the institutions of the state. She then concludes that concepts, formulated by so-called 'pure' scientists and scholars, constitute the backbone of the practices of government. She claims that they are derived from a system of thinking or more specifically a body of ideas about the nature and the control of the 'population' and the 'economy.' Since anthropological findings and knowledge are part of this body of ideas – shaping directly or indirectly the institutions of the state – they cannot work in a value-free area. Yet the involvement of anthropologists in power systems does not necessarily entail a completely uncritical stance of the anthropologist 'collaborating' with the establishment to the disregard of the weak and suppressed groups in society. Wright (1995: 88) thinks the contrary to be truer, namely that anthropologists through applied research are even more able to criticize and reveal injustice and contradictions in society.

> If anthropologists are implicated in a pervasive system of governmentality, they also have the potential to contest the rationality from which government practices and institutions derive. All anthropologists, whether labelled 'pure', 'applied', or 'no longer', are, and always have been, implicated in power relations: the basis for these divisions is dissolved. For a committed stance within a system of governmentality a conception of 'the discipline as a whole' is required with better institutional links between its parts. This is so that as anthropologists working in policy and practice raise issues, which are of central theoretical concern to the discipline, they can be taken

up by anthropologists working in the universities.

The Study of Japan, Anthropology and Postmodernism

Japanology, Japanese Studies, Anthropology

Social research on Japan developed rapidly in the United States after World War II. This trend was also adopted by other Western European countries, where considerable advances were made in the field of 'Japanology.' Japanology, as Bownas (Bownas in Van Bremen 1990: 118) points out, covers multiple fields and meanings:

> The word implies a sweep of studies, at times almost pretentious in its breath; it includes every aspect of Japan, its people, its history, its literature and language, its religions, thought, art and the rest...But at its best, based on a thorough knowledge of the language and original sources, Japanology has everything to teach us.

From the 1960s onwards when researchers studying Japan from a cultural and social perspective started to increase, there was a need for a 'dual competence' (Van Bremen 1990: 118). Henceforth one has to master the Japanese language and gain professional skills in other fields in order to be able to integrate the two competencies. The term of 'Japanese Studies' was coined in order to distinguish the new direction in the study of Japan from the traditional discipline of 'Japanology.' Japanese Studies generally covers the 'Social Sciences' (*shakaigaku*) including Sociology, Social and Cultural Anthropology, Social Psychology, Political Science and Economics. In addition, the need for more intense communication and if possible cooperation with other disciplines was encouraged in order to eschew isolationist and particularistic research confined to a few insiders. Simultaneously, the importance of Japanese scholarship was stressed, implying the mastery of the Japanese language, the body of scholarship developed by the Japanese themselves such as the 'national learning' (*kokugaku*).

In the 1970s the same line of thinking was maintained: how to relate Japanology and Japanese Studies, two complementary but distinct disciplines. One strategy to cope with the precarious relationship between the two fields was to redefine Japanology in a more narrow sense as the study of the Japanese language and literature. A second one was to turn Japanology into an auxiliary scholarship, serving other disciplines. A final but perhaps too radical approach was to scrap Japanology altogether. One of the main preoccupations of the scholars studying Japan in this decade was the question whether Japanese Studies should conduct applied research. At the practical level, this concern was linked with funding purposes as applied research attracts financial support far more easily than 'esoteric' studies. This trend of fund-raising outside the academic institution is reinforced by the ever-decreasing funding situation of universities. However, some, like Van Bremen (1990: 121), think that applied research by its very nature threatens the freedom of expression and autonomy of the researcher.

> ...These forces and activities should not be allowed to dominate, let alone usurp, Japanese Studies at university level. The place and means must be kept for work other than that directed and dictated by immediate and short-term political, administrative and commercial interests, considerations and ends.

In the nexus Japanese Studies/Anthropology the same 'dual competence' is recommended by many Japan scholars. Knowledge of the language and communication with Japanese scholars are quintessential in the production of a meaningful ethnography. Recently, the extensive output of publications on Japanese studies represents an unprecedented dynamic moment of Japan-scholars. This eruption of publications on Japan makes it also difficult to obtain a clear overview of all the current academic activities. Therefore, serious efforts have been made to classify the recently published works according to either paradigmatic approaches and/or certain prevalent themes of research.

One of the first publications is *The Study of Japan in the Behavior Sciences*, edited by Norbeck and Parman (1970). Neustupny (1980), in his attempt to formulate a paradigmatic approach towards the study of Japan, discerns a shift from the Japanology paradigm towards the Japanese Studies paradigm. Mouer and Sugimoto's *Images of Japanese Society* (1990), analyzing the impact of *Nihonbunkaron* on the scholarship of Japan, has received much attention. It contains an extensive list of publications on the holistic view of Japan and a more modest bibliography on the conflict model. By exposing the shortcomings of the holistic approach, they propagate the conflict model in studying Japan. In another publication *Othernesses of Japan: Historical and Cultural Influences on Japanese Studies in Ten Countries*, Harumi Befu and Josef Kreiner (1992) analyze the content of Japanese studies in order to demonstrate the similarities and dissimilarities among the different national approaches of Japan scholars, depending on the particular national preoccupation and orientation. *An Introductory Bibliography for Japanese Studies* consists of nine volumes, covering the works of Japanese scholars in both humanities and social sciences during the period 1974–94. This book has been well received. Terasaki (1994: 27) contends that 'there is virtually no tradition of categorizing and organizing the results of research originating in Japan and the various fields of social sciences and humanities.' Sonoda (1990) divides studies on Japan into three broad categories: Japanology (*Nihongaku*), discipline-focused Japanese studies (*senmon shikooteki Nihonkenkyuu*) and problem-oriented research (*kadai*

23

tsuikyuuteki Nihonkenkyuu). In his classification of all post-war publications by Western social scientists, he includes specifically scholars working in the fields of Sociology, Social and Cultural Anthropology, and Social Psychology, and not Economics and Political Science. Linhart (1994) offers the following classification. He names the first approach 'From the village to the City and the Company.' The 'Village Approach', exemplified by Embree's *Suye Mura* (1939), Beardsley, Hall and Ward's *Village Japan* (1959) and others dominated the first two decades after World War II. This approach is directly linked with the general perception of Japan as an agrarian society by Westerners. The nature of these studies is holistic and essentialist. As the postwar recovery of Japan advanced in an unprecedented rapid pace, it became apparent that the Japanese society in the 1960s did no longer correspond with the general image of an agrarian society but rather with that of a highly urbanized and industrialized one. This prompted the nascence of the 'urban' approach, which emerged in the 1970s. In conjunction with this approach, as a result of the unexpected success of Japanese business, the 'learn-from-Japan's approach' boomed, aptly labeled the 'Companies' study (Rohlen 1974; Dore 1986).

The second approach, which he calls the 'the actors on the stage' approach, is 'biographical.' These works aim to render the account or rather the main actors in the study more tangible and real. Whereas in the past, studies dealt with institutions, practices, and values, these new publications seek to recreate personal lives and life cycles of ordinary Japanese people by allowing them to speak for themselves from their own point of view. To illustrate, the life of ordinary schoolchildren is portrayed by White in *The Japanese Educational Challenge* (1987). In this work she even goes as far as to recreate and evoke from historical data the daily life of Japanese pupils in past centuries.

The third approach concerns the 'actors of different sexes', in which Japanese women, for a long time neglected in the academic world, are singled out as worthy subject for research. This is linked with the changing gender roles in society in general and in Japanese studies in particular (Slawik and Linhart 1981; Hielscher 1980). Women scholars in the field of Japanese studies also introduce new issues on the research agenda, such as gender studies in the Japanese context (Ochiai 1997; Goldstein-Godini 1997).

Finally, the approach 'all is not harmony' is a recent phenomenon of self-reflexivity and the 'unwrapping' of Japanese Studies. Scholars of this school oppose the general trend of emphasizing only the self-congratulatory and self-lauding elements within Japanese study. They vehemently criticize the hitherto 'Japanophile' approach *vis-à-vis* Japan for merely generating sufficient research funding (particularly from Japanese side) but not for contributing to scientific and objective understanding of Japanese society (Befu 1990, 1993; Moeran 1990; Mouer and Sugimoto 1990; Weiner 1997).

This classification is timely but provisional since many studies do not fit neatly into one of these categories. Given the fact that Japanese society has joined the ranks of contemporary complex societies and moreover given the increased number of researchers – with the own inclinations, academic training, interest areas and research agendas – a classification is very much welcomed and urgent. This is necessary not only to understand the historical dimension but also to envision what will and might come in the field of Japanese studies. Or simply said what does the future of Japanology/Japanese Studies entail?

Postmodernism and Japanese studies

At first sight postmodernism and Japanese studies seem strange bedfellows since the study of Japan has for a long time been situated at the margins of social sciences. Moreover, the holistic/functionalist approach of Japanese studies does not seem sympathetic towards postmodernist preference for fragmentation, multivocality and hybridity. Yet postmodernist influences, without being labeled thus, can be found in the works countering and criticizing the Japanese ethnonational identity thesis, variously called *Nihonjinron* (the theory of the Japanese), *Nihonbunkaron* (the theory of Japanese culture), *Nihonron* (The discourse on Japan). Miller (1982), Dale (1988), Mouer and Sugimoto (1990), Befu (1990, 1993) and others can be regarded as postmodernists in the sense of demonstrating sympathy with postmodernist sensitivities of deconstructing 'conventional' Japanese studies. Miller (1982) demystifies the inscrutable character of the Japanese language. Dale (1988) traces the roots of the debate on the uniqueness of Japanese ethnonational identity to Japanese fascism and militarism of the first half of the century. Mouer and Sugimoto (1990) in their relentless effort to unveil the holistic nature of most studies on the Japanese insist that the knowledge and information concerning Japan are processed and presented from a holistic perspective. Recently Weiner and the other contributors of his book *Japan's Minorities. The Illusion of Homogeneity* (1997) provide interesting insights on the 6 principal minority groups in Japan.

Befu, a Japanese-American anthropologist, can perhaps also be seen as a postmodernist voice since he continues to unravel the inconsistencies of *Nihonbunkaron* publications. In addition, he also discerns national differences in approaching Japan and thereby decenters the objectivity of the researcher. In the premise of the publication, *Othernesses of Japan,* which he edited with Josef Kreiner, Befu (1992: 15) notes:

> Differences (in studying Japan) are due to disciplinary, historical, personal and other factors. If we are creatures of our culture, as cultural anthropology instructs us, then it follows that scholars of different cultural backgrounds, as much as anyone else, would manifest different interests, different ways of thinking, different outlooks, and different world views, which should cause them to interpret differently what they behold, be it Japan, China or any other country.

It seems safe to assume that Clifford and Marcus (1986) formally introduced postmodernism in anthropology. In my opinion, the same can be said of Brian Moeran (1990) and his group, who subject Japanologists and Japanese Studies scholars to a postmodernist critique. Not only are they applying postmodernist ideas in studying the Japanese, they also adopt postmodernist terminologies, thereby connecting Japanese studies with the larger community of social sciences. The publication *Unwrapping Japan* (1990) has been both lauded and loathed for the postmodernist approach. In this publication Moeran calls the discourse on Japanism a 'wrapping' endeavor, referring to a mystifying and exoticizing process. The studies on Japan instead of clarifying Japanese culture display a particularistic nature, which feeds the image of an enigmatic Japan. He proposes the term 'Japanism' in analogy with Said's well-known definition of Orientalism. Based on the latter concept, Moeran (1990: 1) defines Japanism as

> A way of coming to terms with Japan that is based on Japan's place in Western European and American experience. Japanism is a mode of discourse, a body of knowledge, a political vision of reality that represents an integral part of Western *material* civilization both culturally and ideologically, with supporting institutions, vocabulary, scholarship, imagery and doctrines.

The difference between Orientalism and Japanism is that in the latter case, Japanese themselves engage in the formulation of the own ethnonational identity. Moeran (1990: 3) states that the 'Japanese indulge in "national myth making", creating and defining their concept of what it means to be "Japanese".' The unwrapping part is an attempt to unravel the multiple layers of studies on Japan in order to reach some new ways in approaching and studying Japan. How does this study of *kikokushijo* relate to this discussion of Japanese Studies, classification and postmodernist influences?

The empirical data consist of voices of returnees and their parents, in most cases the mother, and to a lesser degree their teachers and some school administrators. The rendition of the case studies is essential because they reflect the elastic nature of the Japanese identity and the emergent 'multicultural' turn in Japan. The effort to create channels for the returnees and their family members to speak for themselves during their stay abroad and after return to Japan is a conscious choice. Yet the voices and the life stories are not rendered as 'raw' materials and presented as the main part of the book. This proves to be impossible because the group of returnees is not a geographically confined group living in a small-scale society. On the contrary they are members of a highly complex society, where exchange of goods, ideas and people occurs at all levels and in a multidirectional way. Consequently, the data, obtained in the field, are embedded in processes at the macro and median level. At the macro level the issues of the contemporary notion of culture as flow, the ever-expanding phenomenon of and the concomitant theory-building of international migration and the highly reflexive mood in most disciplines such as the anthropology of ethnicity, the issue of representation and the imbalanced power relationship between the anthropologist and the anthropologized are taken in account. In the case of

Japan, ethnonational identity receives particular attention and more specifically its elasticity.

This is an effort to harmonize the anthropology of ethnicity and Japanese Studies through the case study of returnees. By doing so I attempt to transcend different areas of Social Studies in order to capture and elucidate the issue of the identity-formation and management of *kikokushijo,* a highly mobile group living in the contemporary world. In sum, I aspire to offer the tales of Japanese returnees, living and especially moving around in a globalizing world and in a rapidly changing Japanese society and culture. The different issues concerning the identity of returnees are discussed in detail and should be seen as essential parts of this book.

Judiciously Choosing Ethnography in Contemporary Complex Societies

Ethnography has always engendered criticism because of its small-scope, its inefficiency and alleged randomness. I nonetheless embrace the technique, in particular when working with the Japanese. It would be enormously time-saving if the topic could be approached by a large-scale survey, leading to impressive statistical data. Yet questionnaires do not seem to offer the ultimately viable solution when studying identity formation issues. One needs to observe how returnees live before relevant and meaningful questions can be formulated and solicited in the field. Growing up and living partially abroad and partially in Japan might generate new processes in the identity-management beyond the expectations and imagination of the returnees themselves and of the researcher. Moreover, one can even venture into the prediction that most Japanese would complete the forms conscientiously with answers they think they ought to fill in. An even worse scenario would be if they consult each other on what to answer. In addition, the views, opinions and impressions of the involved Japanese youngsters – strictly speaking the fieldnotes – constitute not the only sources but also the different physical and mental surroundings, in which they interact with other students, teachers, school administrators in school and with family at home, the so-called filed notes, will be included in the ethnographic account.

Battaglia (1995: 11) notes that 'we must recognize that people may argue and persuade not only with words but with sounds and gestures and objects and the images produced by new technologies.' In line with the current trend of methodological experimenting and exploring, Plath (1990: 372) discovers to his own astonishment that of the fieldnotes he gathered during one year of fieldwork in Japan that 'there are not seven pages in it that I now could trace back, even circuitously, to *fuirudo nooto* (fieldnotes) if fieldnotes are the jottings I put into a journal then and there.' He (1990: 374) introduces the term of filed materials, which he loosely defines as 'fieldnotes but they tend to include many more notes that are not of the field provenience, and even vaster amounts of material that is not verbal at all: films, slides, maps, music recordings, artifacts – all the accumulating detritus of our years of trying to document some scene in the human comedy.' He (1990: 375) compares filed work, referring to activity of trying to make sense of the raw data and beyond and the writing-up phase with a 'baking process', arguing that 'once we are home again we have to conduct those shake-and-bake operations that fuse field and filed materials into documentaries that we hope will make sense to others.'

Therefore, a longitudinal ethnographic study of these youngsters seems to be the most appropriate approach. Ethnography provides the core information. Yet the study in-

cludes also literature from a wide range of topics. The literature is consulted in order to fine-tune the questions in the
field and the general direction of the study. Since the group
of study consists of a 'moving' unit in a contemporary complex society, findings in other literature of related disciplines
– ethnicity theories and international migration – will be useful in providing a framework against which the ethnographic
data will make sense. This book is designed to understand
the phenomenon of multiplicity of identity as a contemporary given rather than an aberration or distortion. At the current moment there is a consensus among ethnicity theorists
like Verdery (1994: 51) that difference rather than unity
emerged as a prominent paradigm in the last decade. 'Talk of
"difference" has become ever more prominent in certain academic circles, associated especially with feminist theory and
post-structuralism, and in political circles as well.'

I would like to add that difference has entered the arena of
discussion and appears to multiply at a fast pace. This process has become possible only because difference has become less radical and less absolute in nature and increasingly
comparative and negotiable. To put it succinctly, the enlarged scope of communication and human interaction has
shaped a new consciousness. This means that more people
become increasingly aware of the differences, which in
some instances display a negotiable nature (as in the case of
ethnic minorities, women and others in most Western societies and *kikokushijo* in Japan) and which in other instances
provide the source for conflict and warfare (as in the case of
former Yugoslavia and Rwanda).

Hannerz' contemporary complex societies

Perhaps it has always been difficult and it is particularly so at
the present to find 'pure' cultures and 'pure' representatives

31

of cultures. Movements and exchanges appear inherent in human life and especially in the contemporary world, characterized by among other things the rapid progress in communication means at all levels. Thus, it seems futile and maybe even politically dangerous to see the world as a mosaic of separate and isolated cultures with distinctive cultural properties. Instead, exchange and interaction occur incessantly and at different levels, not exclusively among nations but also within national boundaries between the different regions, ethnic minorities, social class, pressure groups, etc. leading to the fragmentation of the nation state. Consequently, new groups including 'the sons and daughters of migrants' emerged, leading to the blurring of the 'we-them' dichotomy. Barth (1994: 13) notes that

> Whereas radical cultural alterity plays an important role in much Western thought..., ethnic relations and boundary constructions in most plural societies are not about strangers, but about adjacent and familiar 'others'. They involve co-residents in encompassing social systems, and lead more often to questions of how 'we' are distinct from 'them', rather than to a hegemonic and unilateral view of 'the other'.

Instead of perceiving the world as a collection of mutually exclusive, independent cultures and societies, it is more realistic and meaningful to approach most societies in terms of 'cultural complexity.' Contemporary complex societies (Hannerz 1992: 7) refer to societies with heterogeneous cultural inventories against a background of commonality. True, some societies are more complex or multi-layered than others are. However, the question is to what degree this or that society is more complex than another is. In other words, the discussion is conducted in a relational rather than in an absolute context. Hannerz (1992) suggests three dimensions of culture and their interconnectedness: 1. the mental dimension including concepts and values shared by a group of people; 2. the externalization of these ideas and concepts; 3. the cultural distribution or how these ideas and values in the externalized forms are spread, accepted by the members of a group and absorbed in the cultural inventory. The distribution of the ideas and values, also metaphorically called 'cultural flow' takes place along different dimensions, in different layers or frameworks.

The first framework involves the daily life of production and reproduction. This is an important part of life, which is characterized by routinization and repetitiveness of activities. In such a context, the cultural process is shared and implicitly understood by most members of society. As these daily activities are highly adapted to material circumstances, stability reigns.

In the second framework of market forces culture in all its forms manifests in a variety of commodities. These commodities, carrying informational, artistic or emotional signs, are thrown in the market-place, at everyone's disposal for a certain price. It is in this market framework that postmodernists find inspiration to rethink, reinterpret and re-read culture and cultural processes. Whereas in the past, culture with a capital-C shunned material and worldly gains if not in actual life then at least at the ideological level, postmodernists turn our attention to the entrenched market forces in most cultural goods, shaped to carry appeal or signs, appealing to modern or postmodern sensitivities. This seems to explain the emergence of the interest for popular culture, not only in the commercial world for hard currency sake but also in academic circles because of the scope and the impact on other realms of life. Expansion is the main characteristic of this framework.

The third dimension is that of the state, which adheres to the idea of unification and togetherness of all members of society. Due to the creation and management of societal structures, it claims authority in certain parts of these structures such as education and defense. Some states even assume a more ambitious mission of managing the national culture or 'cultural welfare or good culture' (Hannerz 1992: 49). In ordinary circumstances, life is so deeply embedded in existing structures created by the nation state that they tend to last for a long time in normal circumstances.

The fourth framework in contemporary cultural flow is that of movements. Illustrations of this framework are for instance the women's movement, the peace movement, the ecological movement, ethnicity, etc. They come into being when members of a society become dissatisfied with existing structures. The plausibility of this approach of cultural complexity lies in the comprehensiveness of the system. It includes both the mental and the social stage through the externalization process or 'the relationship between cultural and social structure' (Hannerz 1992:10). In addition, this model is able to capture the current 'postmodern' era, without inheriting the relativistic stance of postmodernists. It aims to display diversity against a general background of shared values and structures by working at different levels or frameworks. This paradigm of culture in motion is used in the further course of the analysis of ethnic identity and international migration, more specifically the case of *kikokushijo* in Japan. It should be noted that the cultural complexity theory is an abstract and formal system in need of application by actual cultural processes, which may or may not evolve along the proposed lines.

In order to cope with 'content' in a plausible way, it is imperative to look at the processes and 'actors' situated at the different macro, median and micro levels. The international movements of people and goods are interconnected. As people migrate and re-migrate, ideas, aspirations and commodities, too circulate at the micro level, which in turn affect structures and organizations at the median and macro level. Given the unprecedented intensity and variety of international migration, it is necessary to take a closer look at the phenomenon of international migration and how the returnees and their family fit in this general scheme as skilled or circulatory migrants.

International migration

International migration is a vast discipline. Moreover at the moment the international migratory movements reveal heterogeneous patterns (Zolberg 1989). It is beyond the scope of my dissertation to discuss in detail all the different theories. Yet it seems useful to take a close look at certain migration types. The main rationale is that migration, both outgoing and incoming movements to Japan, accelerates the changing nature of Japanese ethnonational identity and the specific identity issue of the highly mobile group of returnees.

The outward movement of Japanese expatriates, also called temporary transient professionals, has generated the very issue of returnees. Their parents, mostly the father, have been sent by the company overseas, accompanied by spouse and children. These overseas children and youngsters are not only exposed to a different society, culture and language but also to overseas schools, sometimes Japanese sometimes local but at any rate outside Japanese society and culture. The incoming movement of foreign workers in Japan is of a different nature. They constitute the so-called temporary semi-skilled workers, leaving the country of origin to seek their luck abroad in the West and recently also in Japan.

Generally international migration is seen and interpreted against the background of the labor market and national boundaries. A receiving country with a set of 'pull' factors –

including sophisticated production means, the demand for cheap labor, advanced infrastructure, educational and economic opportunities – attracts the labor force of a sending country with push factors – such as inferior opportunities and conditions in terms of work, education, social welfare, low standard of life. In this push-pull framework (Ramakers 1992: 12; van Amersfoort 1998: 14) two kinds of movements are generated: unskilled but cheap labor and brain drain. In the former case, one wants to work harder and for less than someone in the receiving society (this is in the case of unskilled labor) whereas in the latter case one capitalizes on one's special technical skill (this is the case of brain drain). Studies on Japan rarely refer to international migration. This can be attributed to the discourse on ethnonational identity of the Japanese, claiming homogeneity and uniqueness. Yet recently the emergent trend of foreign laborers has captured the public attention in Japanese society. The incoming foreign laborers share indeed many common characteristics with labor migrants in Western countries.

For a long time the push-pull theory has been a satisfying explanation scheme. Recently, more refined theories have appeared since the former theory is situated at the macro level, omitting other mechanisms and influences in migration decisions. Second, since the push-pull theory sought to explain semi-skilled labor migration and since the scope of migration has widened considerably, other explanation schemes have been offered. The typology of Appleyard (1992), adopted by a majority of scholars on international migration, consists of six categories: permanent (settlers), temporary contract workers, clandestine or illegal workers, asylum seekers and refugees and temporary professional transients.

Of particular interest to this book are the categories of temporary contract workers, clandestine or undocumented workers and temporary professional transients. Temporary contract workers are labor migrants recruited for their cheap labor. At this level, the manufacturing sector has relatively declined so that the demand for inexpensive labor in receiving countries has concurrently decreased. Yet in the service and informal sector, the growing demand has attracted increasing numbers of workers, mostly female laborers in the cleaning business. The classification of migration according to the time dimension is problematic. The Mediterranean migrants in Western Europe clearly illustrate this point. This type of migration was defined as temporary by both the governments of the sending and receiving countries and the migrants themselves (van Amersfoort 1998). For a long time Japan could claim to be a homogenous and mono-ethnic society and culture. However, since the 1980s the trend of foreign migrants' inflow has emerged. These migrant workers consist of *Nikkeijin* (Latin Americans of Japanese descent) and workers from neighboring Asian countries. Clandestine or undocumented workers constitute the direct outcome of both the restrictive entry procedures in most receiving countries on the one hand and the risks migrants want to take to escape from poverty, illnesses, and social injustice in the sending country on the other hand. Estimated numbers of illegal migrants diverge greatly.

Most undocumented migrants enter a country in a legal fashion with generally a tourist visa. They become clandestine upon expiration of the visa, when they remain in the country to live and to work. They are the so-called 'overstayers.' In the case of Japan, restrictive immigration policies generate this kind of migration. Although immigration laws in Japan have loosened, reflected in the increasing numbers of foreigners active in the Japanese labor market, constraints for semi-skilled labor abound. In fact, only those of Japanese origin, *Nikkeijin*, are officially invited to immigrate to Japan. The less fortunate workers from neighboring Asian countries enter Japan through the 'back' door such as overstaying tourists, or overstaying interns, etc. Some, the illegal trespassers, simply enter the country illegally.

The movements of temporary professional transients have been subject to numerous labels including CAM (capital-assisted migration); brain exchanges; return of talents (personal communication with an official of the International Organization of Migration); industrial migration, new technology, high-level labor movements (Findlay 1993), etc. As the result of combined factors the flow of the highly skilled is likely to increase in the future. Sassen (1988: 21) argues that these combined factors consist of 'the technological transformation of the work process, the shift of manufacturing and routine office work to less developed areas domestically and abroad...and the ascendance of the financial sector in management.' International flows of a small but significant cohort of elite skilled workers have become essential to the servicing of key production and reproduction activities in both industrialized countries (Böhning 1998) and in the developing countries (Findlay 1991, 1993). In Belgium, the presence of temporary skilled professionals should be underlined. Most Japanese in Belgium except for a tiny minority can be categorized under this type of migration. In spite of the public attention, which is almost exclusively geared towards labor migration of the first and second generation due to ideological, political and social reasons, it should be stressed that in reality professional transients – including EU residents, Americans and Japanese – represent a significant part of the total figure of the foreign population in Belgium. In Japan the recent increase of foreign workers concerns mostly high-skilled workers, who enter the country legally.

At the median and micro level one of the most frequently cited theoretical factors in tracing the origins of migration is the importance of social network. Publications working along the line of the 'push and pull' theory, albeit seemingly viable to explain most (cheap) labor movements such as the Turks and the Moroccans in Belgium and other Western European countries, they do not take into account the differences in size and destination of particular migratory flows. To illustrate the previous statement, why do Algerians tend to go to France rather than neighboring and better-paying Germany? If pure market forces of demand and supply are at play, why prefer France above Germany? In this case, colonial ties rather than economic advantages play a crucial role in the final decision to leave the county of origin. On the whole, Portes and Borocz (1989: 607) insist that 'the onset of labor flows does not arise out of invidious comparisons of economic advantage, but out of a history of prior contact between sending and receiving countries.'

In the case of Japan the largest group of apprehended undocumented workers in Japan is the Korean group. In percentage they made up 29.7 percent of the total figure. In his pioneering work *Migrant Workers in Japan* Komai (1995: 16) explains the presence of Koreans by the following points: '(This is) due to a great extent to the existence of the support network of permanent Korean residents in Japan as well as to the Korean's government relaxation of travel restrictions in January 1989.'

Globalization: between fragmentation and unification

Contemporary complex societies reveal many inconsistencies such as the paradox of opposing forces of segmentation and differentiation on the one hand and unification and an increasing interdependence in the world community on the other hand. This applies especially to those, who belong to (post) modern and advanced industrial societies, often asso-

ciated with the 'West.' In first instance globalization consists of the internationalization of the economic activities
and material commodities. In his endeavor to see through the
ambivalent nature of the globalization process, Iyotani
(1995: 3) reminds us that:

> A modern state comes into being only after it receives recognition
> from the community of nations and thus achieve legitimacy. Modern
> capitalism operates within the international network of trade and in-
> vestment, and the capitalist economy of a given economy is sus-
> tained only through its linkage with a global system based on
> comparative advantage. While politics and culture exist within the
> limits of the time and space of the nation state, economic activity by
> its very nature is part of the worldwide division of labor. What has
> given the modern world its dynamism is the discrepancy between
> these inward and outward orientations.

Generally agreeing with his assessment I would like to add
that the proliferation of commodities, economic activities
and the international migration of people are phenomena
taking place in the international arena with profound impact
on the political and cultural activities within national boundaries. The segmentation, in other words, between the different realms of life is not clear but rather blurred. After all,
commodities are not mere dead material objects. On the contrary they carry messages – implicit or explicit – and furthermore engender novel ideas, insights, lifestyle and social conduct. Whether the messages are inherent to the goods or invented first by their makers is a philosophical discussion
beyond the aim and the scope of this book. Suffice to say that
the increasing proliferation of ideas, lifestyles and habits has
generated two at first sight opposing forces: fragmentation
and unification. One can state without being a convergence
theorist that globalization processes encompass the shrinking of the world community. Dacyl (1995: 226) describes
the phenomenon in the following way: 'Globalization pro-

cesses imply shrinking cognitive and geographic distances between disparate parts of the world, and hence accelerating "standardization of values and rules of conduct".' Similarly Giddens (1991: 21) informs us:

> In a general way, the concept of globalization is best understood as expressing fundamental aspects of time-space distanciation. Globalization concerned the intersection of presence and absence, the interlacing of social events and social relations 'at distance' with the local contextualities. We should therefore grasp the global spread of modernity in terms of ignoring relation between distanciation and the chronic mutability of local circumstances and local engagements...[it is] a dialectic phenomenon, in which events at one pole of a distanciated relation often produce divergent or even contrary occurrences at another.

First, both quotations have used the term of modernity, which corresponds with the term postmodernity /postmodernism, as explained earlier. Moreover, the unifying force of globalization needs to be differentiated from the convergence idea. Convergence contends that all people become alike and ultimately identical as they think, feel, express, work, recreate and consume in the same uniform fashion. Of course, as a cultural anthropologist, I have a spontaneous reflex and professional inclination against the notion of a complete and absolute uniformization process. However, beyond this professional reflex, more profound reasons compel me to refute the previous point. The increased exchange of commodities, information and ideas through ever-advancing communication means cannot be overlooked or dismissed. Material culture has at a very superficial level a homogenizing effect among those who partake in the consumption of the 'global village.' However, much of the contemporary flow of goods and flow occurs at the 'imagined' level and therefore diversity in imagery abounds greatly.

41

In *Imagined Communities* Anderson (1991: 5–6) draws our attention to the imagined nature of nation states:

> In anthropological spirit, then, I propose the following definition of the nation: it is an imagined political community...It is *imagined* because the members of even the smallest nation will never know most of their fellow-members, meet them, or even hear of them, yet in the minds of each lives the image of communion.

Through the intensive use of the printed word a sense of imagined togetherness is generated and nurtured, mediated by the three institutions of the census, the map and the museum. He (1991: 163) clarifies his point:

> But if one looks beneath colonial ideologies and policies to the grammar in which, from the mid nineteenth century, they were deployed, the lineage becomes decidedly more clear...(T)hree institutions of power which, although invented before the mid nineteenth century, changed their form and function as the colonized zones entered the age of mechanical reproduction. These three institutions were the census, the map, and the museum.

Inspired by Anderson's idea of 'imagination', many social scientists (Appadurai 1991; Ginsburg 1995) have further elaborated his theory by allocating the shifting power from the printed word to that of the increased mobility of people and commodities, mass media and especially the image culture. Departing from conventional notions of territoriality, Appadurai (1991: 191) coins the term 'ethnoscape', representing the cosmopolitan cultural forms of the contemporary world. 'The landscapes of group identity – ethnoscapes – around the world are no longer tightly territorialized, spatially bounded, historically unconscious, or culturally homogeneous.' It refers to all 'those on the move' such as tourists, businessmen, academics, refugees, exiles, immigrants and others, who build stable communities and networks of kinship, colleagues, friends, leisure, etc. transcending traditional constraints like geographical limitations, borders, language, etc. They do not diverge from conventional communities in the search for knowledge, human contact, human affection and a general sense of belonging. Yet unlike conventional communities they are different because their stabilities do not tend to be located on one geographical spot but distributed, spread and scattered all over the world for a limited time. After all, migratory movements are potentially multiple, temporary and circulatory. These links are not necessarily tangible or exclusively built on traditional interpersonal ties such as blood, family, profession, community and citizenship ties. Appadurai (1991: 198) states:

> What is implied is that even the meanest and most hopeless of all lives, the most brutal and dehumanizing of circumstances, the harshest of lived inequalities is now open to the play of imagination.

Anonymous individuals in these communities are bound with various 'imagined' linkages including the written word, the images disseminated by majority, minority groups and Aboriginals. Through these linkages, a sense of 'togetherness' or 'sameness' could be fostered and nurtured. Yet the imaginative character of these (post) modern communities depends entirely on market forces, or more specifically the number of individuals believing in the relevance of the '(re) invented identities.' Once the members turn incredulous, the community vanishes. In order to guarantee a long life, one needs to increase its membership, which can be attained to a great extent by bringing the group to the public arena. Applied to the ethnic minorities given the lack of objective norms and values, public attention assumes the role of measuring their validity or success. In other words, the public discourse in the current postmodernist and globalist context or the information society is transformed into a battlefield of diverse groups striving for legitimacy through augmentation of membership and public exposure. Unlike religious and other groups in the past, the distinctive feature of the present time is change and contingency. To illustrate this point, Trouillot (1991: 22) describes the contemporary world as a place '...where the most enlightened are only part-time citizens of part-time communities of imagination.'

The unification force or the ever-increasing information has not necessarily led to global homogenization but ironically to divergence and fragmentation. The important role of 'imagination' in social life has a double-edged effect. On the one hand, it induces a sense of 'togetherness' between otherwise disjointed individuals through the printed word, the media and increasingly so the information highway. At the same time the globalization process also generates, ironically, a growing consciousness of difference. In the increased interaction and communication, one becomes all the more acutely aware of differences.

Verdery (1994) links the new essentialism of 'difference' with the restructuring of world capitalism. Changing demographics, computerization of the workplace, and the processes of product and market differentiation along with other developments resulted into the reorganization of capitalism. These changes altered the traditional all-male labor force and the societal structure built around it. Instead of uniformity and the homogenizing project of society and nation state, the contemporary construction of reality implies difference of all kinds to be 'inherent and imperative' (Verdery 1994: 52). In other words the world is becoming more globalized.

Ethnicity and multiculturalism

The concept of ethnicity, now a widely used concept in the Social Sciences, was introduced in the 1960s. The emergence of ethnicity, and especially the consciousness thereof (Cohen 1994: 59–80) are often explained within the larger global framework of decolonization, structural changes in Western societies and especially the failure of the assimilation policy (Glazer and Moynihan 1975; Roosens 1989, 1998; Vermeulen 1997, Vermeulen and Govers 1994). In the United States, Glazer and Moynihan (1975) unmasked the 'melting pot' theory of America. The assimilation theory assumes that immigrants over time would change into 'decent and proper Americans', while discarding the cultural traits of the own culture. In other words, non-Western or 'indigenous' cultures after contact with industrialized ones would disappear. Culture was then perceived in an essentialist way as a collection of fixed and unchangeable characteristics. However, Glazer and Moynihan and others demonstrated that in spite of an assimilation-oriented policy and immersion in enculturation processes in different arenas of social and public life, ethnic identities were being reshuffled, reorganized, reformulated and sometimes reinvented.

Therefore, culture and cultural identity on the one hand and ethnicity and ethnic identity need to be distinguished. Culture spans a wider spectrum than ethnicity. Perhaps culture can be divided into the objective and the subjective culture (Roosens 1989). The objective culture refers to the entirety of verifiable phenomena, whereas subjective culture is the culture a person ascribes him or herself and thinks to practice. The interpretation of the own subjective culture might not correspond completely with objective culture. Consequently, to use the term cultural identity would be misleading, ambiguous and inaccurate. Ethnic identity results from both the self- and other-ascription act, while containing at the same time genealogical contents, whether tangible or imagined (Roosens 1994). This is to say that a well-integrated 'ethnic' person in the host society may be indistinguishable from a native person in terms of behavior, attitudes, and language but yet s/he prefers to identify him/herself with the own ethnic group in self-presentation. The focal arena of ethnic distinctiveness and ethnic belonging are situated in the more private realms of life such as family, marriage partner choice, food, sensibility for the own popular culture, etc. In analyzing ethnicity Hutnik (1991: 157) reminds us:

> (There are) two distinct but not necessarily related components: (1) a consciously articulated stance or strategy of self-categorization and (2) an underlying system or body of beliefs, attitudes, values, and behavior – or a style of cultural adaptation.

In suggesting the quadric–polar model for the study of ethnic minority identity, Hutnik stresses the need to look at both components. Her model sets forth four types of ethnic minority identity: the assimilative, the acculturate, the dissociative, and the marginal type. In defining who is what, the two dimensions of strategy of self-categorization and the style of cultural adaptation have to be taken in consideration. The assimilative person, embracing the values of the majority group, has a low level of the own ethnic identity. The dissociative person reflects the mirror side of the assimilative person: s/he reveals a weak identification with the majority group but abides by the norms of the own ethnic group. The acculturative person has a high level of identification with the majority and the own group. Finally, the marginal person oscillates between the two groups without knowing what to choose, which results into a weak identification with both groups. It should be noted that she distinguishes assimilation from acculturation, although in most literature on ethnicity, acculturation is linked with the loss of the own culture.

It goes without saying that pure 'types' do not exist. Instead, a person shows a propensity to be more of one style. In other words, it is a matter of degree. Noteworthy is that self-categorization may be relatively independent from the cultural adaptation. In order to cope with the new identity, 'hyphenated identities' are created and used to represent the complex ethnic identity. A refinement in terms is clearly shown by these two separate dimensions. Emic culture is patently broader and universal in scope than ethnic identification, which does not necessarily exclude overlapping areas of meaning. Similarly, Goody discerns (the partial) dichotomy between the actor and the observer. Goody (1993: 16) claims that an outsider is in a better position to observe both consistencies and inconsistencies a particular culture.

> One way in which they are misled is by failing to make a clear distinction between the points of view of actors and those of the observers, an omission which gives rise to some excessively holistic notions of interaction and continuity. From the actor's point of view, the actions in which he is engaged and more especially the thoughts that do or do not guide them, tend to have a certain kind of 'unity' over time. While others may conceive inconsistency, the individual sees consistency. He tries to make sense of the universe, even if the sense is sometimes his own and no one else's.

In a similar way, Mason (1990) underlines the difference of agency between identification and categorization in representing ethnic minorities. The process of group identification, in other words, takes place among co-ethnic members inside the ethnic boundary and the categorization process outside the ethnic boundary. In Great Britain, the well-entrenched term 'black' representing the totality of oppressed people by 'whites', has come under scrutiny for not corresponding with the actual situation in Britain, where (South) Asians form the majority minority group. 'Black' as a category indicating the 'oppressed' or the 'victim of injustices and discrimination' needs to be adapted and changed in order to represent the ethnoscape in Britain, where (South) Asians and not Blacks form the majority minority group.

47

Therefore, according to the former, the black-white dichotomy does not make sense in the British context.

In studying ethnic identity the foremost question to ask is what binds and keeps together the in-group members and simultaneously what renders them different from the out-group members. Two main approaches can be discerned: the primordialist and the boundary view. The primordialist perception of ethnic identity stresses the common ancestry of the members, the shared cultural traits, preserved and transmitted from generation to generation. 'Primordial ties', according to Shils (1957: 113–14), refer to the

> Ties, real or imagery, relating to the historical origin of the community or the ties of kinship that bind a community's members to their common ancestors and second, to the ties of culture shared by members of the community, which tend to be regarded as naturally given.

In contrast, the boundary approach instead of looking from the time perspective points to the space perspective. Ethnic identity arises when one is confronted with other ethnic groups. Although Frederick Barth is generally considered the founding father of this approach, he in fact further developed the idea advanced by Leach, who already in 1954 redirected the attention from the content of a culture to the interactional process among different groups. Yet it is Barth (1969) who firmly established the boundary approach in anthropology, which is still – albeit in altered ways – used by numerous anthropologists. After two and a half decades of his publication on the boundary theory, he (1994: 11) explains in retrospect why he adopted the boundary approach in 1969:

> The empirical strategy my colleagues and I chose was to give particular ethnographic attention to persons who *change* their ethnic identity: a discovery procedure aiming to lay bare the processes involved in the reproduction of ethnic groups.

The primordialist and boundary approaches are related to the instrumentalist and expressivist dimensions of ethnicity. Instrumentalism refers to the use of ethnicity as a tool in order to gain specific advantages such as the attainment of public goods and rights. Already in 1963, Glazer and Moynihan discerned self-serving schemes in the ethnic discourse. In a more extreme version, ethnic minorities are in fact disguised political interest groups (Cohen 1969 in Roosens 1989).

Ethnicity as a weapon can be used by both ethnic minorities and the majority group. The concept of ethnic belonging reveals an elastic nature because the principal agents of the ethnic group are enmeshed in constant negotiations with other members of the own ethnic group, with the representatives of the state and other members of the majority group. Traits can be discarded and added in commensuration with social and economic situations and changes. For instance, the decades of the 1960s and the 1970s in the United States are marked by a grand revival of ethnic identification. This movement gave rise to the formation and conscientization of ethnic groups to organize themselves, to assert their rights and voice their needs (Roosens 1989). The empowerment of ethnic minorities started to take off.

Therefore, from the one side of the spectrum, one can say that ethnic minorities in response to the general forces in society of consideration and sensitivity for their cause of disadvantaged and oppressed minority people, they alter if not invent an own ethnic identity in order to obtain compensations, social promotion and material gains. In other words, the formulation of ethnic identity is self-serving on the part of the ethnic minorities. From the other side of the spectrum, though, members of the host society, they too can use the previous argument of ethnic identity as a rigged fabrication to enhance personal interests – ethnicity as a weapon so to speak – to discredit the merits of minorities in order to maintain the *status quo* in society. More precisely those of the host society can also use the ethnic argument to continue to exclude minorities from prestigious schools and professions and to further discriminate them in daily life. As already noted, the categorization of ethnic minorities by the majority group, disregarding the voices of the former, most likely jeopardizes the emancipation of ethnic minorities, thereby undermining the ideological foundation of a multicultural society. It seems obvious that this double-edged argument shows the fluidity of the concept, which can be manipulated for the own interests by all parties in society. Given its ambivalent, oscillating and highly manipulation-prone nature, it is of capital importance to uncover the divergent processes of ethnic identification and the hidden political agenda behind ethnicity. The use of ethnicity as a weapon so to speak seems inherent to all members of a complex multi-ethnic/multicultural society.

The self-serving dimension notwithstanding, ethnicity also implies affect, warmth and a sense of togetherness and sameness. Yinger (1994: 45–6) states that in an increasingly rational and instrumental world, people have difficultyin

> identifying with a large, heterogeneous, rapidly changing society. They seem surrounded by anomie, alienation, and an unqualified *Gesellschaft*, with its emphasis on universality, rationality, and instrumental values. An ethnic attachment, it is argued, helps one preserve some sense of community, to know who one is, to overcome the feeling of being a cipher in an anonymous world.

This individual or 'characterological' explanation particularly applies to newcomers to a society. Bell (1975) alerts us that more people will become increasingly ethnic-conscious and join ethnic groups. The categorization according to ethnicity appears to be one of the few organizational forms, offering some sort of orientation and stability in the post-capitalistic society, in which authority of all kind has been slowly but surely eroded. Similarly the view that family in terms of a safe haven, creating an enduring connectedness, transposed and extended to the ethnic group has been put forth by quite a few social scientists (Hutnik 1991). Some go even further by attributing a creative dimension to ethnicity and especially the conscientization of the own ethnic identity. After all, as they reasoned, moments of personal confusion and continuous self-reflection and analysis might prompt one to reformulate and reconstruct the own identity. In his article *Ethnicity and the Post-modern Arts of the Memory* (1986) Fisher highlights the shaping of ethnic identity by analyzing contemporary ethnic autobiography. By reading Maxine Hong Kingston's *The Woman Warrior* (1976), Michael Arlen's *Passage to Ararat* (1975) and Marita Golden's *Migrations of the Heart* (1983) against the perspective of the recent findings, he discovers that ethnicity is something reinvented and reintegrated in each generation by each individual. What is discovered and redefined in this self-reflexive exercise of ethnic autobiography is something new and inspiring for co-ethnic members as well as other members of society.

In a similar vein drawing upon his experience as an outsider of a lesser degree, a *sansei* or a third-generation Japanese-American, David Mura (1991: 370) concludes thus after a one-year sojourn in Japan in his publication *Turning Japanese. Memoirs of Sansei.*

> Japan helped me balance a conversation which had been taking place before I was born, a conversation in my grandparents' heads, in my parents' heads, which, by my generation, had become very one-sided, so that the Japanese side was virtually silenced. My stay helped me realize that a balance, which probably never existed in the first place, could no longer be maintained. In the end, I did not speak the language well enough. I did not have enough attraction to the culture. In the end, the society felt to my American psyche too cramped, too well defined, too rule-oriented, too polite, too circumscribed. I

could have lived there a few years more if I had had the money and the time, but eventually I would have left. I would not have become one of those Americans who find in Japan a surrounding society, which nourishes and confirms their own sense of identity. I was American or I was one of the homeless, one of the searchers for what John Berger calls a world culture. But I was not Japanese.

In recent publications on ethnicity, the dichotomy between primordialism and boundary approach on the one hand and instrumentalism and expressivism on the other hand have become blurred. The Barthian boundary approach is still valid as a general scheme, while many concepts and new dimensions have been added. First, the content or more precisely the culture enclosing the boundaries imagined or real is not completely elastic or infinitely reproducible whenever boundaries change. To clarify the previous point, Roosens (1994, 1998) urges us to look at both the content as well as the process, thereby combining the boundary metaphor with that of kinship. Barth himself introduces new dimensions to the boundaries approach through enlarging the scope from the micro level of members belonging to ethnic groups to the median level of institutions and organizations, and finally to the macro level of nations and international organizations (Barth 1994: 11–32). In the same line of thinking, Verdery (1994) proposes to study ethnicity at different interfaces: ethnicity/culture; ethnicity/nationalism and ethnicity/state (1994: 33–58).

The current state of ethnicity studies seems to rest on the following points of consensus. Ethnic identities are not solid or inherent to an ethnic person in all circumstances and at all times. On the contrary, they insist on a pluralist, multi-dimensional concept of the self. The embeddedness of the subject in specific contexts is crucial. Moreover, the dispersed habitation of the self in various forms needs to be taken into consideration because the self borrows concepts and attitudes freely from the different cultures one lives in. The search for an ethnic identity – either a conscious or unconscious activity or prompted by either the others or by the self – may lead to the discovery of a vision. This vision might be ethical in the sense that the new identity fits into the moral landscape of contemporary self-claimed egalitarian society. It might also be therapeutic as by possessing a distinct ethnic identity, one gains a respectable position in society. At the same time the new identity might be rigged and fabricated for self-serving purposes. The therapeutic act refers to the (post) modern struggle for an identity, which gives life and substance to the 'unnamed' in society. As these 'unnamed' may not fit nicely into existing categories and classifications, they engage in a self-reflexive exercise in order to cope with the exigencies and contradictions of (post) modern life. At times the soul-searching can engender self-exploration, self-discovery and strong sentiments of empowerment. Patterson (1977: 79) reminds us that the existing classifications have been inherited from the nation state era, when 'the term nation state has a precise meaning; it is, simply, the state which is based on, and identified with, a single ethnic group.'

In the case of Japan, the consensus on one single ethnic Japanese group in the Japanese nation is still very strong. The unified **ethnonational identity** of the Japanese differing radically from other nations and ethnic groups was the main theme of the *Nihonbunkaron*, a genre that among other things stressed the uniqueness of the Japanese language and the homogeneity of the Japanese people. The Japanese ethnonational identity is not a recent phenomenon, but has been part of the modern nation building project in Japan. It should be noted that in contrast to the identity of ethnic minorities in dominant societies, the Japanese constitute the dominant majority group in their own country. Admittedly many differences exist between the ethnicity of migrants in multicultural societies and the ethnonational identity of Japanese in terms of number, power relationship in society, etc. Notwithstanding this difference one cannot be entirely blind or completely oblivious towards the basic workings of ethnicity in the discourse on the Japanese ethnonational identity including primordialist elements, the importance of boundary, the instrumentality of ethnonational identity used as a weapon such as in trade negotiations with the United States. To illustrate, the existence of an Emperor, whose role has been reduced from divine ruler to the symbolic father of the family nation in the postwar period, reveals many common points with ethnic minorities adopting a similar family metaphor.

Multicultural/multi-ethnic societies

The discussion of multicultural/multi-ethnic societies – not unlike ethnicity – has brought about a state of confusion and obfuscation rather than clarification and elucidation. The basic meaning of 'multicultural' society implies the coexistence of different cultures in one society with a majority group and different ethnic minorities. Then, one can ask what is wrong with the term 'multi-ethnic' society, for it clearly denotes the presence of ethnic minority groups.

Whereas multi-ethnic society is a descriptive term, multiculturalism implies the normative dimension of respect for diversity and hybridity. This project demands efforts from both majority group and ethnic minorities. For instance, Lynch (1983) prefers the term 'multicultural' to other concepts including 'multi-racial', 'poly-ethnic', or 'multicredal' in order to describe the current heterogeneous society in Britain. According to his view (1983: 10), the term 'multicultural' indicates 'a comprehensive descriptor of our society, which embraces the multiracial, multicredal, multiethnic and multicultural composition of that society.' In Belgium, too, the term 'multicultural' is generally preferred, especially in the French-speaking part of the country. It is argued that the term 'multi-ethnic' stresses too unilaterally the existence of ethnic minorities in society. The term fails to incorporate the foremost quintessential aspect of the migrants' experience, namely the very act of migration and the concurrent cultural mechanisms of displacement, deferral, extension, projection, etc. The added value of 'multiculturalism', differing from 'multi-ethnicity' lies in the principle of difference but equality. In addition it calls to issue any assertion of a singular mainstream society, which in the current times of globalization and cultural flow can no longer be sustained. Among its most fervent supporters and advocates, diversity is not merely reality but also a cause for celebration since it engenders cross-fertilization of different cultures and mutually enriching experiences for the different members of society. Multiculturalism is officially embraced because the concept of 'multi-ethnicity' as a mere descriptive term does not inculcate this meaning of fruitful exchange, mutual learning and borrowing.

However, more and more voices (Roosens 1995: 11–12; Vermeulen 1997) point to the normative dimension of 'multiculturalism', which has not been fully attained or perhaps never will be. Roosens (1995: 11–12) assesses the situation as follows:

> Neither parents of immigrant children, nor the children themselves are *de facto, in their praxis*, acting toward the survival of different cultures; neither are the schools nor the authorities; nor do most experts on education. The overwhelming majority of the actors seem to be moving in the direction of an *internally diversified monocultural society*, adorned with the remnants of alien lifestyles and flourishes of symbolic ethnicity.

Although lip service is paid to the 'enriching' nature of a multicultural society, main structures in society such as education, legislation, national languages, etc. are organized along the lines of the mainstream Belgian system. Multiculturalism is pushed to the realm of 'folklore', where all things foreign – food, music, dance, clothing, etc. often reinvented to suit the new 'ethnic' taste – are elevated to the level of 'trendy coloredness' and political correctness.

From the Japanese point of view the assessment of the idea of 'multiculturalism' by Kajita (1993) can be summarized as prudent and critical. The emergence of the idea of 'multiculturalism' (*tabunkashugi*) is in his view the result of the many forms of criticism directed against Europeans and Americans in the aftermath of the World War II with regard to racial discrimination and ethnocentrism. He (1993: 181) argues that

> the advocacy of 'cultural relativism' (*bunkasootaishugi*), which was developed within UNESCO, has become a powerful ideology in the contemporary world...emphasizing the equality between all cultures.

After examining two case-studies in Canada and Australia, where the linguistic and cultural rights of each minority group within the national boundary are guaranteed, the 'bilingualism-biculturalism' (*nigengo-nibunkashugi*) policy, and the acceptance of difference in varying degrees in the different countries of Western Europe such as *droit à la différence* (*sooi e no kenri*) in France, he discerns some major limitations and flaws concerning the viability of 'multiculturalism.' He questions whether the beneficiaries of these policies, 'white ethnics', would apply to non-white groups like the Asians and Muslim migrants as well. Yet while looking at the current picture of multicultural societies in Western Europe such as Great Britain, this question has been dealt with partially as the voices of (South) Asians become increasingly prominent in different discourses. Furthermore, he reflects on the basic function of multiculturalism a 'means' towards the integration of all members into the nation state? Or will it over time become an inherent and unalienable right of an individual to insist on the own culture and/or ethnicity? Is it a temporary phenomenon, which if not solved then at least loose urgency and relevance or is it an unalienable principle or a human right? He seems to suggest that multicultural policies would no longer be necessary once the integration of ethnic minorities into the mainstream society has become a fact. Here, problems of definition and boundary marking arise. To be more to the point, how are the boundaries drawn between ethnic groups qualifying as 'ethnic minorities' in need of social assistance and for whom special programs have been set up and other ethnic groups excluded from such a treatment. Even in the case of a rational explanation, does this kind of differentiation not feed interethnic tension and disjointedness? The ambiguity and contestability of multicultural policies are mainly situated in the decision process of assigning the label of 'ethnic' to certain groups for public policy purposes to the exclusion of others.

Moreover, he alerts us that the link between multiculturalism and nationalist movements should be considered in designing a realistic multicultural policy, without jeopardizing the social fabric of a society. Last but not least, he warns that multiculturalism ultimately requires apart from a large dose of good will also significant means and money.

Globalist ethnography in contemporary complex societies.

It is clear that the merits and the appeal of postmodernism and globalization processes lie mostly in the sensitivity to the world we live in: in Western late-capitalist societies as well as third- or fourth-world societies imagination has entered social life. Therefore, in the shifted cultural dynamics or the emergence of 'ethnoscapes', it is no longer viable to just write a 'thick' description of the local and the particular, dismissing and disregarding transnational flow and continuous international migration. A globalist ethnography is to examine and lay bare the link between space, stability and cultural reproduction, transcending specific territorial boundaries and national identities. The postmodernist critique and insight of global processes are indeed very welcome. However, the suggestions of the postmodernists are rather scanty. After having 'deconstructed' the old, they do not invent the new.

In the field of anthropology, they propose a heteroglossal approach, urging for the inclusion of the different voices in the ethnographic account. In other words, they harbor great doubts towards the representation of the ethnographic account. Representation is not absolute but contingent since it is filtered though the subjectivity of the anthropologist in interaction with other subjectivities. Evidently, one easily detects an honorable attempt to reconcile the gap between the field and the office, between the 'being there' with the 'being here' in the anthropological equation (Geertz 1988: 1–24; 129–52). Indeed, the warning is timely and sound because of scientific and ethical relevance. What is the value of ethnography when the content and the procedure are wholly contested by the involved main actors and general members of that particular culture? Furthermore, is it ethical for an ethnographer to speak for others, even when the others are perfectly able to speak for themselves and have things to say, things that might not necessarily correspond with the ethnographer's point of view?

One can argue that the feedback from the field might be truth distorting if the members of a particular culture deliberately discredit the ethnographer for political and other reasons. Given the oppressive nature of some governments, ideologies, and religions the practice of unleashing the forces and voices in the field seems apt and relevant. The problem, however, is that this strategy of 'framing' and 'being framed', containing both the voice of the ethnographer and that of the observed can only be attained to a certain extent. In the end, no matter how conscious, careful and fine-tuned to contemporary needs and sensitivities the ethnographer may be, the final editing has to be done by him or her alone. S/he will after meticulous consultation and reflection have to throw out some 'irrelevant' stuff, some 'noises' – irrelevant and noises based on his or her own judgement – in order to produce the final ethnographic account.

In sum, the crucial question revolves around the priority in anthropology: research studying other cultures, while bearing in mind the own preoccupations and inclinations. The primary task of anthropology is not to obfuscate but to elucidate the Other or rather others in order to understand the others **and** oneself. Geertz (1973: 16–17) insists that anthropologists should not attempt 'to capture primitive facts in faraway places and carry them home like a mask (but rather) to reduce the puzzlement (and to discover) the informal logic of actual life.' It is suggested by Trouillot (1991: 22–3) that

A truly critical and reflexive anthropology needs to contextualize the Western metanarratives and read critically the place of the discipline in the field so discovered. In short, anthropology needs to turn the apparatus elaborated in the observation of non-Western societies on itself and, more specifically, on the history from which it sprang.

Surely, the reflexive moment postmodernists have introduced in the field of anthropology has urged researchers to engage in individual self-analysis and in collective soul-searching of the entire discipline in the globalizing times we are currently living in. However, postmodernism as a problem-detecting device may be valuable but as a methodological tool, it seems less adequate. It is one thing to be aware of the power relationship between the researcher and the researched; of the intricate and complex reality; of the fact that human conduct is full of ambiguities, multiplicity, contradiction and instability; the blurring between the 'being there' and the 'being here', it is, however, another thing to deal with these discrepancies when actually being confronted with them. What to think of the following situation, Wolf (1992: 137) asks herself: 'A barefoot village kid who used to trail along after you *will* one day show up on your doorstep with an Oxford degree and your book in hand.' Their suggestion to transcend the current contradictions by a literary stance of transforming the single authorship of the anthropologist into a multiple one, combining both the voices of the anthropologist and the 'anthropologized', seems seductive and appealing as an idea but rather difficult to execute. The turbulent times notwithstanding, Geertz (1988: 2–3) warns us not to deviate from the main task of anthropology.

> If anthropologists were to stop reporting how things are done in Africa and Polynesia, if they were instead to spend their time trying to find double plots in Alfred Kroeber and unreliable narrators in Max Gluckman, and if they were seriously to argue that Edward Westermack's stories about Morocco and those of Paul Bowles relate to their subject in the same way, with the same means and the same purposes, matters would indeed be in a parlous state.

Perhaps one needs to use a larger framework than the mere textual and/or aesthetic approach. The paradigm of 'cultural complexity' (Hannerz 1992) is useful since it is embedded in the globalization process of fragmentation and unification projected at the three interpenetrating macro, median and micro levels (Barth 1994). It provides, to my mind, a large and representative model to capture the ever-increasing international migratory movements at the macro level and the intricate webs of ethnicity in contemporary societies at the median and micro level. It is one of the most comprehensive frameworks with the potential of capturing the challenges of the times such as globalization, among other things affecting the formation and management of identities.

Studies on ethnicity along with the recent findings of the postmodernist approach and globalization processes point to the partial truth in convergence theories. Indeed, as a result of rapid progress in technology and communication means, the 'Western' model of late-capitalist consumer society or more correctly societies has been disseminated throughout major parts of the world. Tangible presence of products – material as well as symbolic – of the 'West' can probably be found even in the most remote corners of the world. However, can one thus conclude that everyone becomes 'identical' or at least 'very much alike' as is argued in convergence theories? The apparent unification may be tangible especially when it concerns commodities and sentiments of 'same-ness' but ironically they are to a high degree invented. Here invention should be equated with 'creation' and 'imagining' and not with 'fabrication' or 'falsity.' Trouillot (1991: 22) illustrates in the following 'thick' description of the world from a globalist point of view.

> We, here *is the* West... This is not the West in a genealogical or territorial sense. The postmodern world has little space left for genealogies, and notions of territoriality are being redefined before your eyes.... It is a world where Black American Michael Jackson starts an international tour from Japan and imprints cassettes that mark the rhythm of Haitian peasant families in the Cuban Sierra Maestra; a world where Florida speaks Spanish (once more); where a socialist prime minister in Greece comes by way of New England and an imam of fundamentalist Iran comes by way of Paris. It is a world

where the political leader in reggae-prone Jamaica traces his roots to Arabia, where US' credit cards are processed in Barbados, and Italian designer shoes in Hong Kong. It is a world where the Pope is Polish, where the most orthodox Marxists live on the Western side of the fallen iron curtain.

The 'West' is a contested concept since Western consumer goods, carrying partial symbols and fragmented images of contemporary Western societies, are not only spread but also manufactured everywhere. Thus, the present picture is very blurred as to who becomes who? The problem I have with convergence theories is the monolithic view of cultures as isolated and oppositional entities. In fact cultures should be approached by the 'flow' paradigm, in which the relation between dissimilar cultures is one of negotiation, mutual borrowing, multi-directional influencing, invention, creation and in the worst case of conflict and warfare.

To summarize, the adopted framework of studying the *kikokushijo* consists of the Hannerzian cultural concept of flow embedded in the globalization process at the **macro** level. This framework is clarified by the unifying educational structures of the nation state and family dynamics at the **median** level and the specific sentiments and experiences of the returnees and their family members at the **micro** level. The framework also takes into account the postmodern sensitivities of the blurring between the anthropologist and the anthropologized.

Part One

At the Macro Level

3 In Search of an Ethnonational Identity: The Historical Perspective

General Context

Said's classic work 'Orientalism' (1978) might not mark the inauguration of the shifting notion of culture from the fixity to the flux paradigm. Nonetheless, it has incontestably provided inspiration to postmodernists and others, who developed the notion of culture in flow. Given the overwhelmingly positive reception and the widespread impact of this work, it has become almost redundant to repeat his stance. Succinctly, his thesis evolves around the concept of the 'Orient' (he meant the Middle East), which, as he instructs us, proves to be a construction, made by Westerners. Western thinkers and scholars, of whom some were disillusioned with the own culture and others wanted to insist on the own superiority, attempted to find in the 'Orient' the counter image and agency. This tendency for romantization has transformed the 'Orient' into a part of the European material civilization and culture. Said (1978: 2) argues that the 'Orient' was used

> For display in the museum, for reconstruction in the colonial office, for theoretical illustration in anthropological, biological, linguistic, racial and historical theses about mankind and the universe.

In understanding Japanese culture in general and ethno-national identity in particular, the anthropologist faces the above-described intricate and complex process of cultural description as a particular interpretation rather than the unraveling of the objective reality. Moreover, s/he also has to take into account the plethora of cultural descriptions, produced by the Japanese themselves in terms of national distinctiveness and ethnonational identity.

It has been pointed out more than once that 'Orientalism' – in the sense of the dichotomization between the self and the other through the mystification of the 'other' in order to normalize the self – is not an exclusively Western practice. In a similar way, the Japanese have for a long time essentialized the 'West', too, as a monolithic entity with particular properties. In fact many still do. Moeran (1990) has called this mirror reflection of Orientalism 'Japanism' implying both the practice of both Japanese and Western scholars. Others (Trankell 1996) have called it 'Occidentalism.' The analysis of the development of the *Nihonbunkaron* in the postwar period follows the outline, set forth by Aoki Tamotsu (1990). The primary reason why the term *Nihonbunkaron* (the discourse of Japanese culture) is embraced instead of *Nihonjinron* (the theory of Japaneseness) and *Nihonron* (the theory of Japan) lies in the rather negative connotations of the last two terms. In order to avoid disorderly speech and unnecessary misunderstandings through the usage of different terms indiscriminately and interchangeably, I stick to the term *Nihonbunkaron*, which has been also been the choice of Aoki. In his publication *The Lineage of Discourse on 'Japanese culture': Culture and Identity in Postwar Japan* (*Nihonbunkaron no Hen'Yoo: Sengo Nihon no Bunka to Aidentitii* 1990), he approaches the Japanese discourse on the 'cultural' identity (*Nihonbunkaron*) from a historical perspective. He distinguishes four phases in the postwar development of *Nihon-*

65

bunkaron. The first phase covers the period from 1945 to 1954. In that era the discourse was characterized by a 'negative distinctiveness' (*hiteiteki tokushu no ninshiki*). The second period from 1955 until 1963 is marked by a consciousness of the historical relativism (in perspectives on Japan) (*rekishiteki sootaisei no ninshiki*). The third period can be divided in an early period from 1964 until 1976 and a late period from 1977 until 1983. The third period is featured by a consciousness of Japan's 'positive distinctiveness' (*kooteiteki tokushu no ninshiki*). In the period from 1964 until 1983 a general movement of positive self-evaluation was unfolding. Interpreting this process in Saidian terms, at the height of the *Nihonbunkaron*, some Japanese and Westerners were engaging in the practice of 'Occidentalism.' Finally, the new era starting from 1984 evolved 'from distinctiveness to universalism' (*tokushu kara fuhen e*).

In addition to the current flow paradigm of culture, a shift from 'radical difference' to 'negotiable difference' has taken place in most postmodern societies. The concept of the nineteenth century mono-ethnic nation state, based on the principle of 'one-nation = one ethnic group = one language', has been replaced by that of a 'multicultural' or 'multi-ethnic' society consisting of different groups in terms of race, ethnicity, gender, religion, etc. In the postmodernist and globalist era, difference, fragmentation, disintegration of the whole, hybridity and polyvocality have gained significant importance and meaning in- and outside academic circles. Difference operates perfectly in a complex contemporary society at the material/tangible as well at the imagined level. To phrase this point more blatantly, it is not only OK but also commendable and politically correct to be different. 'Symbolic' or 'imagined' contests can be conducted in an extensively diversified society with a common cultural apparatus. It seems, in other words, more potent when a particular difference is generally acknowledged and understood by all members of a community. One has to master the 'language' and the rules in order to negotiate successfully the differences within one arena. As a result, one cannot approach the other as the ultimately different other but as an other, with whom one can communicate, argue, agree, disagree and negotiate. Last but not least the other has become a person, who is firm on his/her different-ness. In other words, divergence is not only expressed and acknowledged but has become discussible and negotiable in the context of multicultural/multi-ethnic societies. The changing discourse from 'radical' towards 'negotiable difference' seems also to be taking place in Japanese culture and society with regard to the 'other' or the 'marginal', be it a returnee, an ethnic minority group, a women's association, etc. This corresponds with Aoki's new era 'from distinctiveness to universality' (*tokushu kara fuhen e*). For a long time, Japan's ethnonational identity, interpreted as a unique property, was guided and shaped by the other-reference. This is partially due to the voluntary and selective introduction of exogenous cultural elements throughout the history of Japan. During an extended time, Japan looked outwardly to learn and to adopt institutions, technologies, sciences, religions, etc. when they were thought to be useful and necessary for Japan at a particular moment in history.

The symbolic boundary process at play in the process of Japanese ethnonational identity cannot simply be divided in the 'us' versus 'them' realm since the 'us' realm contains a multitude of foreign knowledge and practices, which are subsequently and successfully 'nativized' and incorporated in the 'our own realm' (Yoshino 1992: 123). In the Japanese context, one cannot simply distinguish between the indigenous and 'authentic' institutions, respectively customs and goods on the one hand and the imported goods and ideas on the other hand. The reality is much more complex than one would imagine. Many institutions and artifacts of foreign origin have been adapted in order to suit the Japanese context. The 'central florescence' (*chuuka*) of China constituted the main ideology during the Tokugawa period until 1869 when Japan was threatened by the invading Western colonial powers. The internal political, social and economic problems generated a sense of internal crisis. Moreover, the ambition of the Western colonial powers ready to sail for and invade Japan led to a critical self-reflection on the preservation of Japanese culture in the *Bakumatsu* period (1853–60). In particular, the negative example of China, which emerged defeated out of the Opium Wars and 'humiliated' by the unequal treaties imposed on them by the Western imperialist nations, offered the ultimate proof that Japan needed to modernize the country and its people in order not to fall prey to Western invasion and colonization. Chinese Confucianism, the official orthodox ideology at that time was deemed to be too stagnant and unable to face the new challenges. A 'nativist studies' movement (*kokugaku*) urging for the return to the own roots sprang up.

In the Meiji period (1868–1912), the Emperor, assisted by senior politicians, gradually established a modern nation state with a distinctive Japanese ethnonational identity in the encounter with the technologically advanced Western nations. Priority item on the political agenda was the strengthening of the national cohesion by stimulating a modern economy while 'inventing', promoting and preserving the 'own homogeneous culture.' The description and classification of the Japanese culture and self have been actively conducted by the Japanese themselves, often adopting paradigms from the West and frequently assisted by Westerners in Japan.

In the direct aftermath of the war, the Japanese culture and self became well known in the United States and Europe through Ruth Benedict, the author of *The Chrysanthemum and the Sword* (1946), a much-contested but still renowned anthropological classic work on the Japanese. Drawing upon her earlier works, generally classified as culture and personality study, she uncovers the predominant temperament in the Japanese culture and the specific 'paradoxical' self of the Japanese. Her configuration theory, or as her opponents have termed it 'cultural determinism' has been the target of much criticism for its vagueness, impressionism, relativism (Williams 1947 in Geertz 1988) and lack of fieldwork experiences. Yet it still constitutes one of the most influential works on Japanese society in the immediate postwar period. Recently, a reevaluation of her work has taken place. Her personal life and her career as a woman anthropologist have inspired many to reassess and re-evaluate her work (Geertz 1988; Aoki 1994) and also her personal life (Modell 1989).

A great variety of publications, which can be classified as studies of 'cultural nationalism' or ethnonational identity (*Nihonbunkaron*) have appeared. In reaction, many critical assessments of *Nihonbunkaron* have been published, too. This period, typified by Aoki as the period of Japan's positive distinctiveness, marks a departure from previous cultural debates. This is to say that the other reference in the identity-formation of the Japanese was replaced by a self-centered, Japan-specific identity. This new approach highlights the laudable parts of Japanese ethnonational identity and expresses the pride of being Japanese. For the first time, Japanese identity draws upon the own strength, without having to look at other nations or cultures for emulation.

Recently, to continue the classification of Aoki, in the era of universalism, a more conciliatory mood can be discerned. The insistence on the uniqueness and the homogeneity of Japanese culture and society seems to have lost a great deal of its zeal and fire. Instead it has made room for a view, which displays a higher tolerance towards (more) shared characteristics of the Japanese with the non-Japanese, while discarding a number of inscrutable idiosyncrasies. Japanese as well as non-Japanese scholars have softened their attitude by unknotting the tight dualistic model of the 'us' versus 'them.' Fujitani (1993) equally agrees that a large number of the so-called 'authentic' native practices, beliefs and customs have been fairly recently 'invented' in the late-Tokugawa period. He thus deconstructs 'Japanese tradition and customs' by concluding that they do not date back from time immemorial.

The current line of thinking seems to be the following: the Japanese culture and ethnonational identity have some specificities like other cultures. Yet Japan is definitely not, as ardently argued by some at the height of the *Nihonbunkaron* debate, a unique, particularistic and homogeneous society. In other words, divergence is a matter of degree rather than an absolute and unaltering given. The Japanese preoccupation with national 'same-ness' and distinctiveness is by no means an isolated and exclusive Japanese matter. After all, similar cultural/ethnonational debates on nationalism can also be found among the Turks, the Indians and others (Yoshino 1992). Recent publications, subscribing to a more comparative or universalistic stance in studying Japanese culture and ethnonational identity, seem to reflect the current stance of multiplicity and the erosion of radical differences in the increasingly globalizing world.

Nation building and Nationalism

The emergence of a 'National' political consciousness during the late Tokugawa period

Although the social, economic and political modernization process of Japan started to take off in the Meiji period (1868–1912), it should be noted that the foundations, which had made this process possible, were established in the second part of the Tokugawa reign. Some (Amino 1990) trace the beginnings of the Japanese nation – in the sense of a homogeneous state binding loose individuals into one collectivity of Japanese people – to as early as the seventh century with the introduction of the cursive syllabic writing system (*hiragana*) and the establishment of a central state with civil and penal codes (*ritsuryoo*). The uniform writing system did not extinguish regional differences such as local dialects but smoothened the existing dissimilarities by introducing and imposing the usage of a single standardized written language, and thereby creating a common national language.

It is widely accepted that the birth of the modern Japanese nation state is situated in the second half of the Tokugawa period and in the succeeding Meiji era. Ieyasu, the first Tokugawa shogun, made an end to the 'era of the warring states' (*sengoku jidai*) and subsequently laid the foundation of the Tokugawa government. The shogunate was presided by a shogun from the Tokugawa house, supported by a military officialdom of *daimyoo* (local lords) and *samurai* (warriors). The emperor fulfilled a mere symbolic function. As official ideology, neo-Confucianism was adopted to legitimize the Tokugawa leadership. In neo-Confucianism the cosmic order or the 'heavenly way' (*tendoo*) was fixed, whereas the social organization of society constituted a representation of the natural law. The notion of social order was guided and sustained by the morality of the five relationships, duty and designation (*meibun*). The five relationships included that between father and son, ruler and ruled, husband and wife, older brother and younger brother, friend and friend.

The Tokugawa system, firmly based on the consolidation of family power, distinguished four separate classes: the *samurai*, peasants, artisans and merchants. The four estates were interdependent, as they were all parts of the natural order of things. On the whole, the ruling elite of the samurai maintained a rigid status distinction and enjoyed the highest status in a 'federation' of local communities. Politically, the Tokugawa house and local lords ruled powerfully and autonomously over the local domains (*han*), while tolerating a loosely organized system, comparable to a 'federation.' At the daily level, local dialects divided the Japanese people into separate communities.

Given the Chinese origin of neo-Confucianism, China was seen as the source or the light of civilization. China was referred to as the 'central florescence' (*chuuka*). This view, void of real historicity, was used metaphorically in order to dramatize the distinction between the 'inner' sphere of civilization, represented by China and the 'outer' sphere of barbarism, represented by Japan. Interesting to note were the seclusion edicts, which sealed Japan off from the outside world for the greater part of the Tokugawa reign. Concerning the issue of the uniformity and homogeneity of Japan, Fujitani (1993: 83) concludes that 'in short, politics, society, and especially culture under the ideal Tokugawa system of rule were marked by both horizontal and vertical distinctions and separation.'

During the *Bakumatsu* (the late Tokugawa period), the cosmic order, propagated by the Tokugawa shogunate started to collapse. A growing number of actors in society including intellectuals, peasants and *samurai* became increasingly disenchanted with the shogunal bureaucracy (*bakufu*). The bureaucrats themselves were not sufficiently equipped to deal neither with the internal problems nor with the external challenges. At the domestic level, the policies undertaken by the Tokugawa curbed the power of the local lords in the so-called 'smashing of the daimyoo' (*daimyoo no toritsubushi*) process. In addition, the government imposed taxes on the peasants to such a degree that they were driven to the level of utter poverty. While the upper strata of the *daimyoo* and the *samurai* saw their wealth and status drastically diminished and while the peasants were economically strangled, the enrichment of the socially 'inferior' class of merchants became all the more visible and prominent.

Apart from the internal disintegration, at the beginning of the nineteenth century Japan witnessed an increasing number of foreign vessels off the coast. Disturbing reports reached Japan concerning the adventures of these foreigners in India and China and in particular their ambitions of invasion and colonization. The foreign crisis ultimately brought an end to the Tokugawa seclusion policy (*sakoku*), culminating in the opening of the country (*kaikoku*) in 1854 and the signing of 'unequal' treaties in 1857–8. In intellectual circles, the movement of the 'nativists' (*kokugaku*) sought to change the social and cosmic order. This was in the first stage of the eighteenth century noticeable in the more private realm of social life. The reversal began with a reappraisal of the own, indigenous literature and aesthetics and a return to the institution of a Japanese-style emperor. They found in the great poetic collections of the *Manyooshu* and the *Kokinshu* distinctive native qualities such as *magokoro* (sincere heart) and *mono no aware* (a sense of sadness for the transience of life). These indigenous qualities were thought to be genuine, unadorned and not corrupted by the Confucian didactics and artificial norms.

One of the most influential figures among the nativists (*kokugakusha*), Motoori Norinaga (1730–1801) urged for the political restoration of the imperial authority and the revival of the basic psychological life of the Japanese. Unlike the emperor of China, who had to earn his 'mandate of heaven' and therefore could be dethroned in case of misrule and mismanagement of the empire, the Japanese emperor is divinely appointed. Therefore, he is beyond good and evil. The shift from an emperor as a heavenly principle to a principal of politics or from someone who has absolute power to one who is absolute power does not mean that nativists, Motoori inclusive, demanded a complete reversal of the political order. The principal objective of the restoration was in first instance to conserve and to 'nativize' Japan by dismantling Chinese neo-Confucianist thinking. Harootunian (1970: 29) offers another reason for the establishment of direct imperial rule. 'In his capacity as historical representative of the gods, (the emperor) could induce the ruled, for better or worse, to follow voluntarily the ordinances of the rulers.' As time went by, the domestic social order and the economic situation of the *daimyoo* and the peasants deteriorated progressively. The nativist discourse was continued by the Mito school, who chose to concentrate on domestic problems to the neglect of the foreign threat. The syncretic writers of the Mito school subscribed to the new vision of the nativists but held on to the neo-Confucian moral principles. They pointed an accusing finger to the shogunate, which violated the imperial trust by being morally indifferent to the domains financially and militarily.

To conclude, facing domestic problems and the pressure of foreigners, the nativists found many faults in the political ideology of neo-Confucianism, imported from China. Instead, they promoted a return to the native institution of direct imperial rule and the native values, underlying the Japanese psyche in rediscovering indigenous poetry and aesthetics. Although they had not intended to do away with shogunate autocracy, as a result of their writings and the threat of foreigners, they unknowingly made the Meiji-restoration possible and subsequently the foundations of the modern Japanese nation were established.

Nation building, ethnonational identity and concept of society in the Meiji (1868–1912) and Taisho (1912–26) period

The early Meiji period was characterized by a wholesale importation of all things Western in the general effort to modernize Japanese society. Modernization seemed to be the only viable solution to counter the foreign threat and so preserve Japanese culture. The 1868 Charter Oath marked the formal beginning of Japan's pursuit of modernization. During the first two decades of turbulent institutional change, the national slogans of *fukoku kyoohei* (a wealthy nation and a strong army), *shokusan koogyoo* (encouraging industry) and *bunmei kaikan* (civilization and enlightenment) were seen as emblems and instruments of the national policy. The following description of Storry (1983: 107) is illuminating.

> Banks, railways, harbours, lighthouses, dockyards, telegraph offices, printing presses and newspapers, post offices, cigars and cigarettes – the entire apparatus of Western material civilization seemed to find some reproduction, some kind of an echo, in Japan. Indeed the first two decades of the Emperor Meiji's reign saw a Japan to all appearances intoxicated with the strong wine of Western thought, techniques, and customs.

Along with indiscriminate borrowing, Gluck (1985: 19) in her thorough reading of Japan's modern myth claims that there was also the fickle and capricious attitude of the leadership. She states that 'by 1890 the local government system had undergone three major reorganizations, in 1871–72, 1878, and again in 1888–89, with minor changes in between.' In the decade of the 1880s the fervent mood for institutional and bureaucratic change and the seemingly insatiable craving for all things Western had come to a halt. Indiscriminate borrowing was followed by a call for the formulation of an own ethnonational identity. Gluck links the flaring up of ideology from the 1880s onwards with the consequences of the import of Western institutions, the promulgation of the Constitution in 1889 and the opening of the Diet in 1890. The last two events constituted the crown piece of the early Meiji reforms, preceded by the 1868 Charter Oath. They were the tangible manifestation of Japan as a nation among the civilized nations (*bunmeikoku no ikkoku*). It should be noted that she defines ideology according to Geertz' concept of 'maps of problematic social reality,' as a process which gives meaning to social life for those who must live it. In other words, it concerns a dominant set of values and norms disseminated by different actors and institutions. Their shared efforts help to construct a shared ideological universe. This notion of ideology differs from the Marxist interpretation of ideology standing for the inversion of reality and a product of false consciousness.

The actors shaping the ideological process included government scholars (*goyoo gakusha*), bureaucrats in the central ministries – such as the Ministry of Education – and the *minkan* (meaning 'people') consisting of journalists, intellectuals, public figures and interest groups. Besides individual actors, many institutions contributed to the creation of a 'sense of a nation.' Schools, the army, the local government system and half-public, half-private organizations were among the most influential institutions in shaping 'a collective mind', an ethnonational identity among 'the people of Japan' (*Nihon no kokumin*). In addition, one should bear in mind the rapid development of the transportation system and communication means, changing the material as well as the mental landscape of Japan of the late nineteenth century. As the project of nation building seemed to have taken form by the 1890s, a shift in the concern for the state towards the society took place. It was generally felt that Japan had changed into a complex society. For the first time, the social problems of Japan were brought to the public forum, in which many actors participated for diverse and conflicting reasons. Gluck (1985: 28) describes the consensus as follows.

> Society was in disarray, afflicted with ills, beset by economic diffi-culties, roiled by the struggle for survival, upset by labor problems, exposed to dangerous thought, threatened by socialist destruction, rent by gulfs between the rich and the poor, city and country, worker and capitalist.

The creation of the 'concept of society' (*shakai kannen*) in or-der to foster solidarity among the Japanese people was prompted by economic problems. After the Sino-Japanese war of 1894–5 and especially following the Russo-Japanese war of 1904–5, the economic situation deteriorated drastically. In spite of the average annual growth of 2.5 percent in GNP per capita between 1870 and 1913, government expenditures tripled be-tween 1890–1900 as a result of augmented military costs, the fast growing administrative expenses and increased debt. At the local government level, too, expenses increased seven-fold dur-ing the period of 1890–1910. Consequently, taxes not only went up in amount but also multiplied by type for taxpaying households. By the turn of the century Japan matured into a full member of the international community. The emblems of modernization – the 1868 Charter Oath, the 1989 Constitution, and national education – testified the status of Japan as a full modern nation. Concurrently, a specific ethnonational identity has been developed after an initial period of fervent and fever-ish borrowing from the West. Once the foundation of a modern nation state was consolidated, a sense of solidarity among the 'Japanese people' (*Nihon no kokumin*) was generated and thus the concept of a 'Japanese society' was born. At the end of the first decade of the century, a short-lived eruption of liberalism took place among the intelligentsia. This short-lived creative moment in Japanese literary and intellectual history was prompted by a chain of events. The devastations of the two wars (the Sino-Japanese and the Russo-Japanese Wars), the rural-urban migration of 'the youngsters from the countryside' (*inaka mono*), the growing pollution of the newly built factories and the breaking up of social organizations such as the family were manifestations of the rapid modernization process. When the Meiji Emperor (1852–1912) passed away in 1912, he was succeeded by his son, who adopted *Taisho* as the name of his reign. The new Taisho-era consolidated the major Meiji reforms through Yamagata Aritomo (1838–1922), who made sure conservatism was secured instead of liberalism. Repressive measures were taken such as the inclusion of the Emperor and Shinto cult into the school curriculum, the passing of press laws, etc. On the other hand, there was also a call from the 'public opinion of the people' (*minkan no yoron*) for a 'second restoration' of installing a true constitutional government. By 1915 Japan had developed a vernacular language, shared by the Japanese people. This language included and assimilated all things imported into the daily language, attitudes and look. In the following passage Gluck (1985: 247) ruminates on the swift incorporation of material culture in daily life and in language.

> The model of a 'fire wheeled car' that Putiatin and Perry offered in the 1850s as miniature proof of the might of the West had been domesticated, technologically and linguistically, into the ubiquitous Japanese locomotive which no longer stopped at a *suteishon* (station) but an *eki*. Only fifty years earlier neither railroad nor emperor had yet impinged on the experience of most Japanese. From split-skirted *hakama* to pinch-necked *haikara*; from the privileged learning of *gakumon* to the familiar windowed, wooden village school (*gakkoo*); from the homely native, even regional, sense of *kuni* to the grandly imperial *teikoku*.

In the cities, the sociological landscape was recrafted to sights never seen before. The new lifestyle has been captured by Storry (1983: 166) as follows.

There were to be seen, in sophisticated circles at any rate, the first signs of what was to be known as the *Moga* style. *Moga* was the Japanese contraction of the English words, 'modern girl'. It came to suggest, during the twenties, cloche hats and short skirts, with the 'bob', 'shingle', or even 'Eton crop'. Her male counterpart was the *Mobo*, the 'modern boy' who on leaving university adopted the latest and most flashy Western clothes including, it might be, 'Oxford bags'. *Mobo* and *Moga* might be seen walking down the Ginza in Tokyo hand in hand. This was very daring but it was done.

Concerning appearance, Seidensticker (1983: 257–8) instructs us on the particular Taisho look in people, and more specifically in women.

Men had for the most part taken to Western dress before the earthquake (in 1923) but Japanese dress prevailed among women. The Taisho woman in Japanese dress look more Western, somehow, than does the Meiji woman in Western dress. The bustles and bonnets of the Meiji woodcut are all gay, and, at the remove of a century...seem authentic enough, but the face is of an earlier day. A languorous beauty of Taisho, by contrast, speaks of a world-weariness that has been studied well and mastered, and it is not of domestic provenance.

According to Gluck (1985: 247) Japan had, besides a new vernacular speech, a public language of ideology, which lasted until the end of the World War II.

Produced in the course of the Meiji decades, the ideological vocabulary, meanings, syntax, and usage were now collectively maintained...The language describing state and society, while in unevenly active use among different members of the population, in the passive sense at least was widely and mutually understood.

One recurrent theme in the language of ideology was the omnipresence of the emperor, to whom allegiance was due. Symbols, signs and myths, which were at that moment associated with the *tennoosei* were widely disseminated. *Kokutai*, in its original meaning of the uninterrupted line of the Japanese emperor as Japan's national distinctiveness and *chuukun aikoku* (loyalty and patriotism) became rapidly fixed items in ideological messages. Moreover, the constant evocation of the Great Empire of Japan (*DaiNihon teikoku*) in public discourse made the empire very real and tangible to the great public.

Ideological orthodoxy in the 1930s and the mobilization for World War II

In the late 1920s of the early Showa-period (1926–89) the term *tennoosei* was introduced. The general mood was one of rigidification of the national ideology, culminating into the mobilization for World War II. Whereas in the former periods, suasion and exhortation of the Japanese people by the governing elite and institutions proved to be effective, in the early Showa period disparity between the prescribed ideological formula and the actual living circumstances and livelihood of the Japanese people became manifest. Around this period the emergence of the nuclear family and the professionalization of females changed the traditional family structures to such an extent that the essential virtues of the five relationships became irrelevant and vacuous. The incongruity between ideology and reality resulted into less spontaneous willingness to cooperate unlike in the previous eras. Coercion was sometimes needed to get messages across. Repressive laws were passed such as the 'altering of the *kokutai*' crime against the state in the Peace Preservation Law of 1925, which limited freedom of speech, freedom of publications by organizations and individuals. One of the most representative documents dating from this ultra nationalist period in Japan, was the *Kokutai no Hongi* (the Fundamental Principles of our National Polity), a tract containing the ultimate 'national polity.' The national polity confirmed that Japan, a sacred land, was ruled by a divine emperor. The citizens were members of a large family headed by the emperor and expected to serve the country with absolute and unconditional loyalty. The first paragraph has been translated as follows by Hall and Hauntlett (in Gluck 1985: 283).

The unbroken line of emperors receiving the oracle of the founder of the Nation, reign eternally over the Japanese Empire. This is our eternal and immutable *kokutai*. Thus, founded on this great principle, all the people, united as one great family nation in heart and obeying the Imperial Will, enhance indeed the beautiful views of loyalty and filial piety…This *kokutai* is the eternal and unchanging basis of our nation and shines resplendent throughout the nation and is, together with heaven and earth, without end. We must, to begin with, know with what active brilliance this fountainhead shines within the reality of the founding of our nation.

The *Kokutai no Hongi* tract has been subject to a heated debate in the aftermath of World War II. The consensus was that the tract served as the ideological foundation of Japanese militarism. It glorified service to the state and strongly opposed liberalism and individualism. Two key concepts of *kotodama* and *kotoage* were borrowed from the old Japanese poem the *Manyooshu kotodama*. One of the unique features of the Japanese is the lack of *kotoage* or the lifting (*age*) of words (*koto*). The belief was based on a line in the *Manyooshu kotodama*, and more specifically the line *kotoage senu kuni* (a country where the *kotoage* is not performed). Originally, the *kotoage* was a feature of religious life and belief in pre-Buddhist Japan. It was a kind of magical invocation, mostly related to the request of rainfall, a vital commodity in agricultural societies. Later this was abandoned. As Japan did no longer use this magical invocation, it was assumed that Japan was a country of silence or more correctly non-verbal communication. The mutual understanding among the Japanese was thought to be based on implicit non-verbal communication. Since ancient times, Japanese endured in silence when confronted with crises and hardships. By turning obedience, endurance and passiveness into virtues, the government succeeded in controlling and manipulating the thoughts of the populace. Incessantly the Japanese unique virtues including loyalty, patriotism, ancestor-worship were propagated throughout the media. Befu (1993: 124) argues that

> This self-praise, often in the form of unqualified ethnocentrism, extolling Japan's cultural genius continued until it reached a heightened frenzy, with claims of superiority of the Japanese as against Chinese, Europeans, and Americans.

The ultra-nationalistic doctrine reached a peak during World War II, and came to an end on August 14, 1945.

4   *Nihonbunkaron* in the Postwar Era

General Context

In the direct aftermath of the war, the war ideology of Japanese innate superiority must have sounded unbearably false and hollow, as Miller (1982: 37) eloquently describes.

> (T)hose Japanese who were lucky enough to be alive found their cities and villages overrun by hordes of tall, strong, well-fed, and generally quite genial foreign troops. How, they asked themselves, can we have believed for a moment that we belonged to a race that was in any way superior to these great, smiling hulks of robust pink-faced lads?

In studying the development of Japanese ethnonational identity in the postwar period, Ruth Benedict's book *The Chrysanthemum and the Sword* (1946) stands out as one of the most influential and much contested publications. This work is in many facets original. First, the author Ruth Fulton Benedict was known for her configuration theory of culture-and-personality, her work on the Pueblo culture and Japanese culture and her belief in 'enlightened change' in all societies. During the final stage of World War II, she prepared anthropological reports on allied and enemy countries, of which Japan was according to Geertz (1988: 116–17) 'an enormous something, trim, intricate, and madly busy, that, like an Esher drawing, fails to compute.'

In her book she detects the following patterns shaping Japanese culture: 1. taking one's 'proper station' in a society or the respect for hierarchy and order; 2. indebtedness towards ancestors and contemporary superiors, crystallized in the term *on* (social indebtedness); 3. the repayment of the mentioned indebtedness; 4. the cultivation and codification of physical pleasure; 5. shame culture in Japan versus guilt culture in the West; 6. self-discipline; 7. human freedom and extreme indulgence of children and senior citizens. She summarizes the group-oriented nature of the Japanese through the key concept of *on* (social indebtedness). This principle shapes the Japanese into hierarchical human beings. She singles out *on* as the predominant temperament of Japanese culture.

In spite of the many forms of critique in terms of methodology such as the lack of fieldwork, the holistic methodology and cultural determinism, recently it has been rehabilitated and reevaluated by anthropologists for her powerful language exposing the trope of rendering the radical other into a familiar being and thereby questioning the 'logic' of the own culture. For example, Geertz (1988: 117–21) applauds her effort.

> The great originality of Benedict's book...lies in the fact that she does not seek to unriddle Japan and the Japanese by moderating this sense of oddly made world populated by oddly wired people, but by accentuating it...What started out as a familiar sort of attempt to unriddle oriental mysteries ends up, only too successfully, as a deconstruction, *avant la lettre*, of occidental clarities.

Others, like Modell (1989: 4–5), praise her powerful didactic skills.

> Her work as an anthropologist was pedagogical: she taught her audience the virtues of seeing how other people arranged their lives, the necessity of tolerating individual differences if a society is to survive, the power of culture over nature...By presenting vivid portraits of contrasting cultures, Benedict intended to open the eyes of her readers and compel them to recognize that existing arrangements were not god-given...Benedict never outlined a program for change

beyond increasing cultural tolerance and the awareness of individuals. Her anthropological data and theory constituted the pioneer idea and became a force in shaping our modern world.

Still others, like Aoki (1994: 4–5), hold her up as an example worthy of emulation as she succeeds in linking anthropology and public policy making. The report on Japan after the war was her last assignment at the Office of War Information.

I seriously question whether any anthropologist coming after Benedict has inherited her anthropological attitude. Such people would be valuable. Matters like the economic tensions between Japan and the United States or Europe are said to be the result of 'cultural friction' but anthropologists do not speak out as mediators. Only political scientists, economists, and journalists make themselves heard, while anthropologists, who are supposed to have an 'insider's' understanding of Japan, remain silent. Certainly I know of no anthropologists employed as specialists by agencies in Washington or Brussels or Tokyo.

Notwithstanding the popularity of her book, it was not clear whether MacArthur actually used it (Modell 1989: 4). The fact remains that she has had a lasting impact on the great public and not in the least on the Japanese.

From negativeness to historical relativity: the prelude to the eruption of Nihonbunkaron

In Aoki's classification of postwar *Nihonbunkaron*, the first stage is characterized by a negative distinctiveness. In this period Aoki directs our attention to the works by Sakaguchi Ango, Kato Shuichi and Umesao Tadao. In *Darakuron*, the degeneration theory (of the Japanese) Sakaguchi Ango urges the replacement of the prewar culture and traditions by a new culture and society. Not without irony, he contrasts the chaos and confusion in the direct aftermath of the war with the preceding 'beautiful' period. The negativeness (*hitei*) of the Japanese culture and ethnonational identity lies allegedly in the feudal institutions (*hookenteki na isei*); in the irrational (*higooriteki*), counter-democratic (*han minshushugi*) and 'premodern' (*zenkindaiteki*) society. However, after the initial shock and chaos, a new sense of optimism emerged. As things had already gone so wrong in the 'old Japan' (*furui Nihon*) there was ample room for improvement in the 'new Japan' (*atarashii Nihon*). The decade of the 1950s saw the outbreak of the Korean War and the end of the American Occupation in Japan. In line with these two crucial events for Japan, a new mood emerged in Japanese society. The initial negative self-image made room for a 'consciousness of historical relativity.' In 'the hybrid society', Kato Shuichi poses the thesis that Japan, although geographically situated in Asia, does not necessarily belong to Asia in terms of culture. He puts forth the view that the Japanese traditional society has been thoroughly Westernized and molded after the European society model, and in particular that of England and France. Henceforth, he concludes that the 'hybrid character of the Japanese culture' (*Nihonbunka no zasshusei*) consists of a traditional and a modernized part.

Concurrently but from a different perspective, Umesao Tadao develops the idea of cultural ecology. In his view, one cannot deny that Japan is part of the Asian heritage in terms of lineage, or genealogy (*keifu*). He refers specifically to the Japanese language, customs and traditions. A multitude of tangible artifacts and beliefs reflects the influence and inspiration of the Asian continent. Yet from the perspective of the modernization paradigm Japan shares many more similarities with the Western advanced countries than with the surrounding Asian cultures. To clarify Japan and Western Europe, respectively located at the most Eastern and the most Western sides of the Eurasian continent, display a 'parallel progress' (*heiko shinka*). Admittedly Japan has embarked on the modernization process later than Western European societies. Yet after the importation of Western ideas and commodities, the Japanese has domesticated these thoughts and goods. Through this 'japanization' process the modernization process in Japan has been 'indigenized.'

The Discourse on Japanese Culture or *Nihonbunkaron*

Basic themes

The ascendancy of Japan as an economic power in the world community has been accompanied by an intense soul-searching about the specific and unique characteristics of the Japanese people and culture in the discourse of Japanese ethnonational identity. Japanese economic success has strengthened the national self-confidence. As a result, the positive aspects of the Japanese people and culture are stressed in order to explain why Japan has succeeded in becoming an equal if not a superior actor in the international economic arena. Of course, attempts to explain the distinctive nature of one's nation and culture appear to be a universal phenomenon. According to Yoshino (1992) many nations and cultures engage in varying degrees in self-reflection since 'intellectuals' are concerned with ideas of national distinctiveness. This is by no means unique to Japan's intellectual culture.

Nonetheless it should be underlined that the zeal of the producers of this genre and the equally enthusiastic eagerness of Japanese 'consumers' have not been surpassed by many others, as Befu (1993: 107) puts it in the following way. 'The Japanese manifest a consuming interest in the question of who they are in a cultural sense, so much so that the discourse on Japanese identity may even be called a minor pastime.' The contents of *Nihonbunkaron* genre are vast and

87

multi-disciplinary. The genre encompasses almost all aspects of the Japanese culture in the broadest sense, ranging from ecology, to 'race', to psychology, to social structure and to language and communication. As the genre has become a *taishuushoohizai* (a consumer product), it should not come as a surprise that the output is rather extensive and the sales even more dizzyingly high. In 1978 the Nomura Research Institute published a compilation comprising *Nihonbunkaron* works since World War II. Within that time span of thirty-three years, 698 titles were counted (Befu 1993: 108–9). Befu himself counted 1,048 works as of March 1990 (ibid. 109).

The basic themes underlying each work of this genre remain – the variable contents notwithstanding – constant: the homogeneity of the Japanese people, purity of descent and blood and the uniqueness of Japanese culture. Holism in the sense of functionalism refers to the attempt to see a highly differentiated industrial society as a whole. It aims to analyze order in complex contemporary societies through structural integration. Moreover, there is another form of holism, which seems to fit better the Japanese case, namely 'extensionism' (Yoshino 1992: 88). Extensionism or reproductionism seeks to explain order not through the interdependence of separated and different parts of society but by a binding and all-comprehensive collective consciousness. This consensus on the homogeneity of the in-group members is comparable to that of pre-industrial societies. In simple and small-scale society kinship and community generally constitute the basic units of social order. The kinship system does not necessarily need to be confined to a small group but can be extended to the social group in its entirety. Like other cultures, where the kinship metaphor constitutes an essential part of the discourse on nationalism, the Japanese state, too has often been regarded as a 'family state' (*kokka*) at the national level and the company as a 'familistic institution' at the intermediate level. Eriksen

(1993: 108) elaborates on the salience of the kinship metaphor in nationalism.

> Kinship terms are frequently used in nationalist discourse (mother-country, father of the nation, brothers and sisters and so on), and the abstract community postulated by nationalists may be likened to the kin group...As a metaphorical *pater familias* nationalism states that the members of the nation are a large family: through the national courts, it punishes its disobedient children.

Reproductionism implies a primordialist dimension as references and 'clues' are sought in indigenous traditions. The indigenous kinship institution in pre-industrial Japan was the household. From the genealogical perspective, the *ie* may be translated as 'stem family' with the *daikoku bashira* (lit. principal pillar) as the family head. The *ie* has been defined by Morioka (1967 in Lebra 1984: 20) as 'a vertically composite form of nuclear families, one from each generation', by Beardsley (1965: 78) as 'a patrilineage, a network of households related through their respective heads, comprising main houses, branch houses, and houses of branch houses, and branches of branch houses traced down through generations.' Ideally, the *ie*-unit spans three or more generations of the same family, although this may not always be attained in reality. The rule of unigeniture allows only one child to inherit the house assets including house property, house status, leadership, etc. This child is generally but not necessarily the oldest son. His bride is supposed to move into the household, assume his family name and abide by the rules of his household. However, in case of the absence of a male descendant, the succession of the family can be ceded to a younger son, an adopted son or a daughter. The daughter can maintain the family line by marrying a *mukoyooshi*, an adopted son-in-law. He enters the household of his wife, takes up her family name, and follows the rules of her household. When a child is born from such a union, s/he will adopt the family name of his/her mother's household.

From the functional perspective, the *ie* refers to the household as a corporate body of co-residents, each contributing to the welfare of the stem family. Traditionally, most households in the village function as 'corporate productive units' (Kim 1986: 186), supervised by the household heads. Surely, the genealogical and functional aspects of the *ie* do not differ entirely, it is nonetheless important to point to the preponderance of professional and economic ties in the functional domain and that of blood and descent in the genealogical sphere. When two or more *ie*-units are organized into a kin group, it is called *shinseki* or *shinrui*. Some *shinseki* households are formed into very closely organized groups, a *doozoku*. A *doozoku* emerges when the non-succeeding son, after marriage, leaves the *honke*, the main house of the *ie*, and establishes a *bunke*, a branch family of the main house. If the *honke* has several sons, a series of satellite *bunke* will appear when the younger sons reach adulthood and marry. It is quite obvious that in this scenario, ties among *honke* and the different *bunke* are intertwined.

In sum, the *doozoku* structure is characterized by a group of the main line and collateral households with consanguineous males. In contrast to other full-fledged blood-related male lineage systems such as in the Chinese case, the Japanese lineage system is more a symbolic simulation of the above-described structure. Thus, it allows minor deviations from the ideal-blood-related structure. In analogy to the main house, a *bunke* may be established by the husband of the sister or the daughter of the *honke*'s head. Evidently, in the former case the new head of the *bunke* has to assume the surname of his wife. A *bunke* can also be set up by a non-kin member such as a loyal servant or protégé, who has a record of merits towards the household. Similar to the *ie* metaphor in modern Japan is that of the traditional village community (*mura*). The 'natural village' (Yanagita 1971 in Yoshino 1992: 95) does not indicate the administrative villages under the Meiji period. Instead it denotes the indigenous village consisting of twenty to fifty households as constituent units, enjoying a high degree of autonomy under the Tokugawa period. Given the self-rule, communal solidarity among village members was indispensable for collective survival. The social organization of the village was religiously regulated by *Shintoo* or folk beliefs based on animism, the fusion between the gods and people and ancestor worship. *Matsuri* or festivals were organized to reinforce the bond among the village members. At the economic level, the natural village was based on a self-sufficient economy, in which the results of labor were visible and transparent. The social order is characterized by obedience and docility on the part of the weaker and poorer village members. Given the inequality of family income, the social order was so regulated that the wealthier families would assist poorer families in cases of famine and other forms of calamities. In this social order, docility on the part of the weaker members was the surest guarantee for protection by the stronger and richer members of the village.

Familism within the *ie* household, as explained above, is based mostly on blood ties. Concurrently, there existed also a quasi-parent-child relationship, the *oyabun-kobun* relationship. Most villagers had besides their natural parents, several quasi-parents as protectors. An example of this quasi-parent-child relationship is the relationship between *nedo-oya* (*oya*: parent) and *nedo-ko* (*ko*: child). Young villagers assembled at a lodging place (*nedo*) after a day's work, thus experiencing communal life. The *nedo-oya*, the symbolic father offered guidance and protection to the *nedo-ko*, the ritual son, who in return for the received protection and patronage pledged unconditional loyalty. The former made sure that the latter would gradually grow up to be a full-fledged member of the village. This fatherly attitude of the *nedo-oya* epitomized in the role of the *nakoodo-oya* (a go-between) before and at the *nedo-ko* wedding, although this quasi-parental relationship will be maintained for life. Although no explicit ideology such as the family state or the familistic company has been formulated in relation to the traditional village, the village ethos underlies most *Nihonbunkaron* works. The uniqueness of the Japanese, another prominent theme of *Nihonbunkaron*, represents the boundary approach of *Nihonbunkaron* apart from the above-described primordialist view of common ancestry and shared cultural traits. It is almost superfluous to note that uniqueness is related to particularism. For the most part of history until very recently, Japan was thought to be located at the periphery of the world, far away from the 'center.' In first instance it was China, which assumed the role of the central florescence followed by the West. In other words, this asymmetrical relationship between the 'other' at the center and Japan at the margins has lasted for a long time. It has had a profound impact on the identity of Japan. Yoshino (1992: 12) explains the sense of uniqueness as follows.

> For the Japanese, learning from China and the West has been experienced as acquiring the 'universal' civilization...The *Nihonjinron* or discussions of Japanese uniqueness are, therefore, discussions of 'particularistic' cultural differences of Japan from the 'universal' civilization.

Dale (1988: 39) claims that 'as the anti-image of foreignness, Japanese identity can only be affirmed by stipulating a systematic, if Borghesian, taxonomy of the Other (China, the West).'

Contents

The thesis of Japan's cultural uniqueness has been applied in most disciplines. The main areas include ecology, Japanese language and communication, the social structure and the Japanese personality. Watsuji's well-known work, *Fuudo*, although published in 1935, has had a profound and lasting influence on later *Nihonbunkaron* works. The most important part of his argument was the climactic influence on Japanese society and culture. In his theory Japan's wet-rice cultivation, the conformist social organization, the animistic orientation of Japanese religion and other cultural phenomena could be explained by Japan's specific climate, characterized by the warm and wet winds in the South and the cold wind originating from Siberia over the Sea of Japan towards Japan. As the wet-rice cultivation needed cooperation in sustaining irrigation systems, in rice transplanting and in harvesting, a close-knit social unit was needed for a proper functioning of the society. This is to say that wet-rice cultivation requires cooperation of all members of the community. The wet-rice cultivation economy has been often contrasted with pastoral economy (Ishida 1969 in Befu 1993: 110) in the West. According to his reasoning, Japan's agrarian society favors group orientation rather than individualism as in the West. The Japanese language occupies a very special place in *Nihonbunkaron*. As Miller (1982: 4) puts it, in a rather ironical way though,

> For most modern Japanese, and indeed for modern Japanese society and culture in general, the Japanese language is not simply a language. It is not merely a social convention, something that the society and the culture can use and forget about. Above all, the Japanese language in modern Japan is never regarded as a set of social conventions arbitrarily agreed upon. For modern Japan, the Japanese language is a way of life, and the enormous amount of speculation, writing, and talking about it that goes on at every level of Japanese

life constitutes an entirely distinctive and marvelously self-contained way of looking at life.

Considering that the sense of uniqueness is acutely felt in interaction with outsiders, it should not come as a surprise that the linguistic and communicative modes have been singled out as the key source areas of uniqueness by *Nihonbunkaron* authors. The uniqueness of the Japanese language has been set forth and demonstrated in many ways. The specificity of the Japanese language is reflected in the usage of linguistic particles *wa, ga, no* (Oide 1965: 135–201), the honorific speech, revealing the social status of the speakers in direct speech (Yamashita 1979: 157–222), the impossibility to translate certain Japanese expressions (Toyama 1976), specific cultural terms such as *amae* (interdependence) (Doi 1980), the notion of *kotodama* or the 'soul' of a language, which renders the speaker in the object and the language the subject in the context of a conversation.

Related to the linguistic mode is that of communication. Not only is the structure of the language unique but also the way and the contexts in which it is used, in other words the communicative mode, are unique. In the *Nihonbunkaron* world, Japanese patterns of communication encompass properties such as taciturnity, ambivalence and other non-logical, situational and emotional characteristics in contrast to the Western way, which is eloquent, dichotomously clear, logical, universal and rational. One of the foremost advocates of the unique Japanese communication patterns is Kunihiro Masao (1976). To illustrate how the Japanese communication patterns works, it might be insightful to analyze the expression *haragei* ('the art of the abdomen'). In Japanese culture, the *hara* (the abdomen) contains one's courage, integrity and one's genuine sentiments. Therefore, only in-group members can communicate with each other as they speak not only the same language but they also know all the 'blank spots', which are not explicitly stated but nonetheless expressed. Therefore, an outsider, no matter how well s/he mastered the language, can never become an insider, as s/he does not understand the art of the *haragei.*

The social structure has also been selected as an area where this uniqueness manifests in an overt way. In the 'vertical society' (*tate shakai*) members of the in-group are organized according to their 'frame' (*ba*) rather than their 'attribute' (*shikaku*). Attribute refers to a specific feature of an individual whereas the frame signifies a situational position (Nakane 1973). In Japanese society, there is a tendency to emphasize the situational position in a particular frame rather than the personal attribute. In order to foster cohesion among the members of a particular group, a vertical structure is set up, regulating the personal and professional relations within an institution. An elaborate system of ranking is used to create the 'inferior/superior' positions. 'Inferiors' have the obligation to follow orders, issued by 'superiors', who in return protect and guide 'inferiors.'

Hamaguchi's concept of *kanjin* (1994, 1998) the contextual person, is introduced in order to represent the specificity of Japanese culture. Hamaguchi (1994: 1) advances the view that 'the real cultural character of the Japanese seems to be contextual or corporative, directly reflecting one's own intimate human nexus in a group.' Within the 'contextual' model, he introduces a new paradigm, which seems to suit the Japanese context better than Western dichotomous thinking. In the latter case, social interaction occurs among individuals as individual subjects or atoms. This human model is characterized by the dichotomy between the individual and the group as the analytical frame of reference. In the case of the 'contextual' human model, a person is a 'referential subject', who is essentially connected and conjunct with others. This is the 'common nexus space within each of one's personal area' (Hamaguchi 1994: 4). Consequently, interaction occurs internally in this nexus, the domain of the shared life context.

Japanese psychology has also been cherished as the locus of the uniqueness of the Japanese people. Doi (1980) introduces the linguistic concept of *amae*, which underlies the typically Japanese psyche. Departing from the Western psychoanalytical theoretical framework, characterized by the son-mother-father triangle, he underlines the Japanese psychological functioning in the hierarchical intimacy relationships. *amae* is usually translated by 'interdependence.'

In a similar vein, Okonogi (1978) discards the Oedipus complex in explaining the Japanese personality. Instead, he introduces the Ajase-complex, adopted from a Buddhist myth to define the Japanese self. Whereas in the former myth, the mother-father-son triangle occupies a central position, in the latter it is the mother-son dyad, which constitutes the core of the myth. Succinctly, the myth goes as follows. In the time of the Buddha, there lived a king Binbashara, whose wife, Idaike, feared the loss of her husband's love after old age had dimmed her radiance and destroyed her beauty. Therefore, in order to sustain her husband's affection, she decided to bear a son as soon as possible. A sage came to her and announced that a hermit living on a mountain would die within three years to be reborn as her son. The queen Idaike, however, became impatient and instead of awaiting the natural death of the hermit, she gave orders to kill him. Shortly after, she gave birth to a boy, Ajase. Ajase grew up happily. One day, he was told the secret of his birth. At first he reacted against his father as he saw him as the main culprit and had him imprisoned. However, when he found out that his mother was secretly feeding his imprisoned father, he directed his anger towards his mother by attempting to kill her. However, he was dissuaded from slaying his mother. He

then became inflicted with a terrible skin disease, characterized by a repulsive odor. No one except his mother wanted to
approach him. She nursed him back to health and reconcilia-
tion between the two was the result. In this myth, the son
rages over sentiments of loss of his symbiotic tie with the
mother but later repents after realizing the immense sacrifices his mother was willing to put up for his sake.

Critiques and assessment of Nihonbunkaron

Given the wide-reaching scope of *Nihonbunkaron* publications it should not come as a surprise that the various works
of this genre cannot be simply dismissed as inferior publications. Inferior because the quality is to say the least academi-
cally poor and to put it more bluntly grossly incorrect and
rigged in many aspects. Of course, one should in the first
place be concerned with the veracity or the lack thereof in
published works, especially when they are displayed as accounts of cultural nationalism, reaching a large readership.

Therefore, most critiques (Miller 1982; Dale 1988; Mouer
and Sugimoto 1990) reflect the efforts of academics and
scholars to remain on guard for hidden agendas in publications promoting ethnonational identity. They have pointed to
the most obvious flaws in these publications, namely to use
writing as a means to propagate a certain point of view,
namely the dominant ideology of the ruling class, subscribing to the ideas of Japanese homogeneity and uniqueness.

The sharp critique of Miller (1982) on the myth of *Nihongo*
(Japanese language) is not fixated on the existence of the
myth itself. He admits that in all societies, people need
myths to survive and transcend beyond the daily nitty-gritty.
Miller defines (1982: 7) myths as 'the only fixed elements in
a spiritual and intellectual landscape otherwise filled with
shifting, transitory, and thoroughly undependable elements.'

The activity of myth making is not a purely Japanese phenomenon but a universal one. Yet the difference of the Japanese myth of homogeneity lies in the ubiquitous and persistent nature. This myth-creating exercise of a strong national and exclusive identity, is not only affecting the Japanese life but dictates to a high degree the dealings of Japan and Japanese people with the outside world. The attribution of a 'soul' to the language, the so-called *kotodama,* through which the speaker has become a mere instrument, is a prime example of the *Nihonbunkaron* genre.

In similar ways, Dale (1988) attempts to demystify Japanese uniqueness through the clarification and logical analysis of some blatantly inaccurate assumptions underlying *Nihonbunkaron* publications. These assumptions include racial, linguistic, sociological, philosophical and psychological premises of the Japanese culture and Japanese people. He advises cultural anthropologists to be on guard since native voices are not by definition 'authentic' in the sense of unquestionably true. Dale (1988: 7) alerts us that they too can be influenced by certain *idées fixes,* or ideologies based on shaky and perhaps outright incorrect and false grounds.

> In complex societies like Japan, the 'indigenous' version of how that world is perceived is often deeply coloured by ideological interests. In such cultures, there are no longer 'native informants', but only other interpreters who are subject to the same tendentiousness that inflicts all thought. The outsider, who confuses such interpretations with authentic, 'raw' information, may, far from transcending, merely subject it to the programme of an exotic nationalism. Applied in this way, cultural relativism connives at the importation of value judgments all the more subversive of reality because camouflaged as empirical views. The visible, familiar assumptions of the Western intellectual tradition are replaced by the submerged, ill-recognised and fugitive presuppositions (often substantially analogous in kind) of an ostensibly alien *Weltanschauung.*

One of the most severe and comprehensive critiques on

Nihonbunkaron is undoubtedly Mouer and Sugimoto's volume *Images of Japanese Society*, containing an impressive listing of major works on the study of Japanese society. This compilation categorizes all publications on Japan into two schools: 'the great tradition' or the harmony and homogeneity school and 'the small tradition' or the conflict model. The great tradition model one-sidedly propagates the holistic view of Japanese society for a variety of reasons and consequently obfuscates other aspects like conflict in Japanese society. Besides the many critiques on *Nihonbunkaron*, assessments also emerged with regard to the reasons why this genre has been so appealing to the Japanese; why the demand for these works seems to be infinite; for what purposes they were produced, either intentionally or unintentionally. In other words, instead of assessing the veracity of what is said, one attempts to unravel the underlying rationale for the production as well as the consumption of *Nihonbunkaron* works.

First, the *Nihonbunkaron* genre is more a normative than a descriptive model. Although the works are presented as descriptions of the unique features of Japanese culture and Japanese people, they include all the ingredients of a prescriptive model. If Doi redefines Japanese personality through the introduction of the *amae* concept, he presents this as an empirical finding. When this piece of information becomes a public good and an integral part in the discourse of *Nihonbunkaron*, not before long it assumes an existence on its own. The empirical fact becomes a norm. This is to say that hitherto all Japanese palpably experience the *amae* sentiment. Those, who potentially oppose the notion of *amae*, will be regarded as non-Japanese or at least someone who is not acting and thinking in the Japanese way. Deviations from the norm, in other words, transform one into a marginal, a stranger, a non-Japanese. Thus, non-conformity to this norm leads to marginality and exclusion from the core group. What started out as the factual rendering of Japanese properties turns out to be a prescriptive model. The descriptive/prescriptive cycle works effectively. When Japanese are told that *amae* is a Japanese-specific property by experts, they confirm that indeed they feel as such, after which the Japan-specific *amae* is confirmed as a veritable and particular characteristic of the Japanese.

Often the *Nihonbunkaron* genre is linked with nationalism or at least a 'specimen of nationalism' (Befu 1993: 125). It goes without saying that nationalism is a broad and often-used concept, adorned with vague and blurred meanings. Gellner (1993) contends that the need for homogenization of a shared national culture becomes a necessity in the industrialization process. Anderson (1991) as mentioned earlier regards print capitalism as the binding factor of the different members and groups within the nation state, who through reading publications in the same language develop a sense of 'togetherness.' Hobsbawm (1990) situates nationalism at the economic and socio-political level.

Verdery (1994: 43–4) includes ethnicity and ethnonational feelings in the concept of nationalism. 'As a great deal of current social science literature makes clear...understanding ethnicity at the interface of politics, culture and the state seems to require investigations of this enlarged scope.' Nationalism has been divided by Robinson (in Befu 1993: 107–8) in three major areas of concern:

> The first focuses on sentiment, such as the intense identification of the patriot with the nation-state...The second focuses on 'political and social development'...The third addresses 'an ideology that serves to celebrate and emphasize the nation as the preeminent collective identity of a people.'

Moreover, some (Befu 1993) introduce the notion of active versus passive nationalism depending on the intensity of the nationalist manifestation. The former refers to actions such as the

100

willingness to fight for the own country against an enemy, whereas the latter concerns more muted forms of nationalist manifestations such as an inherent pride in the own culture. The difference in degree of emotional content does not mean that one form is superior to another form but rather that they are complementary. Active nationalism only works when passive nationalism is in place. After all, mobilization of the people for nationalist purposes needs to be preceded by a strong nationalist pride. *Nihonbunkaron* has everything to do with sentiments, strong affiliation and pride in the own culture and nation state. In this regard it can be interpreted as a passive form of nationalism. Similarly, as Yoshino (1992: 225) argues,

> 'Nationalism' refers broadly to the sentiment among a people that they comprise a community with distinctive characteristics and the will to maintain and enhance that distinctiveness within an autonomous state.

His definition implies the feelings of both 'distinctiveness' *vis-à-vis* the out-group members and a sense of 'togetherness' among the in-group members. For obvious reasons nationalism belongs to the more controversial issues in postwar Japan as it has witnessed the excesses of ultra-nationalism in the prewar and the war period. Nonetheless, half a century after the defeat, it is presently argued that some forms of nationalism would be welcomed, a so-called 'wholesome' (*kenzen na*) or 'prudent' nationalism. According to Yoshino (1992), 'wholesome' nationalism consists of two types, notably 'resurgent cultural nationalism' and 'prudent revivalist nationalism.' Resurgent cultural nationalism constitutes the core theme underlying the bulk of the *Nihonbunkaron* publications. 'Cultural nationalism' or the notion of the positive distinctiveness of Japanese culture and people was particularly strong in the late 1960s, the 1970s and the first part of the 1980s. This type of nationalism revolves around the rediscovery, reformulation and the reaffirmation of

Japanese uniqueness. It is situated in the spatial dimension of the 'us-them' boundary. 'Prudent revivalist nationalism', however, draws upon the 'old' prewar nationalism of the emperor system and the concomitant symbols and rituals. Yet, it is a *prudent* kind of revivalist nationalism as only the positive values of some of the symbols and practices would be revived, adapted and updated. It tends to look at the horizontal dimension of primordialism, effecting a sense of solidarity among the members.

Yoshino maintains a differentiation between the two types of nationalism, even while at first sight many common elements can be detected. His findings indicate a fragmented nationalism among the Japanese. For example, younger businessmen are more concerned with the distinctive identity of the Japanese or cultural nationalism. Yet educators of an advanced age tend to value prudent revivalist nationalism. Perhaps prudent revivalist nationalism supports discipline and respect for the elderly in a more pronounced way than in cultural nationalism. The linkage view, subscribing to the merge between the two types of nationalism, is according to Yoshino a too simplistic solution. Yet how justifiable the distinction may be, the difference between cultural nationalism, catering to national identity building and shaping, and prudent revivalist nationalism, soothing the solidarity sentiments of the people, in reality a complete separation of the two types cannot be sustained.

Clearly in *Nihonbunkaron* publications, revivalism of old values is never far or implicit. Although the rituals of old nationalism are not advocated or encouraged explicitly, it is manifest that the underlying framework of *Nihonbunkaron* consists of a holistic view of the Japanese as a *Gemeinschaft*, a pre-industrial form of community. Such a community is characterized by familial ties, of which the emperor system (*tennoosei*) constitutes the ultimate form, and by the *mura* metaphor.

At present the heated debate on the uniqueness of the Japanese has made place for other issues facing Japanese society. To start with, criticizing Japan has turned into another genre, the so-called 'Japan bashing' (*Nihonhihan*) practice referring to publications by James Fallows, Karel van Wolferen and others. It is not within the scope of this book to go into details about this debate. Suffice to say that they have reacted against the extreme views of *Nihonbunkaron* with equal extremity. Furthermore, the multidirectional and incessant movements of commodities and people in Japanese society brought about the change of discourse in Japanese society. In the discourse of 'internationalization', attention has been directed towards the outward movement of Japanese expatriates and their children, the overseas returnee youngsters. Some claim that underlying the rhetoric of internationalization nationalist tendencies can be detected because this 'internationalization talk' heightens the national sentiments and the self-pride in the own achievement and future perspectives. In this respect it is first important to refer to those (Befu 1983), who discern the link between internationalization as a social phenomenon and as a topic of discourse and the 'consciousness of Japan's positive distinctiveness' (*koteiteki tokushu no ninshiki*). The more the Japanese travel and migrate for shorter and longer periods of time, the more the Japanese become aware of their differentness.

Others want to distinguish 'internationalization' from 'globalization', a term gaining more and more influence in intellectual and popular circles. Globalization covers, among other elements, also the increased contact and interaction between two or more different ethnic groups both in depth as in frequency. More specifically certain changes have taken place in Japanese society such as the emergence of foreign workers in Japanese society in the mid-1980s. Due to the difference in economic power and inequality of wealth between Japan and the surrounding Asian countries and the shortage of labor in the Japanese market during the 1980s, migration towards Japan has become a reality. Therefore, the outward movement of the Japanese is discussed first as it lies at the basis of the internationalization process. In chapter 5 a differentiation is made between 'internationalization' and 'globalization.' In the process of globalization, the picture has become more complicated, particularly against the nation state paradigm: instead of Japanese going overseas on a temporary basis, (im) migrants emerged as semi-skilled workers. Of course, the phenomenon of foreign workers in Japan is not a new one. In fact, Japan had already imported foreign workers from the Korean Peninsula as forced workers before World War II. In the 1960s and the 1970s there was already a flow of foreign trainees, followed by females in the entertainment and sex industry. After 1985 foreign male workers became increasingly visible in the construction and manufacture industry of Japan. Yet what is unprecedented is that this new development has captured the attention of the government, the press, the academic world and other opinion makers. Consequently, it has become part of the public debate in Japanese society.

5   Internationalization: the Outward Migratory Movement of the Japanese

General

The discourse of 'internationalization' (*kokusaika*) emerged from the late 1970s onwards and pervaded all realms of society including the spoken and written mass media and academic circles (Mannari and Befu 1983; Kurimoto 1985; Goodman 1990a). Japan has attained a similar if not a more advanced level in terms of economic, social, educational and cultural development.

Throughout the 1970s, Japan maintained higher growth rates than most developed countries. In 1987 Japan found itself achieving the second highest GNP in the Western industrialized world (Statistics Bureau Management and Coordination Agency 1989). In accordance, the number of Japanese 'prolonged-stay' or 'long-term residents' (*chookitaizaisha*), who are in fact Japanese expatriates, increased drastically. As shown in the table below, the grand total of overseas Japanese quadrupled in two decades, notably from 84,050 in 1971 to 340,929 in 1990 (Foreign Ministry in Sato and Nakanishi 1991:14).

Table 1. Development of the Number of 'Long-Term' Japanese Expatriates in the World. Period 1971–90

Year	Number of 'Long-Term' Japanese Expatriates		
1971	84,050	1981	204,731
1972	92,387	1982	204,731
1973	108,488	1983	215,799
1974	124,754	1984	228,914
1975	137,506	1985	237,488
1976	150,068	1986	251,545
1977	160,511	1987	270,391
1978	178,605	1988	302,510
1979	181,008	1989	340,929
1980	193,820	1990	374,044

Source: Ministry of Foreign Affairs (*Gaimusho*) in Sato and Nakanishi (1991) for the period 1971–89 and Japan Overseas Educational Services (*Kaigaishijo Kyooiku Shinkoo Zaidan*) for the year 1990.

Therefore, Japan could no longer embrace the postwar national preoccupation of 'catching up with the West' or 'modernization' (*kindaika*). It becomes apparent that the internal cultural debate of modernization (*kindaika*) has become outdated and not representative of the actual position of Japan in the world community. As a result it needed to be replaced by the new paradigm of internationalization (*kokusaika*). Although the term 'internationalization' is widely quoted and often discussed, an all-inclusive conceptualization of the phenomenon is lacking and its meaning and impact on the Japanese people themselves remain rather vague and blurred.

The Discourse of *Kokusaika* (Internationalization)

The eruption of publications on the phenomenon of internationalization and the omnipresence of this internal cultural debate have made it more difficult to assess the scope and impact of the new international era in Japanese society. In analyzing the phenomenon of internationalization, Passin (1983) discerns numerous paradigms underlying the different concepts of internationalization. In the modernization paradigm the basis idea is derived from the tradition-to-modernization continuum. It is argued that non-Western people evolve from traditional communities to modern industrial nations. In this evolutionary framework, internationalization is thus the logical outcome of the expansion beyond the own national borders or transnationalism. A more narrowly conceived version of modernization is that of Westernization. Since the Meiji period (1868–1912) and some even go as far back as the Tokugawa-period (1600–1868), Japan has embarked on the road of modernization of bridging the gap with the Western nations of that time in terms of technology and economic progress. Iyotani (1995: 2) explains the link between internationalization and nationalism thus.

> First is the phase of modern state formation – a time when the national language, traditions, customs, and other cultural elements, and the norms and rules deemed desirable for modern society are established. Second is the phase of expansion of the nation state, which served as the foundation of industrialization...The homogeneous space of the nation state is transformed to include a space that stretches beyond national boundaries...As outward expansion proceeds, the culture of the nation is transformed into one that extends far beyond the national space.

Befu (1983) alerts us about the interwoven relationship between the so-called new era of 'internationalization' and a growing sense of nationalism. The increasing number of 'Japanese in the world' (*sekai no naka no Nihonjin*) or 'international (Japanese) people' (*kokusaijin*) introduced a new element in the cultural discourse of Japan, namely a reinforcement of the consciousness of Japanese culture and iden-

tity. His thesis reveals the paradoxical effect of internationalization, enhancing sentiments of nationalism rather than
obliterating them. He contests the globalist dimension of the
Japanese internationalization process. He argues contrary to
common beliefs that 'internationalization' (*kokusaika*) is in
fact a mere extension of nationalism (*kokusuika*). Indeed, in
the discourse on internationalization, the theme of economic
interest occupies a dominant position. In this perspective, a
'tough-minded internationalist' (*shitakana kokusaijin*)
(Yamamoto 1981 in Befu 1983: 251) refers to a Japanese,
who can deal with aggressive Western negotiators on an
equal basis. In the Japanese context, internationalization and
nationalism are not mutually exclusive concepts in spite of
the connotation of globalism and cosmopolitanism. On the
contrary, internationalization in Japan, as he reminds us,
should be placed against the background of a worldview
consisting of nations, national boundaries, and national interests (Umesao 1975 in Befu 1983). Befu (1983: 262) clarifies his stance in the following way.

> Yet, as we have seen, results have been the opposite. Instead of free-
> ing Japanese from local attachment (to Japan) and prejudices against
> foreigners at home and in foreign countries, it seems to renew their
> attachment to their fatherland and even awaken their prejudices
> against locals or foreigners (such as Southeast Asians) to whom their
> leading sense of prejudice in the past was at best merely dormant. In-
> stead of leading directly by the surest and shortest road to the cosmo-
> politan world, internationalization process is a U-turn, returning to
> renewed nationalism.

In a similar vein, Kurimoto (1985), an international diplomat,
distinguishes in the interpretation of internationalization between the official (*kan; oyake*) and the people's (*min*) or the private (*shi*) point of view. The official stance is situated in the
framework characterized by two distinctive properties: the 'inside the country' part (*kokunai*) and the 'outside the country'

part (*kokugai*). In order to illustrate his point, he uses the metaphor of the 'boiled egg shaped view of nations' (*yudetamagokei kokkakan*), in which the egg yolk represents Japan, the 'inside the country' element and the egg white the outside world, the 'outside the country' element. In this view, internationalization means a thorough understanding of the 'outside world' while solidly and unambiguously maintaining the own culture and identity.

Saito (in Kurimoto 1985: 12) refers to an international person as 'someone who interacts (with foreigners) in a natural way but he does not forget (the fact that) he is Japanese.' Similarly, Yamamuro (in Kurimoto 1985: 12) thinks that 'there are no internationals without an unclear nationality.'

Or according to Yamazaki (in Kurimoto 1985: 12-13) s/he is someone who,

Grasps the difference in thinking between a Japanese and a foreigner and assesses both the congruencies and discrepancies of opinion based on the understanding of the stance of each other and therefore able to decide on how to solve (the discrepancies) through consultation.

Miyachi (1990), defining the discourse of internationalization in Japanese society as a 'boisterous dance' (*ronbu*), also reminds us of the economic factor behind the discourse on internationalization. The foremost essence of internationalization does not rest on an ideal, a humanitarian act or 'virtue' (*zen*) but rather on the existence, the development and prosperity of Japan, 'a business-oriented nation' (*bijinesu orienteddo na kuni*). The general notion of internationalization among the Japanese is a 'Japan, turning outward in multiple ways' (*soto ni muku koto no ooku naru Nihon*).

None of the above-presented definitions seems to inculcate the mutual enriching experience of cultural exchange. The overseas experience and the contact with non-Japanese people are based on instrumental grounds rather than on genuine mutual learning process. Of course, there is nothing intrinsic or uniquely Japanese in this practice of minimizing conflict and contact abroad. Most expatriates usually live in privileged enclaves. While seeking social contact and emotional warmth within the own group, their relationship to the people around them hardly impinges on their consciousness. Yet perhaps one can speculate that the degree and the uniformity of this aloofness towards the host society distinguish the Japanese from others. The many challenges facing a global and multicultural society are absent in the Japanese definition of internationalism. One of the most pressing issues facing traditional nation states is the emergence of foreign workers and other (im) migrants. A multicultural society both in the descriptive and normative terms challenges the nineteenth century notion of the nation state and the concomitant accoutrements like a singular national language, a homogeneous culture, a mono-ethnic society, etc.

Internationalization and Globalization

Passin (1983: 22–3) provides a more plural definition of internationalization and refers to it as an 'awareness of interdependence, the process of adjusting to the involvement that arises from it, and the conditions that facilitate or impede the capacity to engage in these interactions.' In the contemporary world, no culture can afford to seal itself completely off from the rest of the world. In this framework of interdependence, the Japanese display a seemingly paradoxical attitude. On the one hand, Japanese demonstrate a genuine eagerness, far more prominent than other people do, for learning about other cultures and a keen willingness of keeping themselves incessantly updated. Moreover, Japanese consumers have developed one of the most 'international' tastes. There is a pronounced interest for foreign goods, especially the luxurious and the prestigious ones. According to Passin (1983: 15), the Japanese are deeply entrenched in the consumption of international goods.

> The Japanese tourist has almost replaced the American tourist of an earlier day as the symbol of the rich materialistic provincials. A great deal of attention is given to foreign languages: English is a required subject in junior high school and university.

Yet at the behavioral level in terms of tangible contact and exchange, the Japanese seem to lag behind. The particular case of Belgium is discussed in a later chapter. Suffice to mention here is that Japanese tend to confine their professional and private life to a particular neighborhood. Moreover, it is noteworthy that most of the knowledge and experiences about the outside world have been filtered through a Japanese lens. Information has been translated, transformed and thus 'processed' in order to fit the Japanese language and culture. Group travels are organized by Japanese tour operators. Individual travelers leave home armed with Japanese-language guidebooks. Most Japanese learn foreign languages in Japan, etc. The paradox can be clarified by the fact that economic activities are situated in the international network, a space transcending the nation state boundaries, while politics and culture operate within the realm of the nation state. As profusely discussed in the chapter on globalization and culture in contemporary complex societies like Japan, it is no longer possible to see nation states as unique entities exclusive from others through safely guarded national borders. Instead, the movements of commodities, information and people mark the new era of globalization. In contrast to internationalization, this process cuts deep into the structures of nation states and generates irreversible changes in society. The exchange and communication between people and commodities and between people and people are multiple. According to Iyotani (1995: 2) globalization destabilizes nationalism. 'Third is the phase when globalization begins to rock the nation, shaking the foundations of its culture. At that point the homogeneity of the nation state and its national culture is revealed to be an illusion.' Concerning genuine exchange and in-depth interaction, Kurimoto's 'private' (*shi*) or 'people's' (*min*) interpretation of internationalization is embedded in the framework of the current globalization process. To explore further his boiled egg metaphor, Japan again constitutes the yolk amidst international societies, situated in the egg white part. Kurimoto's (1985: 15) reformulation of the internationalization concept stresses concrete and tangible contribution of the Japanese to host societies.

> The very image of the existence of Japan depends for instance on the contribution of Japanese with excellent skills to countries all over the world, where they (the Japanese) are scattered around and working (diligently), dripping with sweat and stained with oil.

He seems to suggest that internationalization so far has been dictated by the exigencies of the internationalization of production processes. The people involved in this particular migration process see the overseas sojourn as a temporary phenomenon and therefore invest a minimal amount of time and energy in host societies. This contact-avoidance leads to inter-national rather than globalizing tendencies. The former is represented by insularity, encapsulation and in-group solidarity abroad, whereas the latter includes contact, interaction, communication and even conflict. He suggests a more meaningful form of internationalization, in which Japanese immerse themselves in the host society through fruitful work, genuine social contact and mutual understanding. His view of internationalization, generated by 'Japanese from all over the world working in all sectors while dripping with sweat' (*sekai no kakuchi de aseshite hataraku Nihonjin*) seems to be inspired by the idea of globalization. In most studies dealing with internationalization, major attention has been given to the outward Japanese (mostly circulatory) migratory movements to the neglect of the 'internationalization towards Japan.' The increasing number of labor migrants in Japan is hardly noticed or mentioned in the discussion on the increasing international trend of Japanese society. Though part of the same process, the emergence of non-Japanese in society and in the labor market has simply been omitted in the discussion on internationalization, except for some. Only recently an increasing number of authors touched upon the issue of the emergence of foreign laborers in Japanese society. For example Miyachi (1990), apart from stressing the 'business-orientation' of Japanese society, also mentions the relative recent influx of foreigners including both legal and illegal labor migrants, foreign professionals and the existing minorities and foreign groups in Japanese society. Ideally a multi-ethnic environment provides fertile ground for the 'internationalization of people' (*hito no kokusaika*). This is a process in which people through continuous interaction and exchange with the other develop a more global identity. In his view, this phenomenon is at the current moment virtually non-existing in Japanese society. In contrast to the still general practice of approaching foreigners as the ultimate other, who needs to adapt him or herself completely to the mainstream Japanese culture in a one-directional mode, the concept of 'the internationalization of people' or called differently globalization process, supports mutual and even multi-directional borrowing and understanding. These exchange processes will therefore make the *modus vivendi* in complex contemporary societies possible and in the most ideal circumstances fruitful and meaningful. Despite intense and overheated discussion of the internationalization phenomenon (*kokusaika*) in Japan, Miyachi seems rather pessimistic about the globalization process in Japanese society.

In a similar way Nakajima (1988) reminds us of the blind spot in the debate of international understanding. She underlines that internationalization process is not only represented by the Japanese leaving for other countries but also by the foreign people in Japanese society. This diverse group of foreigners includes the North and South Koreans, refugees, permanent residents from China, the *Nikkeijin* and others. She contends that the discourse mainly focuses on the outward migratory movement of Japanese towards all parts of the world. The main actors in this movement include the 'long-term' expatriates, their dependents, tourists, students and scholars, etc. Yet in analyzing the etymology of the word, it consists of both an outward and an inward movement of members belonging to different nations.

Finally Iyotani (1995: 4–5) singles out two major challenges facing Japanese society, namely the notion of culture of flow and the issue of multiculturalism.

> What does it mean to talk about the globalization of Japan's economy and the flow of culture? Many of us think of culture as something that endures changelessly, rooted deep in people's lives, immune to the vagaries of shifting ages. We see it as an undercurrent impervious to the flow of history, something closely tied to tradition...Even though the forms of such institution remain the same, however, their meaning changes with the passing of time from one era onto another. Manners and customs that allegedly have been passed down for hundreds of years hold a different meaning in each historical period... My second point concerns the coexistence of cultures, or multiculturalism, a theme that has attracted increasing attention as the pre-eminent force of Western culture fades. In Japan, it is the ever-increasing numbers of foreign workers here that have prompted serious thought about living together with non-Japanese

and cultural coexistence. Multiculturalism and pluralism are frequent themes in international conferences and exchange programs. Yet discussions about the coexistence and symbiosis of cultures often are tinged with the tacit conviction that the differences between cultures make mutual understanding between them impossible. Accordingly, arguments supporting 'respect for other cultures' may help avoid cross-cultural friction, but they also risk premature closure of any possibility of mutual understanding. In effect, arguments for cultural coexistence and those for cultural exclusion often boil down to the same thing.

Assessment of the Discourse on 'Internationalization/Globalization'

In analyzing the previous descriptions of the international person and the process of internationalization, one can safely assume that the foundation of the Japanese culture and identity in international exchanges remains solid and the identity boundaries clear-cut and well-defined. What is new in the 'international' person is his/her ability to move into the world as a self-confident Japanese without inferior feelings, who does not feel uneasy in the company of foreigners. In short, s/he is someone 'who acts in a natural way' in an international environment. The nationality concept in Japan clearly appears to constitute an essential and unalienable part of being Japanese. The generally accepted notion in Japan is that the nation equals the Japanese culture, which equals the Japanese language and which finally equals the Japanese people. Therefore, any form of ambiguity in the nationality issue is undesirable in the Japanese context. The modernization/Westernization paradigm is problematic because of its Eurocentric connotations. The framework implies exclusively the unilateral direction of non-Western cultures attempting to modernize, in the sense of changing along the model of Western development and therefore becoming like the West in terms of systems and modes of production. This model does not allow for mutual influencing. An example of a two-way interaction between the 'West' and non-Western countries is the 'Learn from Japan' boom in the West (meaning Europe and the United States) during the 1980s. Examples are mostly situated in the specific nature of Japanese management styles.

To recuperate the internationalization process is above all the direct result of the Japanese national project of modernization. The movement of the Japanese throughout the world is in first instance guided by the interests of the Japanese nation and (economic) concerns of business and industry. In addition, the internationalization concept is interpreted in realistic terms. As disagreement dominates in the international discourse and indeed inflammable issues need to be neutralized from times to times, the international person is supposed to act as an efficient but friendly problem-solver, a seasoned diplomat without getting involved at the personal level. As Japanese businesses expand beyond Japanese boundaries, it is necessary that Japanese businessmen and diplomats adapt themselves in the international community by learning how to deal with foreigners and in particular how to conduct negotiations with Westerners on equal terms. The entire discussion of the internationalization applies to the Japanese circulatory migrants and not the incoming foreigners to Japanese society.

To assess the impact and the development of the discourse on internationalization, a link should be made between the internationalization debate and the quest for a Japanese identity in the genre of *Nihonbunkaron*. Of particular interest is the third stage of the consciousness of Japan's 'positive distinctiveness' in Aoki's theory. In the two decades of the 1960s and the 1970s, Japan has transformed itself in a major economic power (*keizaitaikoku*). Concomitant with the economic success, Japan as a nation was in search of a 'self-consciousness' (*jikoninshiki*) or a self-identity.

Aoki (1990: 83, own translation) argues that 'as the number of the Japanese working overseas increased, the demand for a *Nihonbunkaron* genre became a necessity (*hitsuyoobutsu*) in the international community.' He underlines the necessity to formulate a strong Japanese identity serving as 'moral support' (*kokoro no sasae*) to Japanese working overseas. He indicates that the growing economic power of Japan and the concomitant internationalization of Japanese business and the expanding group of Japanese expatriates have reinforced the creation of a well-defined and bounded Japanese identity, characterized by groupism (*shuudanshugi*), the culture of shame (*haji no bunka*), etc. His view seems to correspond with the discourse on internationalization.

This argument supports the view of Befu (1983) that internationalism is a parallel phenomenon in time and in content with the period of Japan's consciousness of 'positive distinctiveness.' Similarly Kurimoto (1985) detects in the official version of internationalization many properties of nationalism. This version is based on the dichotomous worldview, consisting of two mutually excluding parts, Japan and the outside world. Briefly, the process of 'internationalization' is in fact the complementary part of the discourse of Japanese self-identity. Given the link between internationalization and nationalism, the international experiences of Japanese returnee youngsters certainly require rethinking and reformulating. Elsewhere I have already called the internationalization process of the returnee youngsters controlled instead of full-fledged (Pang 1995). 'Controlled' because it is part of an internal cultural debate on the specificity of Japanese culture and society. This ethnonational identity is reinvented, refined and managed by certain empowered groups in society including the academics, the press and the government. Given the fixity idea of Japanese ethnonational identity, returnee youngsters, who have lived extensively outside Japan, need to be 'readapted' upon return in Japanese society through special educational provisions.

In order not to fall unwittingly into the trappings of Japan-bashing, I hasten to add that in no culture, this globalization process has been attained. Therefore, it is not a uniquely Japanese problem of dealing with the new exigencies of the times of cultural flow and globalization. Recently a new phenomenon, unseen and unprecedented, has taken place in Japanese society, namely the emergence of migrant workers in a self-proclaimed mono-ethnic society. Critical voices, quite rightly, would reject the previous point because of the presence of ethnic and indigenous minorities in Japanese society predating the recent development. Yet these oldcomers have been forced to assimilate, while their presence has always been silenced. Even in the current debate on migrant workers, all attention and potential public policies are geared towards the newcomers and not the oldcomers. Following this new phenomenon, the globalization aspect of internationalization has become more salient. Iyotani informs us that Japanese society, and especially since the 1990s becomes increasingly aware of the ongoing globalization process. The process is mainly manifested through the presence of migrant workers in Japanese society.

6   Migrant Workers in Japan

General

The issue of foreign workers, the leading actors in international migratory movements, is part of the (post) modern reality of the global mobility, and poses major pressures and challenges to host societies in terms of public policy and the general *modus vivendi* in society. The import of semi-skilled labor does not only concern the recruiting of labor force in a robotic sense. On the contrary, the process implies human beings with a specific culture, ethnicity and religion, and often accompanied by wife and children. All these actors seek a way to live and survive in the host society through negotiating new identities and fostering new bonds and relationships. Most Western countries are confronted with these issues when foreign workers start to settle. Japan has long claimed to be a mono-ethnic nation and thus free from the (post) modern challenges of ethnic minorities. For a long time, the existence of ethnic minorities such as the *Zainichi* Koreans and Chinese, the *burakumin* and indigenous people like the *Ainu* people, the so-called 'oldcomers', have been neglected and not dealt with in the public arena. This can be explained by the 'insignificant' number but perhaps, most of all by the fact that ethnic minorities do not fit in the consensus on Japan as a homogeneous and unique culture and society.

The Oldcomers

The Koreans constitute the largest ethnic minority in Japan. The first Koreans, now almost all residents in Japan entered the country during Japan's rule of Korea, along with their descendants. Currently their number amounts to approximately 600,000 (Miyajima 1994). They should be distinguished from the 'newcomer' Koreans, who migrated to Japan after World War II. Past Japanese policies towards minorities need to be projected against the background of the Japanese colonization process. Ethnic minorities were forced to assimilate in all realms of cultural life implying even the adoption of Japanese-sounding names. Examples of the assimilation policies are the 'creating family names and changing names' (*sooshi kaimei*) policy, carried out on the Korean peninsula and 'the movement to change names' (*kaiseimei undoo*) in Taiwan. At the same time, they were nonetheless denied political and social rights. This 'social stratification' policy (*kaisoka taipu*) (NIRA 1993: 267) of assimilation and discrimination by forcing ethnic minorities into certain classes has not changed significantly. Their high level of assimilation is reflected in their native ability of the Japanese language and a level of education, equal to that of ordinary Japanese. Moreover, according to a 1986 survey, the overwhelming majority, some 75 percent, changed their names into Japanese sounding ones (Kimbara et al. 1986: 175 in Miyajima 1994: 4). Although assimilation was accepted and carried out, naturalization and citizenship rights were major barriers for Korean residents to become full citizens with equal rights and duties as the Japanese. Until 1984 when the Nationality Act and Family Registration Act were amended, non-Japanese who intended to become naturalized were required to adopt a Japanese name, or at least change the existing name into a Japanese sounding one together with the denouncement of the original nationality. As a result very few members of ethnic minorities became naturalized Japanese citizens. Creighton (1997) argues that these oldcomers or '*uchi* others' have been denied an 'identity' in order to sustain the master narrative of Japanese homogeneity.

Yet changes have occurred along. First, the postwar generation of Japanese have developed attitudes and values, which are more tolerant and less discriminatory towards Koreans and other ethnic minorities in Japan than during Japan's colonial rule of Korea. A sign of the new era of relative tolerance and openness is perhaps the enormous ascent of mixed marriages between Japanese and Koreans. The number of mixed marriages made up 71.6 percent of the total marriages within the Korean community (Miyajima 1990 in Miyajima 1994: 23).

The Newcomers

Recent inflow and some (divergent) numbers

Due to the rapid rate of economic growth, Japan alongside with the newly industrialized countries – South Korea, Taiwan, Singapore and Hong Kong – have attracted labor attraction from other countries in East and Southeast Asia. The recent surge of labor migration in Japan can be attributed to a combination of labor shortage in Japan and a large labor pool of workers in the neighboring Asian countries in search for a better life. The revaluation of the yen after the Plaza Agreement in 1985 widened even more the gap in per capita GNP between Japan and the surrounding developing countries. Labor shortage in Japan is caused both by the economic sustained growth, a negative demographic growth and the unwillingness of the educated youth to do the '3K' (*kitsui, kiken, kitanai*) or in English the '3D' (difficult, dangerous and dirty) jobs.

According to some estimations (Inoue in Stahl 1991: 168), job vacancies exceed jobseekers by 35 percent. Labor shortage is especially acute at the skilled, semi-skilled and unskilled level. The construction industry in particular has a shortage of 100,000 workers (Inoue in Stahl 1991). Komai (1995: 2) traces the emergence of the newcomers to an earlier date. The harbinger of the current situation was the flow of trainees into Japan during the late 1960s and early 1970s. However, the first significant flow started only fairly recently, in the late 1970s, with the large-scale influx of women into the sex and entertainment industry. In the 1980s males began to make their appearance, coming to work as manual laborers in the manufacturing and construction industries.

Table 2: Figures of Registered Foreign Nationals in 1987 and 1992

Nationality	1992		1987	
Korean	688.144	(53.7%)	673.787	(76.2%)
Chinese (Incl. Taiwanese)	195.334	(15.2%)	95.477	(10.8)
Brazilian	147.803	(11,5%)	2.250	(0.2%)
Philippines	62.218	(4.9%)	25.017	(2.8%)
American	42.482	(3.3%)	30.836	(3.5%)
Peruvian	31.051	(2,4%)	615	(0.07%)
British	12.021	(0.9%)	7.754	(0.9%)
Other	102.591	(8.0%)	48.289	(5.5%)
Total	1,281.644	(100%)	884,025	(100%)

Source: Ministry of Justice in Tanaka H., 1993

Table 3: Figures of Undocumented Foreign Workers

Nationality	May, 1993	July 1, 1990
Thai	55,383 (18.5%)	11,523 (10.8%)
South Korean	39,455 (13.2%)	13,876 (13.0%)
Philippine	35,392 (11.9%)	23,805 (22.4%)
Chinese (Exc. Taiwanese)	33,312 (11.2%)	10,039 (9.4%)
Malaysian	30,840 (10.3%)	7,550 (7.1%)
Iranian	28,437 (9.5%)	0,764 (0.7%)
Other	75,827 (25.4%)	38,940 (36.6%)
Total	298,646 (100%)	106,497 (100%)

Source: Tanaka H., 1993

The above figures are official estimates. Stahl notes that in official sources approximately 260,000 illegals were counted by October 1992. In unofficial statistics, however, the illegal presence is estimated to attain as high a figure as 500,000 (Stahl 1993:350). According to the Far Eastern Economic Review, the total number of illegals has – starting from the mid-80s – risen 'from almost nil to 100,000 to 150,000 during the last part of the decade' (do Rosario 21/06/1990:62).

Table 4: Changes in Numbers of Apprehended Undocumented Foreign Workers

Country of origin	'87	'88	'89	'90	'91
South Korea	208	1,033	3,129	5,534	9,782
	(109)	(796)	(2,209)	(4,417)	(8,283)
Iran	0	0	15	652	7,700
			(13)	(648)	(7,611)
Malaysia	18	79	1,865	4,465	4,855
	(15)	(265)	(1,691)	(3,856)	(3,892)
Thailand	1,067	1,388	1,144	1,450	3,249

Country of origin	'87	'88	'89	'90	'91
	(290)	(369)	(369)	(661)	(926)
Philippines	8,027	5,386	3,740	4,042	2,983
	(2,253)	(1,688)	(1,289)	(1,593)	(1,079)
Mainland China	494	7	39	481	1,162
	(210)	(5)	(26)	(428)	(981)
Pakistan	905	2,497	3,170	3,886	793
	(905)	(2,495)	(3,168)	(3,880)	(793)
Sri Lanka	0	20	90	831	307
		(20)	(87)	(821)	(295)
Bangladesh	438	2,942	2,277	5,925	293
	(437)	(2,939)	(2,275)	(5,915)	(292)
Others	150	762	1,139	2,618	1,784
	(70)	(379)	(664)	(1,957)	(1,198)
Total	11,307	14,314	16,608	29,884	32,908
	(4,289)	(8,929)	(11,791)	(24,176)	(25,350)

Notes: 1. Figures in parentheses are for males; Mainland includes both Taiwan and Hong Kong
Source: Ministry of Justice in Komai 1995: 17 and Kajita 1994: 36.

Channels of entry

Japan has since long opted for exporting capital rather than importing labor. Therefore, unlike Germany, Japan chose to encourage capital-intensive production at home, and invest in labor-intensive production in nearby countries with low-cost labor. Known as 'job exports, it was preferred to bringing foreign workers in Japan' (Appleyard 1993: 266). Currently, Japanese immigration policy still reflects very much this closed-door policy. The Alien Registration Law stipulates that foreigners, who stay in Japan for more than 90 days, must register at a local government office. The December 1989 Amendments to the Immigration and Control and Refugee Recognition Act, reinforced in June 1990, allowed foreign 'professional transients' or high-skilled foreigners. The increased number of non-Japanese with legal residence status in Japan concerns thus mostly the capital-assisted, high manpower migration (Muto 1993: 349).

Table 5: Expanding Figures of Legal Residence Status for Foreigners in Japan (1990–1)

Residence category	1990	1991
Investor/BusinessManager (*tooshi,keiei*)	3,807	1,523
Professor (*kyooju*)	591	750
Entertainer (*koogyoo*)	75,091	89,572
Engineer (*gijutsu*)	1,338	3,166
Skilled Labor (*ginoo*)	1,510	2,381
Artist (*geijutsu*)	1,202	52
Religious activities (*shuukyoo*)	1,958	2,073
Journalist (*hoodoo*)	410	401
Legal/Accounting services (*hooritsu,kaikei gyoomu*)	42	7
Medical services (*iryoo*)	73	4
Researcher (*kenkyuu*)	458	823
Instructor (*kyooiku*)	4,092	2,651
Specialist in the humanities/International Services (*jinbunchishiki,kokusaigyoomu*)	2,756	6,416
Intra-company transferee *(kigyoonaitenkin)*	1,540	3,780
Total	94,868	113,599

Source: Ministry of Labor, Japan and International Migration, Quarterly Review, Vol. XXXI 2/3, 1993.

Table 5 indicates a surge of legal immigration at the onset of the 1990s in Japan. There has been a marked growth of 'foreigners' in Japan. The most dramatic increase occurred within the 'international' realm: the specialist in humanities and international services, intra-company transferees and investor-business managers. They certainly belong to the newly emerged and growing group of capital-assisted high-level migration manpower migration. Exceptions to this rule are the categories of entertainers and artists. As these concepts are elastic and open for interpretation, it offers possible loopholes for immigration of the less-educated and special-skilled people, who are not of Japanese descent and who nonetheless want to migrate to Japan. It is important to note the high numbers of foreign entertainers entering Japan *vis-à-vis* other groups. In 1990 and 1991 they make up 79 percent of the total number of legally allowed foreign entries.

Concerning unskilled labor only foreigners of Japanese descent (*Nikkeijin*) are legally permitted to work in Japan. They are mostly employed in the car manufacturing industry and its small and medium-sized affiliates. Recently, three centers have witnessed a remarkable surge of these U-turn migrants, more specifically in Aichi, home basis of Toyota; Shizuoka, home basis of Honda and Suzuki; and finally Kanagawa with Nissan and Isuzu (Tanaka 1993).

Although legally other manual workers are denied entry in the country, the persistence of illegal immigration testifies that no restrictive immigration policy is completely waterproof. Illegal immigration is not only sustained but it shows a mounting trend, too. Some authors think that the presence of undocumented foreign workers is even tolerated passively by the industry and government in the form of foreign traineeship. Undocumented migrants can be divided into many subcategories: those who enter without the appropriate documents such as ship-jumping migrants; those who enter with a tourist visa and who do not return at the designated date, the so-called 'overstayers'; *shuugakusei* or immigrant workers entering Japan under the guise of students in language and technical schools lower than the four-year university level. They enter through the so-called 'side door' (Kajita 1994: 32) and are thus 'dual purpose migrants' (Nagayama 1993: 429). This is to say that they enter the country legally but most work illegally. In the different entries of undocumented workers, brokers play a crucial role. The term 'broker' refers to a job broker, who makes profit by assisting foreigners to find work, whether legal or illegal. According to Muto (1993: 349) the official objective of the 'training program' is to provide foreign workers the occasion to improve their technical skills in Japan.

> Many entrepreneurs throughout the world say that the success that the Japanese have had in improving the quality of their industrial output derives from the efficient technical training provided within each company, and some of these Japanese companies have opened their doors to foreign trainees. There are also those, who believe that while it is still premature to accept unskilled workers, it would be worthwhile to provide the same opportunity for unskilled foreign workers to improve their technical abilities. Some ministries in Japan are now considering the possibility of establishing new mechanisms to promote the smoother acceptance of foreign trainees.

The official rationale of the system involves the teaching of Japanese language and special skills to the trainee. Yet Komai (1995: 37) and Stahl (1993: 353) claim respectively that *de facto* foreign trainees are often used as cheap labor migrants under the guise of a traineeship in order to alleviate the acute labor shortage in certain sectors.

> In order to find a resolution to Japan's serious labor shortage, both the business world and the government agencies have begun considering permitting the use of foreign unskilled labor, and the trainee system is one branch that has opened up in the traditional barriers.

127

The use of the 'trainee' adopts the pretext that these are not unskilled workers, and thus avoids infringing on the wall.

One veiled attempt to permit this type of immigration has been the extension of 'training programmes' through which workers from other Asian countries are brought in for a period of time, part of which, if not at all, is spent in 'on-the-job-training'...For many foreign 'trainees', their 'training programme' has proved to be a euphemism for long hard hours of factory or construction work at sub-standard wages.

In order to curb the abuses of the traineeship, the Japan International Training Cooperation Organization (JITCO) was established in 1991 by the Ministries of Justice and Labor, in cooperation of the Foreign Ministry and MITI (Ministry of International Trade and Industry) to coordinate and implement the original objective of the program.

The undocumented originates mostly from neighboring sending countries except for the category of Iranians. The reason for the high presence of Iranians in Japan was the existence of a mutual agreement between Japan and Iran allowing travel without visa. This explains the sudden increase in 1991. This agreement was suspended in April 1992, accompanied by a sudden drop in entries by Iranians. There are many disincentives obstructing newcomers to enter Japan. Examples are: the 'exclusive' character of Japanese society, the menial and unpleasant nature of the jobs done by illegals, the high penalty of employers for hiring illegals – fines that go up to as high as 300,000 yen and three years of imprisonment (Stahl 1991: 169) – and the recession (Iyotani 1995: 1). Notwithstanding these obstacles, there is clearly a large supply of and a high demand for cheap labor either legal or illegal. Generally, the small-to-medium-sized companies employ undocumented workers. Whereas large-sized companies recruit Japanese college graduates, the small and medium-size enterprises (SMEs) cannot attract the latter as

Table 6: Changes in Numbers of Overstayers According to Nationality/Place of Origin

	1 Jul. 1990	1 May 1991	1 Nov. 1991	1 May 1992	Perc. of total as of May '92
Thailand	11,523	19,093	32,751	44,354	15.9%
Iran	764	10,915	21,719	40,001	14.4%
Malaysia	7,550	14,413	25,379	38,529	13.8%
South Korea	13,876	25,848	30,976	35,687	12.8%
Philippines	23,805	27,228	29,620	31,974	11.5%
China	10,039	17,535	21,649	25,737	9.2%
Bangladesh	7,195	7,498	7,807	8,103	2.9%
Pakistan	7,989	7,864	7,923	8,001	2.9%
Taiwan	4,775	5,241	5,897	6,729	2.4%
Myanmar	1,234	2,061	3,425	4,704	1.7%
Sri Lanka	1,668	2,281	2,837	3,217	1.2%
Others	16,079	19,851	26,416	31,856	11.4%
Total	106,497	159,828	216,399	278,892	100.0%

Source: Ministry of Justice in Komai 1995: 1

129

they prefer to join the official sectors with attractive conditions such as promotion, life-long employment, overseas work, benefits for family, social prestige, etc. In the more informal sector of the economy, gearing towards the potential workers of housewives, students, older people and unskilled foreign labor (Kajita 1994: 56), the foreign workers seem to be the most efficient, submissive and hardworking category.

Kobayashi's (1987: 21) interview with a 'disappointed boss' after the raid of the police at the car-plant in Toda City demonstrates the desperation of SME owners. 'It is hard to find young Japanese men willing to do this kind of work these days. Those (= the arrested ones) were good, strong and dependable.' To summarize, the government is very reluctant toward the import of unskilled labor. The expanded categories include only foreigners with special expertise. Yet the idea of creating training programs for foreign workers is generally accepted following the needs of certain industries.

Current discourse on migrant workers

The official stance towards the emergence of foreign laborers in Japanese society is one of moderation and caution. Whereas more foreigners were allowed in recent years to enter Japan, it concerns mainly those who possess special knowledge and/or skills and not the low-level manpower or unskilled migrant worker, except for the group of *Nikkeijin*. Within the current debate on this issue, pro's and con's exist. Those opposing more relaxed entry policies point to the potential social disruptive character of migrants to the social, cultural and ethnonational fabric of Japanese society.

Nishio Kanji (1989) ardently defends protectionism of the Japanese internal market against foreigners in his publication *The Case of Labor Market Seclusionism: Foreign*

Workers are Crippling Japan (*Roodoo Sakoku no Susume: Gaikokujin Roodoosha ga Nihon o Horobosu*). The basic line of his argument is that the Japanese society cannot absorb a sudden inflow of (Asian) foreign workers. Especially the threat of one billion Mainland Chinese entering Japanese society seems effective as horror device. Should this take place, it would undoubtedly change the 'Japanese way of life' and the social fabric of Japanese society. It is argued that the discrepancy of social class – the Japanese being the middle class and the foreigners the blue-collar workers – will after some time transform Japan into a society with two opposing social and 'racial' groups. This development is potentially disruptive and even explosive for the current *status quo*. In order to solve the shortage on the labor market, proponents of this school suggest to recruit from the reservoir of the own people, such as females and elderly people.

Defenders of opening Japan for unskilled workers can be divided into two camps. At the more general level, it is argued that it is the responsibility of Japan to absorb foreign laborers in the era of internationalization and globalization. This stance has been put forward by Kawai (1993: 284). The question of foreign migrant workers in Japan needs to be viewed from a variety of perspectives. Ultimately, the question of Japan's responsibility towards the world and the global community has to be considered. The flow of human resources throughout the world will continue to increase in the future. Japan cannot isolate itself from these flows. Thus, we can expect to see an increase in the number of foreign workers in our country.

At the more practical level, there is a consensus among the leaders in industry and business that the current labor shortage in Japan forms a new challenge. Whereas the shortage of the 1960s could be alleviated by the influx of the countryside people and through automation in the production process, the current situation concerns first a shortage in the service-sector, where automation cannot solve the problem. Second, the SMEs, which constitute the backbone of the Japanese economy, cannot attract sufficient numbers of young Japanese to do the 'lesser' jobs in the informal sector. Furthermore, they argue that Japan cannot continue to seal off the country while Japanese businesses expand on an ever-rapid global scale.

Besides the pro and con debate, there are some, who have gone one step further. Assessing the two camps, Komai (1995) concludes that those against the presence of foreign workers refuse to look at the reality. Whether one is for or against foreign workers, either stance cannot deny or dismiss that foreign workers are already working and living in Japan. In other words they are a reality. He is equally harsh towards the 'open door' school since importing cheap labor is a form of brain drain on the part of developing countries. As a long-term solution to curb migration the most laudable option seems to be development. Migration robs the skilled and young labor away from these poor countries, through which their development is even more hindered. In the meantime, Komai argues, Japanese government needs to change its attitude towards foreign workers. Instead of perceiving them as a temporary phenomenon, as labor force, they should be seen as foreign laborers with a high probability of remaining in Japan, of building family and other social networks. The Japanese authorities should bear in mind, he continues, the example of Western Europe, where the process of guest workers has evolved into the issue of settled migrants. Therefore, a rethinking in many areas is urgent: housing, health facilities, family reunification, the education of the children and the pension arrangement of elderly foreign workers (Komai 1995: 253–65; Miyajima 1995: 123–7).

Part Two

At the Median Level

7 Centrality of Japanese Education

General

Education as an institutional tool to shape and bundle the social behavior and the minds of future generations into a basic form of national cohesion occupies in most nation states and industrial societies a central place. It is an organizational form, which engages in the activity of binding loose individuals into members of a geographically, culturally and linguistically well bounded entity. Apart from strict instruction in the sense of transmission of knowledge and technical skills, it is also the place *par excellence* of socialization: particular forms of behavior, social manners, and in short human relationships. In *Reproduction in Education, Society and Culture*, Bourdieu and Passeron (1977: 118–19) uncover the continuation of class differences not only through formal knowledge but also through language and modes of behavior.

> Methodical observation of the linguistic and gestural behavior of the candidates in an oral examination enables us to bring to light some of the social signs by which professorial judgement is unconsciously guided, and among which we must count the indices of the modality of the use of language (grammar, accent, tone, delivery, etc.), itself linked to the modality of the relation to the teacher and the situation which is manifested in bearing, gesture, dress, make-up and mimicry. The analysis required for the purposes of experimentation reveals that nothing, certainly not the appreciation of even the most

technical knowledge and know-how, goes uncontaminated by the system of convergent or, more precisely, redundant impressions bearing on one total disposition, that is, on the system of manners characteristic of a social position.

In the Japanese case, Sabouret (1993) claims that the school is the primary locus of socialization for children and youngsters, even more than the family. Education as in most other countries occupies a central place in Japanese society. One can even go further by claiming that in the Japanese case the firm control of the government over the young generations through the formal educational system has been unsurpassed. In Japan the priority lies in the formation of a competent workforce and citizens of good conduct in order to ensure industrial development and cultural continuity of the Japanese identity or the sense of 'we, Japanese' (*wareware Nihonjin*). Apart from the average high score of intellectual skill and knowledge in Japan, the high degree of orderliness and diligence has captured the attention of many Western education specialists (Rohlen 1983; White 1987; Duke 1986). Some contend that the socialization process in school and certain courses like Japanese history and moral education have a deep impact on the particular Japanese mode of behavior. White (1987: 16–7) explains in detail how 'moral education' should be seen as a process fostering the youngsters becoming Japanese, the so-called *nemawashii* (digging around the roots) process.

> Japanese common sense, taught along with Japanese history and culture, is most evident in what is called 'moral education.' In its current manifestation, a child studies behavior and relationships within the family and community...Among the goals of the school syllabus are those, which a Westerner would recognize, such as 'respect for another's freedom' and 'acting according to one's beliefs.' There are some that are very Japanese: 'it is desirable that, in the lower grades, one should learn to bear hardship, and in the middle grades, to persist to the end with patience, and in the upper grades, to be steadfast and

accomplish goals undaunted by obstacles or failures.' Furthermore, 'in the lower grades, one should learn to listen to the opinions of others and admit frankly one's own mistakes or faults, and to behave unselfishly, and in the middle grades, to live a life of moderation, and in the upper grades, to reflect always one's words and behavior, to act with prudence and to live an orderly life.' Zeal, striving, and self-abnegation are to be combined with cheerfulness and sensitivity to others – all within the context of learning 'to love one's hometown and to protect the land, the culture and traditions of the motherland, and ... to be aware of one's responsibility as a Japanese.'

Generally the primary concern of Japan's educational system is to provide a high average level of basic skills like literacy and high competence in mathematics on a universal basis rather than to nurture a handful of exceptionally gifted individuals. Rohlen (1983: 322) and Reischauer (1986: xviii) explain respectively,

> The great accomplishment of Japanese primary and secondary education lies not in its creation of a brilliant elite (Western industrial nations do better with their top students), but in its generation of such a high average level of capability.

> Japan has undoubtedly outpaced all the major nations of the world in what should be the fundamental task of schooling, imparting to virtually all students adequately high levels of basic skills, such as literacy and high competence in mathematics.

Educational system and ideology in the Imperial Period (1868–1945)

Prior to the centralized education system, notably during the Tokugawa-era (1600–1868), there existed many schools and various types of instruction depending on social class, gender and rural-urban location. In general, learning was highly valued. Within the Confucianist ideology, the official doctrine of the *samurai* ruling class, virtue is attained through study and learning. The most common school experience of the majority of Japanese children was the parish school or temple school (*terakoya*). It was attached to a temple, where Buddhist monks taught children to read and write. Later, it was organized by the local village or town. In the Meiji-era (1868–1912) Western models of universal schooling were introduced as part of the general movement of modernization and Westernization. The Meiji reformers displayed an eclectic attitude towards the wholesale import of all things Western. They borrowed what they saw as the most suitable features of several western educational systems and altered them in order to fit in the Japanese situation. Consequently, a highly centralized administrative structure with a focus on state-run normal schools was imported from France. The system of higher education was, however, based on a handful elite school following the example of Germany. The English model of character-building preparatory schools found fertile ground in Japanese society. The model of elementary education, some practical pedagogical approaches and an outspoken interest for vocational education were clearly American influences.

The formulation of education was in the hands of the state bureaucracy, in cooperation with the gerontocracy (*genroo*) and the military. The 1872 Fundamental Code of Education (*gakusei*) and the 1879 Edict on Education (*kyooikurei*) formally abolished a class-based educational system by nationalizing the school system for the first time in the history of Japan. Henceforth, schooling was open to all those with intellectual capacities, at least theoretically since *de facto* members originating from the own clan or region were favored according to Horio (1993: 218, own translation).

The new Meiji government subscribed to the egality of the four social classes, which had been established under the feudal Tokugawa rule. In descending order of social prestige they consist of the warriors, the peasants, the craftsmen and the merchants. It made an effort to promote the chances of all members of society...The leaders, however, displayed a tendency to favor people from the same region and from the own clan.

The Edict on Education was largely based on the ideas of Fukuzawa Yukichi (Yasukawa 1989). Recognized as the Japan's foremost educator, Fukuzawa stressed the importance of an educated mass to successfully modernize Japan and so retain the national independence *vis-à-vis* the powerful colonial powers of the West. He discerned a direct connection between education and the preservation of the nation. In his view, the promotion of individual enhancement should be embedded in a moral system promoting loyalty and filial piety (*chuukooitchi*) of the individual towards the Emperor and the state. Education was never seen as an inherent and unalienable right of the individual but as a means to strengthen and serve the nation. This is to say that the people's sovereignty (*minken*) and that of the nation (*kokken*) were intricately interwoven.

The ideology of the new educational system was based on two pillars: namely the *bansei ikkei* ('line for ages eterna', referring to the uninterrupted line of the Emperor since time immemorial) and *kokutai* (the essence of the nation). The official document, which outlined the new educational policy based on the two key ideas of *bansei ikkei* and *kokutai*, was the Imperial Rescript on Education (*kyooiku chogoku*) promulgated on October 30, 1890. The Rescript was in first instance an education document and according to many also the key document for the development of ultra nationalism in Japan. As an education document, it contained very little concrete information on the actual organization of the educational system. It was rather a moral manifest urging Japanese subjects to abide by the Confucian virtues of filial piety towards one's parents; of maintaining harmony between husband and wife; of developing affection between brothers and sisters and of demonstrating absolute loyalty towards the State and in particular the Emperor. This special relationship between the Emperor and his subjects as a 'one-family-nation' (*kazoku kokka*) has been explicitly stated not only in the Rescript on Education, but also in the Imperial Constitution of 1889 and the Imperial Rescript for Soldiers and Sailors of 1882.

The Rescript has been subject to a series of rereading and reinterpreting, mostly situated at the criticizing end. Education serves as one of the key structural elements in the Imperial nation building project during the Meiji period. The document contained the seeds, out of which ultra nationalistic tendencies germinated and bloomed. The use of education as a tool for propaganda proved to be extremely effective in imbuing the Japanese with nationalistic ideas and values. In fact, it provided a legal and moral basis for an educational system, which supported the rise of ultra nationalism in the 1920s and the 1930s culminating into the mass mobilization for the war. Following the spirit of the Edict on Education, the foremost *raison d' être* was its utility to foster national cohesion and to collectively modernize in a rapid pace. Therefore, education was not seen as a process of nurturing students into individuals with an autonomous mind. Instead, individuals were subordinated to the good of the state and expected to obey blindly to instructions issued from above. At least, that was the case for the majority of Japanese. A clear distinction should be made between the ruling elite and the masses. Whereas the elite engaged in learning (*gakumon*), the masses needed to be instructed (*kyooiku*). The schism *gakumon* and *kyooiku* reflected the implicit class distinction in spite of the official policy of equality.

The Taisho era (1912–26) is characterized by the general climate of intellectual freedom in a more democratic society and the short-lived movement for a more liberal education in private schools. However, this trend was abandoned in the beginning years of the Showa era (1926–89). In 1937 the *Kokutai no Hongi*, published by the Ministry of Education, reiterated and reinforced the primordial importance of loyalty and filial piety. This document, in which education was linked with national interests and in which individuals were subordinated to the greater good of the nation, personified by the Emperor, played a direct role in the mass mobilization of the Japanese for the war. In 1941 in the midst of the war, the Edict on national schools (*kokumin gakkoorei*) was promulgated to safeguard and to solidify national unity. Yet despite all the critique on the utilitarian and potential dangerous nature of Japanese education, containing seeds of ultranationalism, White (1987: 16) and others relativize the original motives of the educators.

> Education, during the Meiji period, was developed in part to institutionalize and perpetuate Japanese cultural identity. Thus, the centrality of Japanese history and culture in the curriculum has to be tied to the rise of modern nationalism. But a more benign reading of the Meiji and Taisho (1912–26) period curricula shows that the development and perpetuation of the national identity were used to forestall cultural colonization by the West, not to create aggressive aggrandizement.

Furthermore, one cannot possibly deny the positive outcomes of this policy. Given the relatively weak economic position of Japan at the end of the nineteenth century, it was opted for the middle road of advocating the enforcement of compulsory education in primary schools. The systematic organization of compulsory (primary) school on a legal basis was introduced in 1888 through the Edict on Primary School (*Shoogakkoorei*) by Mori (Horio 1993: 66). Although the Imperial educational system is often associated with the creation of a political and technological advanced elite, educational mobilization was carried out in rural as well as in urban areas. Children of farm families, and in particular the younger sons with no inheritance seized upon the possibility to obtain an education. The overall success to produce a select group of intellectual elite and to provide a general education for the mass has been lauded by Reischauer (1976: 169).

(This policy is) closely tailored to national needs as the leaders saw them. It eventually created a literate mass of soldiers, workers, and housewives, ample middle-level technical skills – an aspect of education that many of today's modernizing countries have failed adequately to appreciate – and a stream of highly talented young men emerging from the universities to occupy positions of leadership in government and society. In retrospect, however, even the most benevolent reading of history cannot deny that in the mobilization of the Japanese into the World War II the national education did play a role.

Postwar Development and Objectives of the National Educational System.

The occupation of Japan (1945–1952)

When the Emperor's representatives formally signed the document of surrender on September 2, 1945, Japan became an occupied nation under the supervision of General MacArthur, the Supreme Commander of the Allied Forces (SCAP) until 1952. Major reforms in education were proposed in the direct aftermath of the war. First, the educational system was seen as one of the key mobilizing factors in the rise of ultra nationalism and militarism culminating into Japan's involvement in World War II and its subsequent defeat. Furthermore, in the direct aftermath of the war, the entire system was destroyed, the personnel demoralized and the students idle as there were no schools to attend. The document Educational Situation at the End of the War (in Beauchamp and Vardaman 1994: 52) describes the following situation.

> Surrender day found the Japanese educational system at a standstill; 18,000,000 students idle; 4,000 schools destroyed; 20 percent of the necessary textbooks available; military officers occupying responsible educational positions; textbooks impregnated with militaristic propaganda; teachers dispersed; the Ministry of Education a tool of the militarists; liberal educators hiding from the Thought Police.

The two most important documents, shaping the postwar educational system, include the School Education Law (*gakkoo kyooiku hoo*) and the Fundamental Law of Education (*kyooiku kihon hoo*). They were promulgated respectively on March 29, 1947 and March 31, 1947. The School Education Law was an extensive document outlining the organizational structure of the regular school system; education for the handicapped, kindergarten; special course school. The regular system adopted henceforth the 6-3-3-4-school track universal for the entire country replacing the multi-track system of the prewar period. Compulsory education covered primary school and secondary school. Consequently, the school age was extended to the age of 15. The Fundamental Law of Education was in content and in tone a complete reversal of the 1890 Imperial Rescript. At that time the principal aim of education encompassed according to Beauchamp and Vardaman, (1994: 52)

> The full development of personality, striving for the rearing of the people, sound in body and soul, who shall love truth and justice, esteem individual value, respect labor and have a deep sense of responsibility, and be imbued with the independent spirit, as builders of a peaceful state and society.

Compulsory education was extended to middle school. Henceforth, youngsters were officially obligated to attend school until the age of 15 instead of 12. Political education was banned as the prewar 'morality' course (*shuushin*) was regarded a propaganda channel for the militarist government. Perhaps the most radical and therefore most controversial article was article 10 (in Horio 1993: 91–2) stipulating that 'education shall not be subject to improper control, but shall be directly responsible to the whole people.' It marked the formal rupture with the prewar system of Imperial Ordinances. The new system established the principle of passing education laws through the parliamentary channel. These two legislations have changed the educational system in a significant way. They still constitute the legal basis of the current educational system in Japan. Another legacy of the Occupation policy was the creation of the Japan Teachers' Union (JTU or the *Nikkyooso*). Against the background of the democratic climate and the reform zeal in the aftermath of the war, the the left-to-the-center members of socialists and communists saw a unique chance to ally themselves against the government in general and the Ministry of Education in particular. This marks the beginning of a continuously antagonistic relationship between the JTU and the Ministry of Education. By 1949 as the United States was more drawn into the problems of the Cold War, the American influence and eagerness for reforms in Japan started to diminish accordingly. On the whole, it seems that the SCAP succeeded in transforming a system, which was traditional and feudal, into a modern and democratic system.

Yet the decentralization issue, as reflected in article 10 of the Fundamental Law and the establishment of the Board of Education Law (*Kyooiku Iinkai hoo*) could not elicit much support in Japan. This American ideal of decentralization fundamentally clashed with the concerns of most Japanese leaders in the field of education.

The Post-Occupation Period (1952–60)

After the Occupation when the Japanese regained their sovereignty, the first point on the political agenda was a critical assessment of the occupation reforms and thus also of the education reforms. This 'reverse course' or 'counter reformation' aimed at abolishing the excesses of the Occupation educational reforms, which have proven unfit in the Japanese context. Among the new reforms, which could not find root in Japanese soil, was the 1948 Board of Education. It was an attempt of the Occupation Administration to decentralize the education administration by transferring the power from the Tokyo-based Ministry of Education to the communities through the locally elected school boards. The education of morality (*shuushin*) was abolished by the Occupation policy as it was seen as the backbone of the prewar ultra-nationalist and militarist regime. It was according to Beauchamp and Vardaman (1994: 11) 'a primary vehicle for inculcating prewar ideas of racial supremacy, the righteousness of Japanese overseas expansion, and the divinity of the Emperor.'

Yet the Japanese thought the cancellation to be too radical and urged to reformulate the content and to rename the course. In 1958 the Ministry of Education incorporated a course of moral education in the compulsory curriculum. This course was henceforth called *dootoku* instead of the discredited term *shuushin*. The counter reformation movement was supported by the consensus that the Occupation policy had gone too far at some points in the democratization process. Furthermore, according to *Nikkeiren* (the Japan Federation of Employers), grouping the largest industrial firms, the new educational reforms stressing democratic ideals did not sufficiently prepare Japanese youngsters for the workplace. In other words, they demanded more vocational schools and the professionalization at the college level. The *Nikkeiren* issued the following points in the document 'Opinion on Technical Education to Meet the Needs of the New Era' (*shinjidai no yoosei ni taioo suru gijitsu kyooiku ni kansuru iken*) (in Beauchamp and Vardaman 1994: 141–6),

The promotion of technical education is a pressing matter...There-
fore, to reform industrial technological education to meet the demands of the new era and to systematically cultivate scientists,
technicians and engineers, we urged the government to take the following measures: systematic training of engineers and technicians to
cope with future economic development; promotion of science education and vocational education in compulsory education; promotion of technical education of working youth; enrichment of
technical high schools for the training of first-grade engineers and
supervisors; reform of education in science and engineering universities for the education of engineers.

This particular demand marks the beginning of the link between big business and education, in which students are
transformed into competent and skillful workers for the sake
of industry and business through education. Again, Japanese
were mobilized through an industry-serving educational system to contribute to the national enterprise of rebuilding Japan in the postwar period. On the whole, a 'reversion course'
was deemed necessary to make the reforms acceptable in the
Japanese context. The basic democratic framework, however, laid down by the Occupation administration has fundamentally remained intact. Some reforms were abandoned as
they were felt to be dysfunctional such as the Education
Board. Others were adapted to suit the Japanese situation including the introduction of a new course of moral education.

Expansion in the 1960s and the 1970s

The unprecedented economic growth from the 1960s until
the oil crisis in 1973 and the surge of the student population
have influenced the educational system profoundly. Already
in the second half of the 1950s, the industry requested the educational system to shape and transform students into capable workers, engineers and other scientists. The Occupation
administration in fact disrupted the special relationship be-

tween the school and the industry. The increase of young-sters, putting a severe strain on the university system will become clear by the following figures (Beauchamp and Vardaman 1994: 178).

University education in this period was still a matter of the happy few since only 17.9 percent (166,761) of the entire group of high graduates (933,738) planned college entrance. Furthermore, the discrepancy between the number of applicants (197,847) and the actual entrants of university (166,761) shows the difficulty of passing the entrance examination. Roughly 85 percent succeeds while the remaining 12.5 percent of the applicants fails. In addition, these figures are general, as the differences between universities are not entered into the statistics. One can extrapolate that the percentage is significantly lower for the most prestigious national universities.

One of the most influential documents of this time was the 'image of the ideal Japanese' (*kitai sareru ningenzoo*) of 1966. Although the left thought it to be a reinstatement of the prewar Imperial period, it was emphasized in the document (in Beauchamp and Vardaman 1994: 166) that 'the economic prosperity, which Japan has been enjoying, has produced hedonistic tendencies and a spiritual vacuum.' The ideal Japanese has different roles to play in society, notably as an individual, as a family man, as a member of society and as a citizen. The ideal Japanese as a citizen should strive to reinstall, though in a much more moderate way, a sense of 'proper patriotism' and 'respect for symbols.' These symbols included the Emperor, the national flag, the national anthem and the development of the 'Japanese character.' Given the mild yet definite presence of the Emperor in the document made the left very uneasy about the new situation.

To facilitate the search for the best and the brightest out of the increasing pool of youngsters, the prewar hierarchical system of ranking schools was reinstalled. In spite of the increase of the student population, government did not create new national universities accordingly. On the contrary, it preferred to invest in the industry and delegated the foundation of (private) schools to the private sector. During the period 1960–75 only 9 new national universities were established, which paled in comparison with the 165 newly founded private institutions. This process had its effect on the students, who were eager to comply with the system and to compete for the most prestigious universities. At the university level, the most prestigious were the national universities, followed by private universities, a ranking that has been preserved until today. Within national universities the government has differentiated the newly established postwar universities including upgraded versions of former high schools, organized like the American-style course system and the 7 most prestigious imperial universities, maintaining the prewar chair system. Prestige goes hand in hand with funding, superior equipment and higher salaries for the teaching and technical staff.

There was a consensus on the 'ability first principle' (*nooryokushugi*) because it was believed that not descent, class or wealth but educational background, which plays the decisive role in one's social position. After all, the current examination based education is a plausible and meritocratic way to develop, select and mobilize Japanese to fill the appropriate jobs in society, each according to the personal ability while serving the economic prosperity of Japan. It is not only widely accepted in Japan but it also elicits praise from educational experts. In this ability first ideology, prestige is not (directly) associated with money in the Japanese educational establishment. As school success equals ensuring good social status or ideally in an ability first ideology promoting social mobility, there are certain ways to obtaining this goal. Schools in Japan are divided in three categories: national (*kokuritsu*), public (*kooritsu*) and private (*shiritsu*) schools. The most prestigious schools are the national ones, which make up 0.5 percent of the grand total (Goodman 1990a: 81). During the compulsory education most pupils are found in the public schools (*kooritsu*), supported by both local and central governments. At the senior high school level, the private schools attract the majority of pupils.

A second but more select channel to get into the best schools is the so-called 'escalator system.' At the top of the pyramid are the national universities along with a few private universities including Keio and Waseda. In order to enter these universities, the selection procedure already starts at kindergarten through primary, secondary, high school to one of the previously mentioned elite universities. Besides a handful, most private universities with steep enrollment and tuition fees are considered less prestigious and therefore less desirable than national universities with less enrollment and tuition charges. Passing the university entrance examination cannot be simply attributed to mere natural talent or intelligence. On the contrary, the success rate is highly dependent on a meticulous school planning – carried out by the parents and in reality by the mother – and personal sacrifices of the mother and the child. Those, who passed the university entrance examination are assured of a much-wanted job after graduation in government, diplomacy or big business, offering a high salary, job security, significant bonuses, overseas travels, social security, pension arrangements and prestige.

In the ability first ideology, teachers in Japan generally enjoy a high status, which is reflected in their title *sensei*. One can compare this term with the title of 'doctor' in Europe (Goodman 1990a: 87). The profession of a teacher in Japan is characterized by security. Most teachers enter the profession when they finish college and remain to teach in the same school until retirement. The main function of a teacher is to instruct students how to pass examinations successfully to the negligence of inciting the intellectual curiosity of the students and the development of a critical mind. It should be noted that the Japanese educational system, although extremely competitive at the entrance level, rarely fails a pupil during course work in contrast to for instance the European system. Moreover, much conformity and teamwork are required in Japanese schools. Goodman (1990a: 86) elucidates this paradoxical situation.

> One of the apparent contradictions of the Japanese educational system is that while demanding competition among individuals, it also instills into those individuals the ideals of conformity which are so important to Japanese employers. Essentially this can be *between* one stage of the system and another, which may be from as early as the age of 3, while *within* each establishment they will find the emphasis on conformity.

Critical assessment of the ability first ideology

At first sight the system appears quite waterproof. Indeed, the principle that students with excellent scores enter the prestigious universities and obtain first-rank jobs does not sound typically Japanese. All educational systems encompass processes of selection and exclusion, in which competition takes place in the form of examination. Examination, upholding the image of neutrality and objectivity, has been subject to severe critiques. Bourdieu and Passeron (1977) claim that the inequality among the different social classes is reproduced by the examination system. This is to say that working-class youngsters eliminate themselves by not participating in the exams rather than failing them.

Thus Bourdieu and Passeron (1977: 153) argue that:

> In every country, the inequalities between the classes are incomparably greater when measured by the probabilities of candidature (calculated on the basis of the proportion of children in each social class who reach a given educational level, after equivalent previous achievement) than when measured by the probabilities of passing.

Applied to Japan, recent surveys have shown that in spite of the meritocratic ideal money does matter in getting ahead in the educational career of youngsters. For example, Sabouret (1993: 26 own translation) reminds us that the parents of *Toodai* (University of Tokyo) students, ranked as the best university in Japan, belong to the upper strata of society.

> According to recent surveys the income of the family of students at the University of Tokyo ranks among the highest in Japan. This proves that economic power is nonetheless one of the conditions for succeeding in school and university and therefore one of the key factors of professional and social success.

Given the fact that the choice of the right high school determines university entrance, which again determines the professional life in an irreversible way, parents, aspiring the best for their children, are eager to pay private tutors, costly cram schools and expensive private universities. The youngsters are willing, for example, to put up with sleeping only a few fours per night during the examination period. Sabouret (1993: 25) continues his critique.

> The cost of education puts more and more a strain on the family budget. A good university implies a good private school with fees or instruction by a private tutor (*kateikyooshi*), cram and prep schools (*juku* and *yobikoo*) of which the fees are as high as the results they claim to produce. The cost of schooling and the problems of housing are the main factors of the decreasing birth rate in Japan.

A more fundamental criticism of Japan's educational system comes from a prominent Japanese pedagogical expert, Horio Teruhisa (1993), who denounces the ideological basis of 'ability first' principle. First, only children of relatively wealthy parents with a university degree have access to the system. Moreover, rote learning does not really engender the growth of the personality of the child. As the current system subjugates the educational values to the economic development of the country and reflects the social structure of Japanese society, Horio (1993: 205) thinks that it counters the very idea of egalitarianism.

> The act of turning one's back to egalitarianism in schools and considering economic inequality to be natural means the acceptance of a well-defined hierarchy. One gives up the pluralist values, typical of the educational reforms in the direct aftermath of the war in order to reinstall – in a new form – the standardization and the abusive control of the educational system, prevalent before the war. Gone are the sacred personality of the human being and the recognition of the differences of individual personalities.

Western observers, too, have pointed out the boredom and the lack of inspiration of a Japanese class. Instruction in Japan is a necessary nuisance; one has to go through as Goodman (1990a: 87) testifies.

> Subject-teaching often consist of no more than reading the teacher's copy of the school textbook and setting and marking endless examinations to ensure students are keeping up to standard. Lessons are not exciting and students not encouraged to ask questions. If they do, then they risk being labeled disruptive.

Rohlen (1983: 241) thinks classes to be boring: 'Frankly, sitting in class day after day I found it hard to believe that such a monochromatic and monotonous kind of reality could inspire so much intellectual fervor and political heat.' In sum, by the end of this period the increase of the total student population in conjunction with the rise of private educational establishments *vis-à-vis* the stagnating number of public schools, has led to a dual system. The official system existed in ambivalent symbiosis with private institutions, which pursued blatantly commercial and profit-making objectives. It has also created two sorts of equally unfortunate youngsters: the pupils, preparing for the university entry, the *moyashikko* ('bean sprout-children') and the *boosoozoku* (the dropouts) roaming the streets.

New challenges and problems

Whereas the previous period was featured by a quantitative expansion of the educational system, this period was characterized by a decreasing school population and a critical reflection on the quality of the system, the excesses as result of a fiercely competitive system, high uniformization, and the changing times of internationalization. For the first time, Japan's education system was confronted with problems and issues not unlike those of other industrially advanced countries. These issues include a (comparatively) higher rate of dropouts, bullying (*ijime*) in school, the decline of the meritocratic nature of education, the increasing numbers of children of expatriates (*kikokushijo*) and foreign children and youngsters. Sometimes, these side effects of the Japanese school system are called 'diseases of an advanced nation' (*senshinkokubyoo*).

The 'school refusal syndrome' in Japan has caused indignation and concern in Japanese society when the first statistics were collected in the 1970s. Some youngsters simply refused to comply with the system and dropped out of school. In absolute terms, the number was relatively low. In 1983 the percentage of dropouts in relation to the total of senior high school students was merely 2.4 percent. In the same year, the percentage in the US was 23 percent. Yet it should be noted that the number in Japan has been increasing since 1974. This alarming phenomenon has been explained by the Ministry of Education (in Beauchamp and Vardaman 1994: 27) as the negative outcome of 'the rapidity of social change, the proliferation of the nuclear family, loss of community feelings, affluence and urbanization.' Others saw many faults in the rigid and inflexible nature of the educational system, in which the principal preoccupation was uniformization and schooling in function of the industry rather than the development of the personality of the student. School violence forms another headache of Japanese educators. The NPA (National Police Agency) reported a steady increase of school violence. Nishimura (1985: 19) attempts to explain this phenomenon. 'The sense of crisis springs primarily from the rising number of violent incidents involving junior high school students. Gangs of students smash windows and doors at their schools and assault their teachers.' A very particular problem is bullying *(ijime)*. Bullying acts are reported (in Beauchamp and Vardaman 1994: 29) as 'inflicting bodily injuries, blackmailing, being burnt with cigarette butts and a cigarette lighter, forcing victims to drink sour milk, poking hot needles under a victim's fingernails, and forcing them to eat insects.' Bullying in Japanese society, admittedly a grave problem needs to be relativized. Duke (1986: 190) reminds us that, when comparing Japan with the United States, 'bullying takes on a completely different dimension from the bullying that goes on in many a lower ranked American inner city school facing problems of school vandalism, intimidation, gang feuds, not to mention the severe problems of drugs and teenage pregnancy.'

It has also be pointed out (Roden 1980) that the phenomenon of 'bullying' is deeply ingrained in the Japanese educational system and needs to be seen from the historical perspective. In the prewar system, 'bullying' was not called or experienced as deviant behavior or violence towards the co-students. It was part of the 'initiation' process. The ability first principle, even the staunchest supporters of the system would recognize, has revealed inherent problems. While

153

having lauded the meritocratic nature of Japan's educational system, Rohlen (1983: 312) discovers that 'the meritocratic principle is threatened. The rise to pre-eminence of a set of private schools...marks a significant change in which money appears increasingly significant to the pursuit of educational advantage.'

Rohlen (1980: 207) argues that along with expensive private schools, the cram schools (*juku*) and preparatory schools (*yobikoo*) were created as 'tactical weapons in what is frequently referred to as "college entrance war" (*juken sensoo*).' Since universal elementary education was achieved in the nineteenth century, the term *juku* has shifted to private-run preparatory schools, which coexist with the official system. *Juku* serves the target group students from grade one to grade nine and *yobikoo* students from grade ten and above (higher middle school), preparing them for the college entrance examination. *Juku* (cram schools) offer a wide variety of course subjects. There are the *gakushuu keikoo juku* (academic-oriented cram schools), offering courses as mathematics, science, English and those that provides training in non-academic matters. Students attend *juku* for a variety of reasons. In order to get ahead of others, they enroll themselves in *shingaku juku*. Those who have fallen behind in middle school (*ochikobore*) attend a *hoshuu juku* in order to catch up with the fellow students in the regular system. These cram schools, an unaccredited and unregulated education system, which coexists in an ambivalent symbiosis with the official one, have become a lucrative business. In 1976 a poll of thousands of Japanese children showed that 60 percent of the total number of students in the 7th, 8th and 9th grade were enrolled in a *juku* (White 1987:76).

Cram schools are not a uniquely Japanese phenomenon. Similar types of preparatory schools operate in South Korea, Taiwan, Hong Kong and Singapore. Yet the high student rate and the *de facto* recognition of the *juku* phenomenon render

154

the Japanese case particular. Cram schools have become the target of criticism by both Japanese and Western educators. According to Rohlen (1980: 214) and others they reflect the excesses of the exam-based system in Japan 'one of the most exaggerated forms of the "ant hill" aspect of contemporary Japanese society.' As they represent the apex of a mechanical pragmatism, they contradict the ideals of a humanistic education. Ironically, the exam-based system safeguarding a meritocratic system has developed some not-so-favorable side effects such as the examination hell. It has been generally denounced as being inhuman, rigorous and pedagogically unsound. Then, one can ask why it is still existing if not flourishing at the current moment?

How to explain the *juku* phenomenon?

First, there is the practical issue of the number of students surpassing the actual available slots in universities. In this perspective, the organization of a grand-scale exam seems to be a plausible selection instrument. Second, there is the Confucian legacy, which underlies and legitimizes the examination procedure based on rote learning. The Confucian legacy prescribes the memorization of the classics, in which the wisdom of the ancients is crystallized. Although the subject matter differs fundamentally, the way in which the learning process is perceived and implemented is still very much the same, namely rote learning. Moreover, one can see that the outcome of the examination system such as the cramming of a large amount of information and the regurgitation upon demand is not the only component why the system is still maintained. The process through which the student needs to pass has an intrinsic value. That is to say that if a student wants to succeed, s/he has to build up a large dose of willpower, a strong sense of self-discipline in order to attain the goal. This Spartan experience of character building and persistence is seen as a sound preparation for all future challenges in life, professional as well as personal. Third, the examination system has created a new 'business.' Most students preparing for the entrance examination enroll themselves in cram schools. In addition, materials ranging from traditional books and manuals to audiovisual products have been launched in the 'education market.' The supporting 'education market' would collapse if drastic reforms were introduced in the education policy. Last but not least, most of these students, who are considered the victims of the system, they themselves make a 'quick yen' out of their situation by tutoring primary or secondary school children and youngsters. In other words, the lucrative education market consists of intricately interwoven interest groups, ardently opposing its abolishment. Important to note is that a system can only be sustained when the actors involved are willing to cooperate, comply and play by the rules of the game. Rohlen (1980) introduces the *tatemae/honne* principles in Japanese culture to explore the *juku* phenomenon. The *tatemae* principle refers to the public consensus whereas the *honne* principle covers the inner reality. Applied to education and especially the *juku* phenomenon, the proliferation of the latter can be explained through the *honne* principle of Japanese parents and youngsters. No parent in his/her right mind and for that matter no student would ever imagine to jeopardize the social opportunities by defying the system. Society is viewed as an extensive arena where all members strive for similar things, such as a good education and well-paid jobs. Therefore, most actors are willing to abide by the rules of the game in order not to fall behind and preferably to get ahead of others. This explains why parents do not hesitate to pay huge fees for *juku* and youngsters prepared to sacrifice their leisure time to get instruction in these cram schools. This is the *honne* principle or how parents approach and cope with the educational 'rat race.' When asking the Japanese to assess the competitive, rigid and fact-cramming nature of the exam-based system, they would acknowledge the shortcomings and the futility of the system. This is the *tatemae* perspective. Not unlike the staunchest critics of that system, they want their children to have more time to play, explore and develop their talents as part of the growing up process instead of imposing all the rigidities and constraints of adult life to them. These constraints imply meticulous time management. Youngsters have to stuff their minds with facts and figures, which need to be regurgitated during the entrance exam but allowed to be forgotten thereafter. The students themselves too prefer to relax and to postpone adulthood filled with obligations and nerve-racking schedules to a later date. The *tatemae* perspective sees many disadvantages in the *juku* phenomenon. Interesting is that this specific social order is not created by the *juku* but by the meritocratic principles of the official system. The *juku* lives and thrives by grace of the official system. As long as the current exam-based system is maintained and as long as the Japanese people see the official system as essentially meritocratic, the *juku* phenomenon and its aberrations will persist.

The third major reform

It is important to note that this period is called 'the third reform period' (1978–present). The first reform period was the nationalization of education during the Meiji period (1868–1912) through the introduction of compulsory education. The foremost priority was to build an educational system, which would produce a capable workforce to catch up with the Western industrial nations. The second reform period occurred after Japan's defeat by the SCAP. The main rationale was to turn Japan into a democracy and to install an educational system, which reflects the ideals of a democracy: the development of the individual into an independently thinking human being instead of the absolutely loyal subject of the Emperor.

The third reform reflects the changing times. At the end of the 1970s Japan had joined the ranks of the advanced nations. In addition, given the new changes in the world community such as internationalization and the emergence of the information society, it was felt that the Japanese educational system was no longer equipped to cope with the new realities. Two major documents have been the underlying forces of calls for reforms. They were successful in generating a nationwide debate on educational reform. The first important document was the report issued by the Organization for Economic Cooperation and Development (OECD) on Japan's educational system, issued in 1971. It praises the accomplishment of the educational system of producing a competent workforce, the backbone of Japan's postwar economic success. Yet it had many question marks concerning the emphasis on uniformity and competition to the neglect of the development of the total personality of the student. Beauchamp and Vardaman (1994: 25) claim that 'the time may have come to devote more attention to such matters as cooperation, in addition to discipline and competition, and creativity, in addition to receptivity and imitation.' The contributors to the report seem to defend a humanistic approach, which links education with human development rather than the existing economic dictum of the auxiliary function of education *vis-à-vis* the industry. The second document, dating from 1972, is one issued by the Central Council for Education, an advisory organ of the Ministry of Education.

In a very candid way, transcending both conservative and leftist arguments of pro's and con's of the system, it declared the following (in Beauchamp and Vardaman 1994: 24),

> Education is rapidly falling behind the times because vested interests protect the *status quo*, because idealists oppose reforms without pay-

ing attention to their actual contents, and because much time is spent wastefully on the discussion of the reforms, which have no possibility of being implemented.

The proposals recommended in this report concern the upgrading of the quality of education. Suggested measures were: free public education to 4- and 5-year-old children; increase of the teachers' salaries; providing teachers with more time for teaching by curbing administrative work; larger subsidies for private universities, etc.

In sum, the Japanese educational system has never aspired to produce renaissance figures. Instead, it chooses to generate capable workers, contributing to the greater good of the nation. In the universal educational debate between 'instruction' and 'education', or the choice between the dissemination of knowledge and the development of the total personality of the student, it is patent that the Japanese system has opted for instruction. Given the completion of the national project of 'catching up' with the West, it is recognized that a reorientation of the educational system towards a more all-round education is needed to an educational system, prioritizing rote learning to the development of the individual.

Overseas Education and Reception Policy upon Return

General

Internationalization concerning *kikokushijo* revolves mostly around the issue of education in the host society as well as in Japan. The growing number of the overseas returnee youngsters, who are sometimes labeled 'little internationals' (*chiisana kokusaijin*) or 'new internationals' (*shin kokusaijin*), has introduced new themes in the education debate such as 'international understanding and intercultural education' (*kokusai rikai, ibunka kyooiku*).

Table 7: Development of Overseas Children/Returnee Children (*Zaigai kikokushijo*)

Year	Number of Overseas Children/Returnee Children	Year	Number of Overseas Children/Returnee Children
1971	8,662	1982	33,333
1972	11,106	1983	35,663
1973	13,372	1984	36,223
1974	15,390	1985	38,011
1975	16,316	1986	39,993
1976	18,092	1987	41,155
1977	19,489	1988	44,123
1978	21,386	1989	47,118
1979	24,289	1990	49,336
1980	27,465	1991	50,773
1981	30,200	1992	50,977

Source: Foreign Ministry (*Gaimusho*) in Sato and Nakanishi (1991) for the period 1971–90 and Japan Overseas Educational Services (*Kaigai Shijo Kyooiku Shinkoo Zaidan*) for the period 1991–2.

Table 7 indicates that as the number of 'long-term' Japanese expatriates (*chookitaizaisha*) increases, so does the number of accompanying children. To be precise, the number augmented by more than five times during the period 1971–90 from respectively 8,662 to 49,336. The number of Japanese expatriates has been increasing since the 1970s as the result of the expansion of Japanese industry and business. In accordance the children of these expatriates have augmented. Japanese education has always had a special relationship with national goals. Education often means the preparation and the mobilization of the nation's young and talented for the national project of catching up with the West. Since Japanese youngsters abroad are severed from the Japanese educational system for several years and often more than once, it is claimed by their parents and Japanese education experts that after return they encounter problems in terms of language and cultural readaptation. The rupture in the school career of the youngsters is seen as the main rationale for setting up an extensive network of Japanese schools abroad to cater to the particular needs of this group of overseas returnee youngsters (*zaikaigai kikokushijo*). Japanese overseas education can be divided in three categories: the full-time Japanese schools (*Nihonjingakkoo*), supplementary schools (*hoshuukoo*) and local schools (*genchikoo*) including international schools.

The full-time Japanese school is organized from grade 1 to grade 9. This corresponds with the compulsory education of elementary and middle school. In principle, these schools do not differ from those in Japan. The only particularity of *Nihonjingakkoo* is situated in two areas: the teaching of the foreign language(s) of the host society and the organization of activities fostering intercultural exchange with members of the host society. These measures clearly demonstrate goodwill on the part of the Japanese to the host society to avoid critique of exclusiveness and insularity.

In 1990 there were 84 Japanese schools in the world. In absolute figures, there were 26 full-time schools in Asia, 3 schools in Northern America, 17 in Central and South America, 19 in Europe, 3 in Australia, 11 in the Middle East, and 5 in Africa (*Monbusho* in Sato and Nakanishi 1991: 130–6). In the same year, 22.5 percent (or in absolute terms 11,081) of the total overseas Japanese youngsters (*zaigaishijo*) sojourned in Asia, 44.4 percent (21,913) in Northern America, 4.2 percent (2,048) in Central and South America, 23.5 percent (11,600) in Europe, 3.1 percent (1,509) in Australia, 1.2 percent (580) in the Middle East, and 1.2 percent (605) in Africa (*Gaimusho* in ibid. 16).

To compare the two sets of data, the total number of overseas youngsters in each area will be divided by the number of schools in each of the geographical areas to obtain the number of students per Japanese school in the respective geographical region. In Asia, there is 1 school for 426 youngsters; in Northern America 1 school for 7,304 youngsters; in Central and South America 1 school for 120 youngsters; in Europe 1 school for 610 youngsters; in Australia 1 school for 503 youngsters; in the Middle East 1 school for 52 youngsters, and in Africa 1 school for 121 youngsters.

Hoshuukoo are supplementary schools. They are created as an addition to the regular school system in the host society. They are usually organized on Saturday and Wednesday afternoons. The coursework in supplementary school consists of Japanese language (*kokugo*), mathematics (*suugaku*) and social studies (*shakaigaku*). In 1990 there were 146 supplementary schools worldwide. In that year only 0.7 percent of the total overseas Japanese student population in Asia was enrolled in supplementary schools; in Northern America the percentage reached a high 76.8 percent; in Australia 17.6 percent; in Middle and South America 7 percent; in Europe 32.7 percent; in the Middle East 15.2 percent and in Africa 19 percent (*Gaimusho* in Sato and Nakanishi 1991: 17).

Noteworthy is the geographical distribution of these schools. The highest percentage is located in the United States and the lowest in the Middle and South America, the Middle East, and in Africa. Europe scores relatively high. The high number of supplementary schools corresponds with the low number of Japanese schools. The case of the United States illustrates this point manifestly. Given the limited number of Japanese schools, most Japanese youngsters consequently attend local schools. This can be easily explained by the use of English, the contemporary *lingua franca*, in the local schools. Yet parents still want their children to maintain the link with the Japanese language and culture. Therefore, youngsters have to sacrifice their free time, as they have to attend supplementary schools outside the regular school hours to keep up with the Japanese language, mathematics and social studies. Contrary to the situation in the so-called developed, prosperous and advanced countries, a high percentage of Japanese schools are found in developing countries. This is embedded in the official view that education in developing countries is of a lesser quality than the Japanese system. Thus, Japanese schools have to be set up to accommodate the educational needs of the overseas returnees there. It is officially stated by the *Monbusho* (1985 in Goodman 1990a: 32) that 'this is in line with the 1976 Japanese government policy statement of support for *Nihonjingakkoo* mainly in countries where educational provision was considered poor by Japanese standards.'

Tailored return education for *kikokushijo*

Special educational provisions for returnees have been established to facilitate the return of these youngsters for the 'recovery of scholastic ability' (*gakuryoku no kaifuku*) and 'adaptation to the lifestyle education' (*seikatsu no tekioo kyooiku*). At the compulsory education level, the reception of returnees is concentrated in the public schools (*kooritsu gakkoo*). In 1989 80 percent of the total returnee youngsters studied in these schools (Sato and Nakanishi 1991: 226). There was especially a great concentration at the primary level. Several methods are employed in the reception schools (*ukeirekoo*). The 'returnee education standard' (*kikokushijo kyooiku gakkyuu*) provides for separate instruction in the first year. In the succeeding years, when returnees have adapted to the educational system and the overall lifestyle, they study together with non-returnee pupils. The 'method of the mixed reception towards the general standard' (*futsuu gakkyuu e no kongoo ukeire hooshiki*) is mostly adopted in regular schools, accepting a limited number of returnees. The rationale is to allow this small group of returnees to readjust to the Japanese school environment in a 'natural' way. There are also the 'cooperative schools' (*kyooryokukoo*), supporting research on returnee education.

At the high school level, most returnee high school students (70 percent) were enrolled in private schools in 1990 (Sato and Nakanishi 1991: 235). The oldest ones are the ICU (International Christian University) High School, Doshisha International School, Nanzan International High School and International Middle School. In some schools, such as the Tokyo Metropolitan High School and the Nanzan International High and Middle School, only returnees and non-Japanese foreign pupils are allowed to enroll. The international component of the student population has an impact on the curriculum, which in addition to the usual courses also offers foreign languages including English, French, Chinese, Spanish, etc., and courses fostering international understanding.

At the university level, private universities were the first to respond to the needs and demands of the returnees by establishing a special college entrance system for returnees, the so-called *tokubetsu waku* (special quota system). Sophia University in Tokyo was the first to accept returnees on the criterion of having studied abroad instead of the usual college entrance exam in 1971. In 1976 Keio Gijuku University, a private university in Tokyo and Nanzan University in Nagoya started to have special entrance exams for returnees. Among the national universities Tsukuba University was the first to organize a special 20 percent quota program for prospective students based on recommendation rather than competition in the standard university entrance examination. In 1976 returnees could apply for this program. In 1982 the Law Department of Kyoto University opened its doors for returnees.

Currently, the reception policy for returnees at the primary and secondary level is destined for those children and youngsters, who were abroad for at least a continuous period of two years in the company of their parents. Like all other children, they need to have a certificate of a Japanese school in Japan or an equivalent diploma acquired overseas in a Japanese school or a local school. At the university level, along with the above conditions, one has to have reached the level of 12 years of education, completed partially or entirely abroad. Those, who return from the United States, are required to have taken the scholastic aptitude test (SAT), the achievement test (AT) and the test of English as a second language (TOEFL). Returnees from England have to take the general certificate of education and the general certificate of secondary school. Those from France have to pass the Baccalaureate. In most other countries, including Belgium, the International Baccalaureate is recognized as a valid test.

The aim of setting up full-time Japanese schools is to create a school environment similar to that of Japan to minimize the occurrence of a culture shock upon return to Japan. Consequently, they are not excessively inconvenienced by the overseas experiences in the competitive schooling system in Japan. Moreover, some schools at different levels have special entrance provisions for returnees so that they gradually reintegrate in the Japanese school environment in terms of scholastic ability and social adaptation. The underlying principle of the different educational policies – overseas as well as the reception education upon return – is to neutralize major upheavals in the mental condition and the identity formation and management of these youngsters.

Ebuchi (1987: 4) describes the function of the Japanese school and other Japanese organizations as follows:

> Ethnic organizations/institutions such as the Japan Club and the Japanese school provide members of the community with not only organization services but also basis for further expansion of informal human relationships. Among these organizations, the school plays a tremendous role in helping to reduce a fair amount of sociocultural difficulties and psychological tensions that the Japanese families, especially children of school age, meet in the course of adaptation to a new environment and behavioral system.

Investing a minimal amount of time, energy and affection in the host society seems to be based on the return-intent and the related return problems of Japanese expatriates and their families. In this perspective, overseas education is seen as temporary and preparatory for the educational system in Japan. Therefore, I have argued elsewhere that the internationalization of the Japanese is not full-fledged but 'controlled' (Pang 1995).

8 Social Construction of *Kikokushijo*

The 'Non-Han-Shin' Flow in the Theory of Handicap, Singularity and Metaculturalism

Academic concern and research do not occur in a vacuum. Often, it responds to social phenomena in need of clarification and analysis. Concerning returnees, one of the basic questions is when and why it has become a social 'issue' at all. This leads us to the first approach, in which the overseas education and experiences are considered an obstacle or 'handicap' when returning to Japan. Consequently, this approach is called 'the handicap theory' (*handikyappuron*), in which the returnees have lost their 'Japanese-ness.' They are perceived as 'non-Japanese' (MacDonald 1995). First, the problem is acutely experienced by the returning youngsters and their parents. Most of the complaints center on difficulties of language and social attitudes upon return. They feel less well equipped to compete for the good schools, thereby possibly jeopardizing their chances to succeed in school and by extension in professional life. Another set of ill adjustment is situated in the general school environment. Some do not feel at ease in socializing with other children in school, who bully them for their different and 'odd' behavior. Since these personal problems were shared by a great number of returnees and as their parents – in most cases the mother –

167

and educational specialists, many who are themselves parents of returnees, have brought these issues into the forum of public discussion, these items have been transformed into social problems.

One of the most prominent scholars, who has detected or as some claimed created the problem of *kikokushijo*, is incontestably Kobayashi Tetsuya, professor at the Department of Education at Kyoto University. Together with his team researchers he was commissioned by the *Monbusho* to explore and uncover the difficulties facing returnees were confronted with in order to provide recommendations for policy guidelines purposes. In addition, one must not forget that returnees, who themselves through the personal experience and training in disciplines, participate in the discourse on *kikokushijo* like Horoiwa Naomi and Nakatsu Ryoko. Last but not least teachers of returnees also entered the discussion through their daily contact with returnee children and youngsters. In explaining how the different forms of ill adjustment arise, Hoshino (1990) examines the outcomes of 'intercultural contact' (*ibunka sesshoku*), which he has defined as 'overseas sojourn, education received abroad' (*kaigaitaizai, kaigaide uketa kyooiku*) (1990: 111). Ordinary Japanese pupils and their counterparts abroad are not exposed to the same experience. Overseas children and youngsters have to learn and speak a foreign language in daily life and in school abroad. After a while, this process brings about the phenomenon of 'a child who suddenly has become fluent in English' (*aru hi totsuzen eigo ni natta ko*). This child after intense socialization in the host society becomes increasingly disconnected from 'common knowledge, consciousness, and Japanese language' (*jooshiki, chishiki, Nihongo*). Other frequently cited problems are: lack of 'groupism' or team spirit (*shuudankunren no ketsujo*); an overdeveloped self-consciousness (*jikoshuchoo ga tsuyosugiru*); forgetfulness (*wasuremono ga ooi*); violating easily school regulations (*koosoku ihan o okashiyasui*); lack of competitiveness (*kyoosoo ishiki no ketsujo*) in exams and other areas. It is reasoned that if they do not overcome these problems, they will suffer from 'culture shock,' which is brought about by non-adaptation in Japanese society after intercultural contact abroad. Nakabayashi (1981: 214) indicates that 'there is a stereotype that *kikokushijo* are undisciplined, stuck up, argumentative, express clearly what they like and what they don't like.'

Table 8: Culture Shock Scale

Culture-acceptance (C)		
ABROAD	family life (H)	JAPAN
(f)	school life (S)	(j)
	Level of development (D)	
CS= f [(Aj.Dj) (Af.Df)] A=C, H, and S		

Source: Takahagi 1982: 67

The culture shock scale, advanced by Takahagi (1982) consists of three major elements including culture content (c, h, and s), level of development and the two settings of Japan and foreign country. If a returnee lives by the content (c, h, s) of the foreign country and that of Japan, s/he is highly vulnerable and prone to a culture shock. In other words, the juxtaposition of the two cultures, Japanese and non-Japanese is impossible, ambivalent, contradictory and might cause mental health-disturbances, the so-called 'conflict within' (Horoiwa 1987). Certain age groups are especially vulnerable for a difficult re-entry or 're-entry shock' (*fukki shokku*). According to Minoura (1984: 168) children older than nine most likely experience such re-entry problem. This age is in her theory crucial and therefore has been termed 'the nine-year-old wall' (*kyuusai no kabe*). It is contended that children beyond that age have the capacity to absorb cultural elements of the host society. The 'consciousness of being a Japanese' (*Nihonjin de aru to iu ishiki*) or the Japanese cultural grammar (*bunka bunpoo*) gradually decreases to the increase of the foreign cultural grammar. In her study she contrasts the Japanese cultural grammar with the American cultural grammar. The major difference between the two systems lies in the point of reference: in the former case the point of reference is the other and in the latter case the self. Given the incompatibility of these two cultures, one can either live by the Japanese cultural grammar or by the American cultural grammar. As the formation takes shape and solidifies in the age range from nine to fifteen, Japanese youngsters, who have lived in those crucial years in the States, are said to be particularly vulnerable to re-entry difficulties.

Apart from the age-linked factors, the duration of an overseas sojourn also has an impact on culture shock occurrence. Those, who sojourned abroad for more than five years are especially susceptible to a return shock (Minoura 1984: 87). Since the overseas experiences are considered a handicap in Japanese society, re-entering in this kind of reasoning implies the process of 'peeling off the foreign-ness' (*gaikoku hagashi*). It has also been called the subtraction model (*kezuritorigata*) (Horoiwa 1987). As the term already reveals, one has to discard or 'subtract' the experiences and ideas acquired overseas.

From the 1970s onwards education of *kikokushijo* both in terms of content and method has been singled out as the foremost urgent research topic. The main objective of these studies was therapeutic. The main concern was how to dispel the 'foul-smell-of butter' (*bataakusasai*) and to transform these

170

children into Japanese, behaving like a Japanese (*nihonjin-rashiku*). Certain anthropological findings (White 1988) even go further and claim that they have been socially 'polluted' by going overseas as they have left the boundary of the Japanese cultural realm and therefore susceptive of exclusion from mainstream Japanese society. White (1988: 106) explains,

> When Japanese leave Japan, their membership is suspended. Every year they are away, re-entry as members of the group – re-establishment of relationships to the satisfaction of those at home – becomes more difficult. It is particularly difficult if after re-entry they betray their exposure to foreign ways, which reminds others of the severing of bonds. Re-entry raises questions of identity that can be silenced only by strict conformity and virtual denial of the foreign experience.

In the singularity theory, there are two extreme views: a) the default theory underlining their deficiencies and shortcomings and b) the theory of merits stressing their valuable assets and potentials. The common element between these two divergent views lies in the fact that returnees are treated as special or particular, different from the 'mainstream' Japanese, who have never left Japan. The difference in the marginality of the returnee between the default and the handicap school is a matter of degree. In the former theory, the sense of marginality is experienced as less dramatic and less irreversible as in the handicap theory. Instead of being 'non-Japanese' (*non-Japanizu*), they are seen as 'half Japanese' (*han Japanizu*). In both instances returnees are perceived as deviant actors from those, living at the center of Japanese society. Complementary with the previous default theory, is that of its contrary, namely the positive approach. The returnees are perceived as 'little ambassadors' (*chiisana taishi*) (Iwama 1992). In this perspective, returnees develop a more critical view of the foreign and the own culture during their overseas stay. While living abroad, they

171

have the opportunity to develop an international consciousness. This allows them to develop a more balanced view of extreme ideologies. They also harbor a higher sense of public civility and universal love than 'ordinary' Japanese do. On the basis of the own experiences and self-reflections, they can foster ties with foreigners on a solid and mutually enriching basis, resulting into a better understanding between people from different cultures. This is because first they have acquired knowledge of foreign languages. Some (Hara 1982, 1983, 1986 in Ebuchi 1994: 489, Hoshino 1990) even argue that by living abroad, returnees become even more conscious of the own identity in a more critical way. This is to say, that through their overseas experience, they have developed an 'international consciousness', through which they can evaluate the shortcomings of Japanese culture in a more objective way than ordinary Japanese (Hoshino 1990: 125). This school developed a different strategy to cope with re-entry, the addition model (*tsuketashigata*) (Horoiwa 1987). One simply adds the overseas sojourn to one's self and adopt all the positive overseas experiences. According to this reasoning returnees are not ill and therefore do not need to readapt themselves to the Japanese educational system in particular and Japanese culture in general. On the contrary the educational system should see the returnees as the representation of the changing times. It is the Japanese school system, which needs some basic rethinking and reforms according to the new condition (Inui and Sono 1977 in Goodman 1990a, and Kobayashi 1981: 180). In contrast to the above two theories, some regard the experiences of a returnee as 'identity-transforming', resulting into the creation of a new identity, a 'new type of Japanese' (*atarashii taipu no Nihonjin*), who lives in the 'metacultural world.' This 'new' Japanese (*shin Japanizu*) is often called a 'bicultural' person (*nibunkajin*). This term, however, does not only mean that one speaks two or more languages and acts comfortably in two or more cultures. It is rather a process, in which after an initial stage of self-questioning and self-reflection, one attains a 'self-crafted' identity. One recognizes it as such and feels a strong 'empathy' with other individuals, who have lived and still live in contexts, different from the own. As become clear, a certain kind of transformation or reshaping of the own identity has taken place, leading to a new and integrated one. This process is called the way of self-determination (*jiritsukata*) (Horoiwa 1987).

The 'metacultural' world refers to the reality, where any kind of representation and expression of the 'metacultural self' has to be reinterpreted and even recreated by the individual. This stands in contrast to the 'cultural' world with its long-established material manifestations (such as architecture) and deeply embedded spiritual rituals (folklore, customs, etc.) and expressions (music, visual arts). Said differently, in the 'metacultural realm', cultural traces, inherited from the past, are not readily available for reference and use (Ebuchi personal communication). This new type seems to share many characteristics with the definition of 'cosmopolitan' as a type, offered by Hannerz (1992: 252): 'A genuine cosmopolitan entails a certain metacultural position–willingness to engage with the Other, an intellectual and aesthetic stance of openness toward divergent cultural expressions.'

The above-described modes (Ebuchi 1994) should not to be interpreted in an 'evolutionary' way, although a chronological development can be traced. One can argue that the process of increasing acceptance in Japanese society of the 'foreign nature' of returnees is reflected in the handicap theory, the theory of singularity and finally the third 'metacultural' theory of the 'new' Japanese. At the same time this flow coincides with the major internal cultural debates in Japanese society. Yet this does not mean that all returnees in all possible variations in terms of age, duration and place of sojourn, etc., have become 'new' types of Japanese. That would be too deterministic a view, downplaying and neglecting the freedom of choice of each individual and the informal and multi-faceted logic of 'culture.' It is rather a framework, which attempts to analyze and interpret the manifold of publications conducted by academics, journalists, and opinion leaders. It aims to capture the changes in the other-ascription and in part also the self-ascription concerning the 'different nature' of *kikokushijo*.

To recuperate, in the 'handicap theory', returnees are seen as 'non-Japanese', completely alien and thus badly in need of foreshortening the cultural distance and ironing out all the differences. In the second theory of the singularity, it is clear in both cases – negative and positive likewise – that returnees are regarded slightly peculiar, or somewhat off. They are only 'half Japanese' (*han Japanizu*). In the two instances of non- and half-Japanese, the view of Japanese society and culture is that of a monolithic entity. The third 'metacultural realm' is a departure from this stance since it introduces a self-creating element by the individual, who should be recognized as a new variant in the multi-ethnic/multicultural society rather than deviant element (Ebuchi 1994).

However, Goodman (1990a: 208–9, 220) critically evaluates the manifold of publication on returnees and comes to the following conclusion.

> The work that Kobayashi and his group produced between 1975 and 1978...served...the established view of *kikokushijo* – that they have problems on their return to Japan as a direct result of having spent time overseas... It is important to point out that...just as many of the members of the original *Monbusho* Committee had belonged to the pressure group, so had some of the more important figures in the creation of this research work *stressing the need of an adapted overseas and return education for kikokushijo* (italics own addition)... the parents of *kikokushijo* played an important role in bringing the problems of their children to a wider audience and ensuring that something was done to help them. Indeed, they may have exaggerated the problems

of their children in order to ensure that special treatment was forth-coming and that their children were not disadvantaged in Japanese so-ciety. These parents are greatly aided in their efforts by the Japanese media, a large section of which it sees itself (in the absence of an effec-tive political opposition) as the defender of the people against the gov-ernment. The media are often fiercely critical of the establishment in Japan, and the left-wing press, including the powerful *Asahi Shinbun*, is a virulent opponent of the post-war educational system. The prob-lems from which *kikokushijo* are said to suffer have offered the anti-establishment section of the media an ideal platform from which to attack Japan's monolithic educational system.

He furthermore observes that the different pressure groups did not only transform the status of returnee youngsters into a social issue. Moreover, they have essentialized the image of the returnee. The other-ascription is one of conscious fab-rication, which in many cases has little relation to the actual situation and the personal identity of the involved actors, namely returnees. This is the point of view of Goodman (1990a: 223–4).

The important point to emphasize, however, is how little the images of *kikokushijo* which are utilized in these debates on the nature of Japanese society actually pertain to the real individuals. They are simply Weberian 'ideal types.' Those who perceive the *kikokushijo* as in need of 'rejapanization' also support the general *status quo* in Japan and the so-called 'traditional' concepts of groupism, consen-sus, and homogeneity. Those who support the idea of *kikokushijo* as agents of change see them as valuable assets in emphasizing con-cepts of individualism, creativity, and heterogeneity in Japanese so-ciety. Those who take the former conservative line would tend to see Japan as a rather closed society. Those who take a more dynamic po-sition would see Japan as a society which is as receptive as possible to influence from the outside world.

Reading and analyzing Goodman's assessment, one can safely state that the status of 'returnees' like ethnic minori-ties in other societies is to a certain extent created and (mis) used in certain circumstances on order to prove some points of a particular hidden agenda. He discovers that this 'recrafting' of a specific identity may come from involved people such as academics, whose own children are returnees or from the returnees themselves (like the Horoiwa's and the Nakatsu's) or from outside groups. Furthermore, besides the different actors in society, 'promoting' the cause of returnees, including their teachers, researchers, certain sympathetic ministries, the media, Goodman (1990a: 220) finally ascribes the high status of the returnees' parents as a decisive factor in negotiating special educational provisions for returnees.

> Access to the media, on the one hand, and to the important establishment figures who control educational policy, on the other, was only open to the parents of *kikokushijo* because of their high status in Japanese society.

It is certainly not inaccurate to point out to the high status of the parents – although some (Ebuchi, personal communication) contest the elitist status of all returnee youngsters – as the reason for the acceptance of a specific returnee identity and special treatment. In fact, this idea is quite new and daring as the explanation of most other studies is situated not in the structural but in the culturalist-essentialist realm: the island mentality of the Japanese, the cultural grammar of the Japanese, etc. But many questions remain without answer. For instance, if they belong to the upper strata of Japanese society, why did the issue arise at all and fought out in the public arena? As members of a privileged group, why do they continue to justify the shifting notion of the own specific identity? In attempting to give an adequate reply to these questions, it might be helpful to take a closer look at the issue of marginality and belonging in Japanese society.

Marginality and belonging in the Japanese context

In the discourse of Japanese ethnonational identity the homogeneity idea has been stressed and reiterated by Western and Japanese scholars. The homogeneity equation of 'one country = one people', the notion of the mono-ethnic nation (*tan'itsuminzokukoku*) is an ingrained and widely accepted reality. Logically, the homogeneity concept engenders a strong sense of belonging. Yet at the same time in order to make 'belonging' possible, one needs to create its mirror reflection of 'non-belonging': the (belonging) insider versus the (not belonging) outsider. Furthermore as belonging is not always clear-cut and complete, ambiguities create the 'in-between' or the peripheral status – depending on how the center is mapped and interpreted – namely the marginal.

In classical anthropology marginality has long since been a central subject. In viewing culture as a network of classifications, marginals are those who find themselves in the 'betwixt-and-between' position. Turner (1977) calls this marginal state 'liminal' (*limen*: 'threshold'). The liminal phase constitutes one important moment in the *rite de passage*. Building on Van Gennep's concept, Turner (1977: 94–5) discerns three phases in the process: separation, the margin or the *limen*, and reaggregation or incorporation.

> The first phase (of separation) comprises symbolic behavior signifying the detachment of the individual or group from either an earlier fixed point in the social structure, from a set of cultural conditions ('a state'), or from both. During the intervening 'liminal' period, the characteristics of the ritual subject ('the passenger') are ambiguous; he passes through a cultural realm that has few or none of the attributes of the past and the coming state. In the third phase (reaggregation or incorporation), the passage is consummated. The ritual subject, individual or corporate, is in a relatively stable state once more and, by virtue of this, has rights and obligations *vis-à-vis* others of a clearly defined and 'structural type.'

In her theory on purity and pollution – in which the former represents order and the latter chaos – in small-scale, so-called 'primitive' societies, Douglas (1991) introduces the marginal period as a point in time, 'which separates ritual dying and ritual rebirth.' During the transitional period, controlled by ritual, the novices live as temporary outcasts, where they are exposed not only to danger but also to the source of power. This ritual guides them into the ritual rebirth, which transforms them into new full-fledged members of the social order. She discerns an element of power and danger in the state of marginality within a ritual context. She (1991: 98) continues that in a secular society, however, a marginal person, who does not have a secure and clear-cut place, experiences a situation, in which 'all precaution against danger must come from others.' This is to say that regular members of this society continue to see him/her as a being at the margins. Examples are ex-criminals, recovered mental health patients, etc. 'With no rite of aggregation, which can definitely assign him a position he remains in the margins, with other people who are similar credited with unreliability, unteachability and all the wrong social attitudes' (Douglas 1991: 98).

In the Japanese context, the notion of the us/them dichotomy is not only existent but perhaps more marked than in other cultures. This is reflected in the *uchi/soto* categorization, which governs all forms of natural and human/social categories ranging from the most abstract such as the order of the universe to the tangible realm of social interaction. Said differently, the *uchi/soto* schism is not a mere philosophical/geographical category but it underlies the basic workings of Japanese society, culture and language.

Within the tradition of Japanology and Japanese Studies, most studies on Japan are situated in the *uchi* realm of the zero-sum schism, making only vague references to the *soto* side as the mirror reflection. When actually dealing with 'non-belonging', the involved actors, or more precisely those who are labeled 'non-Japanese', mostly stand at the other side of the equation. The liminal phase, the zone of the 'betwixt-and-between' of the *uchi/soto* pair has until now not received the same degree of attention as in anthropology. The reason why the liminal has escaped the attention of most Japan scholars so far can be explained by the monolithic and essentialist paradigm of the Japanese people and culture, leaving no room for in-between, undecided, 'middleish' and at the border lingering actors and entities.

Exception to this general trend includes Ohnuki-Tierney's study of *Illness and Culture in Contemporary Japan* (1984) and Valentine's interest in the significance of marginality in Japanese society (1990). Ohnuki-Tierney (1984: 47) equates the marginal with the 'outer margin' in her analysis of the 'outside.'

> There are two kinds of 'outside' – the clear-cut outside, which is the opposite of the inside, and the outer margin. In terms of meaning, the former is assigned dual power, beneficial and destructive, whereas the latter is designated as 'impure.'

Valentine's study of the significance of marginality in Japanese society is one of the few works in this area. On the basis of a combined method of content analysis, participant observation and (unstructured) interviews, he (Valentine 1990: 40) makes an extensive classification of 'potential types of marginality in Japanese society, grouped tentatively according to the supposed source of marginality.' The marginalizing categories include foreign blood – not of 'pure Yamato race'; foreign contact, pollution through illness/damage; deviance: criminal and/or ideological; association with the liminal; unusual family and work circumstances. He examines the semantics of the Japanese term for 'marginality.' He concludes that apart from the loanword *maajinaru*, a transliteration of the concept, Japanese terms including *kyookai* and *shuuhen* are both used in the Japanese academic world. The former refers to the state of being betwixt-and-between and the latter to the peripheral situation of the marginal *vis-à-vis* the center. He notes, however, that the term *shuuhen* is used more frequently. The term reinforces the idea of the edge, the external boundary separated from the center at a significant distance. He relates the periphery notion of marginality to the specific Japanese view of the own society as a circle. By doing so, he explains why the use of the periphery metaphor is preferred to the 'betwixt-and-between' status. The latter refers to groups living between two cultures – the own and that of the host society – such as ethnic minorities in most Western societies. Underlying this status is the 'difference but equality' among cultures.

The Japanese preference for the peripheral implication of the marginality might be explained by the 'centrality' concept. This idea was developed in the Tokugawa period (1600–1868). At the onset, Confucianism was embraced as the source of official morality and the basis of education and social organization. In the *chuuka* (central florescence) concept China represents the sphere of civilization and Japan the outer sphere of barbarism. However as China progressively declined, a reversal of the dichotomy took place. Henceforth Japan, once a 'barbarian' country, was transformed into a center of civilization, the center of florescence (Harootunian 1970). In contemporary Japan, the centrality concept is reflected in the idea of a single center, the metropolis (*miyako*). Taira (1993: 183) states that 'borders, frontiers, fringes, peripheries – such images evoke only fear of contempt...the *miyako* (metropolis) is the source of pride for everyone.'

In locating returnee youngsters in the triptych 'insider/marginal/outsider', those who claim the Japanese to be polluted by the foreign contact, obviously situate them in the outsider sphere. Those who accord special traits to returnees see them as half-Japanese or marginals lingering at the border, displaying of both powerful (international understanding and knowledge of foreign languages) and dangerous as they possibly pose a threat to the *status quo* in society. Those who think that they constitute a new kind of Japanese situate them at the insider sphere after a reimmersion or reincoporation process of (educational) reception measures after return.

9   The Host Society

Some Statistical Data on the Japanese in Belgium

According to the Japanese Embassy (Section Consulate Services) in Brussels, the total number of Japanese in the territory amounted to 5,112 in October 1994. The table below gives a summary of the development of Japanese people and Japanese companies in Belgium starting from 1979.

Table 9:   Numbers of Japanese Companies and People in Belgium

Month/Year	# Prolonged Overseas Japanese	#Japanese Companies
October 1979	2,141	125
October 1984	3,792	132
October 1989	4,643	162
October 1990	4,551	185
October 1991	4,595	202
October 1992	4,935	217
October 1993	5,418	225
October 1994	5,112	221

Source: Embassy of Japan, Consulate Services in Brussels, Belgium 1995

It is perhaps illuminating to point out that the category 'prolonged' or 'long-term' overseas Japanese refer to those, whose stay extends beyond three months in the host society. They differ from the category of tourists by the relatively long sojourn and from Japanese emigrants and permanent residents in the host society by the temporary character of their stay.

Table 10: Age, Gender and Profession of Long-Term Overseas Japanese and their Dependents

Profession	Expatriates		Dependents		Total
	man	woman	man	woman	
Employees of large companies	1,295	91	699	1,576	3,661
Journalists	9	0	6	7	22
Free entrepreneurs	18	30	14	12	74
Student, Researchers, Teaching Personnel	128	117	38	78	361
Government Officials	88	14	45	111	258
Others	173	261	131	171	736
Total					5,112

Source: ibid.

In consulting the Belgian statistics, issued by the NIS (National Institute for Statistics) the most recent figures date back from the last census of 1991. In 1990, the total amount of Japanese was 3,070. This figure does not correspond with the Japanese figure of 4,551 in October 1990. Difference may be due to a variety of contingent reasons such as the negligence to respond to the census or simply not knowing how to fill out the forms for the national census by the Japanese, the incompatibility of the year, etc. What is more important, though, is to note the same tendencies in the two sets of statistics concerning the composition of the Japanese population in terms of gender and age. In the Belgian statistics, 1,587 or 51.7 percent were men and 1,483 or 48.3 percent were women. Within the male population the two age groups of 35–9 and 40–4 reveal the most elevated figure, notably 244 and 213 members. This means that the majority consists of high-skilled male employees of large Japanese companies. Generally, the 'long-term' Japanese expatriates live for three to five years in Belgium. Afterwards, they either return to Japan, with a high probability to be sent abroad later or they are directly transferred to other countries.

A large number of dependents are concentrated in the category of expatriates. What should be mentioned is that in the age range of 15–18 one encounters a rather low number of male students, notably 699 versus 1,576 female students. This group of overseas returnee schoolchildren (*kaigai kikokushijo*) between the same age 15–19 constitutes the core of this book. Analyzing the discrepancy between female and male student population, one can assume with rather great certainty that Japanese parents prefer boys to stay behind in Japan for educational reasons. The same trend is noticeable in the Japanese statistics. The majority of prolonged stay expatriates is situated in the expected category of those, who are employed in large Japanese firms. The majority of this category is male. The gender discrepancy among the dependents (a total of 933 male dependents versus a total of 1,955 female dependents) illustrates again the same assumption that Japanese parents consciously decide to let male children study in Japan. Although official statistics of returnees usually present boys and girls together as one category, many indications show an overrepresentation of girls. For instance in a survey conducted by Onoda Eriko and Tanaka Kazuko (1988: 26–7 in Goodman 1990a: 22), parents are more likely to take girls overseas than boys and that they keep them there, on average, one year longer.

Geographical Setting of Brussels and the Japanese

The agglomeration of Brussels consists of 19 townships. Recently the publication *Multicultureel Brussel*, conducted by Van der Haegen et al. (1995) attempt to map the numbers of Belgians and foreigners in Brussels. The total number of foreigners in the capital in 1995 amounted to 285,617 or 30 percent of the total population (915,580) (ibid. 4). Unfortunately they analyzed only the largest foreign groups: Moroccans, Turks, Italians, Spaniards, Frenchmen and Englishmen and the Portuguese. Concerning the smaller groups of Americans, Japanese and the Swiss, the authors (1995: 20) considered them too small to be mapped.

> The Americans, Japanese and the Swiss can be grouped together. Their presence is linked with the international nature of Brussels, both economically and politically. They are generally affluent, working in high rank positions in Brussels. Given their high to very high socio-economic position it is not surprising that this group lives in the posh suburban areas South and Southeast of the center. In 1991 the number (of this group) was 5.552. Due to the relatively low figure they are not mapped separately.

The total number of Japanese in Belgium amounted to 3,070 in 1990, of which 72 percent lives in the agglomeration of Brussels (NIS 1991). The majority of the Japanese is concentrated in the southeastern part of Brussels, more specifically in Ukkel (11 percent), Watermaal-Bosvoorde (17.3 percent), Oudergem (14.5 percent), Sint-Pieters-Woluwe (18.5 percent), Sint-Lambrechts-Woluwe (14.2 percent). These are the wealthy residential areas of Brussels. Concerning social and economic position it is not possible to measure exactly which group is the most well to do. Yet certain indicators – such as the type of migration and living condition measuring the number of luxurious amenities – provide clues. Van der Haegen et al. (1995) have chosen the living condition as the measurement of social economic position. The situation of the Belgian is taken as the standard and measures 100. As for foreigners, Japanese rank number one with a living condition indicator of 188, followed by the Germans with indicator 149, the Swiss with indicator 147 and the Americans with indicator 135. The lower end of the scale is occupied by the Portuguese with indicator 49, the Greeks with indicator 34, the Turks with indicator 14 and Moroccans with indicator 7 (ibid. 21).

The educational landscape in Brussels is largely shaped by the increasing numbers of foreigners and the complexity of the native Belgian population. Most Belgian people in Brussels are officially supposed to be more or less bilingual (Leman and Byram 1990). Most of them speak both French and Dutch with varying degrees of fluency and mastery of the two languages. Currently, it is estimated that about 20 percent (possibly more) is Dutch-speaking, and 50 percent French-speaking (Leman and Byram 1990). In addition to the 'natives', there are also the foreigners and the newly naturalized Belgians, constituting 28.6 percent of the total population (NIS 1990). As the combined result of the Flemish commitment to establish education in the own language and the relatively strong economy in Flanders (the northern part of Belgium), the Dutch language spoken by the Flemings has gained importance in the capital over the years. Yet discontent and strife between the two language groups remain strong and at times eruptive.

It is quite obvious that in such a complex linguistic context, the majority of Japanese youngsters, whose parents came as long-term expatriates, do not attempt to enter local Belgian schools at the primary and secondary educational level.

Educational Facilities for the Japanese in Brussels

Due to a combination of factors and circumstances Japanese children in Belgium follow a similar school route. First, the temporary nature of their sojourn in Belgium does not encourage long-time investment in the local language. Moreover, the second language they have learned in Japan, namely English, proves to be difficult enough, let alone studying an additional language. Last but not least, there is the tacit agreement that Japanese youngsters need to study in a Japanese educational system to become a full member of society and to be able to work in a Japanese work environment. Japanese parents take the socialization process in school very seriously. Even abroad, they find it essential to let the children grow up in a Japan-like environment. Therefore, the recommended and generally followed school path of a Japanese child is to attend Japanese School (*Nihonjing-akkoo*) during the compulsory school age comprising primary and middle school. Youngsters beyond that age either return to Japan or attend boarding schools in London or the different international schools in Brussels. When parents decide to keep the children in Belgium, they mostly send them to the International School of Brussels. Only a handful of Japanese youngsters attend Saint-John's, the British School or the Lyçée Français.

Like other Japanese schools in the world, the Japanese School of Brussels is a full-time school, partially financed by the Ministry of Education (*Monbusho*). The school was founded in 1979. The supplementary school or also called

187

the Saturday School, has been in operation since 1974. The Japanese School is currently for 50 percent subsidized by the Japanese Ministry of Education (*Monbusho*) and the other half by donations of Japanese companies (personal communication with a school administrator). The school is located in Oudergem. In form and content the school does not differ from an ordinary Japanese school in Japan. Pupils are all Japanese. The school year starts in April and ends in March. All the festivities of a Japanese school are maintained such as the 'Day of Culture' (*bunkasai*) and the 'Day of Sports' (*undookai*).

Teachers at the school are selected and dispatched by the Ministry of Education. Concerning the content of the courses, the curriculum is identical to that of an ordinary school in Japan. Schoolbooks are mailed directly from Japan through the Japanese courier service and bookstore OCS, a few footsteps away from the school. The only difference is that students need to learn the language of the host society and to participate in intercultural activities and exchange programs with its members. In Brussels Japanese children learn two foreign languages: English and French. In 1995 there were 323 pupils, among whom 177 female and 146 male pupils. In primary school there were 252 pupils and in middle school 71. In the same building classes are given on Saturdays. This is the 'Japanese Supplementary School of Brussels' (*Burasseru Nihonjin gakkoo hoshuukoo*). Pupils study mathematics (*suugaku*) and Japanese language (*kokugo*). The students attending the supplementary school are Japanese, who live in cities at a relatively far distance from Brussels including Ostend, Antwerp and even Maastricht (personal communication with the president of a Japanese company in Ostend).

In short, the main objective of the Japanese school is to create a school environment similar to that in Japan. This is reflected in the content of the curriculum, the recruitment of teachers from Japan, the Japanese school year (starting in Spring), celebration of traditional festivities and the creation of a Japanese atmosphere in school. In 1993 I attended the Cultural Day in the Japanese School. From the moment I set foot in that school I felt the general Japanese 'mood' in the school. First, everyone spoke Japanese. Most of the people there were Japanese. Even the few non-Japanese I have seen there fit very well in the general picture because they spoke and acted like Japanese in terms of body language and gestures. Furthermore, there was a 'boisterous' (*nigiyaka*) atmosphere in the air. The secretary of the school, a middle-aged man, was running back and forth busily and nervously, while wiping vigorously the sweat from his forehead. Many smart-looking children, dressed up in cotton *kimono*'s for the occasion, were excited playing the different games, while munching large quantities of food their mothers had prepared. These mothers, all very *onna rashii* chatted among themselves or with the teachers. It was all very gay, merry and very Japanese.

The case of the Japanese school of Brussels seems a successful simulation of Japan. It is in the first place a school, where children come to learn and socialize like their counterparts in Japan. Moreover, it also functions as a microcosm of the Japanese community in Brussels. It is the arena, where exchange of information at the practical level occurs. In addition, it is also a place where mutual support and warmth can be found and developed among the parents of the children.

Although it would be interesting to do fieldwork in such an exclusively Japanese network from many perspectives like the self-perception of the Japanese, how they view Brussels and the Belgian society, I consciously did not choose to work there. I was not interested in reporting how close-knit the

Japanese are, how they segregate themselves from others, in short stressing their unwillingness to 'integrate' in the host society and their insistence on the own ethnonational identity. I did not want to write another 'Japanophile' work, underlying the uniqueness of the Japanese in preserving their culture and ethnicity. Nor did I aspire to produce a Japan-bashing book, condemning the insular character of the Japanese overseas. There exists already an abundance of such publications. What interests me is to look, study and perhaps learn from life-course events and transitions of individual Japanese youngsters such as schooling, work, relation with the family members and possibly entrance into sexual relationships and marriage.

Given the planned four- to six-year period of my research, I had to interview and follow youngsters from age fifteen or older at the beginning of the research period. Only then would I be able to observe the different life stages. Youngsters in the age range 15–18 are increasingly confronted with major transitions of their life: the change from adolescence to adulthood. They start to think – in close cooperation and sometimes coercion of the parents – about university life back in Japan. Besides the entrance examination, a major headache for most youngsters and their mothers, there are many practical problems such as housing. Since the best schools are located in the Tokyo area, most youngsters, who have never lived in the metropolis, move from the hometown or indirectly from overseas to Tokyo. Furthermore, it is also a period when some enter relationship with members of the other sex and the concomitant changes in the personal life. Finally, the entrance in the job market is also an essential part of their life.

Major Japanese Formal Social Organizations In 1

979 Japanese business leaders founded the *Nihonjinkai*, the Japanese Association in Belgium (literally: the Association of Japanese people). At first, the principal objective was to organize and sponsor the education of overseas returnee children (cf. supra). As the Japanese community increased, the scope of the activities of the *Nihonjinkai* became more diversified. For each activity, a commission has been set up. The activities include common business issues organized by the committee of commerce and industry, culture-oriented events and conferences organized by the committee for culture, multicultural activities, organized by the committee of cultural exchange and support to local charity organizations.

The main rationale of these committees is to bridge and strengthen the ties between the Japanese and the local Belgians and local organizations. Every year a Japanese speech contest for Belgians is organized to promote the learning of the Japanese language in the host society. The Belgium–Japanese Association and Chamber of Commerce, previously two separate organizations, reunited in 1991. Their main objective is to promote trade relations between Belgium and Japan. The EU–Japan Club is an organization, set up to foster ties between the EU and Japan. It should be noted that in Brussels there are Japanese ambassadors, representing respectively Japan in the host society of Belgium and in the European Union as Brussels is also the capital (or one of the capitals) of Europe. Concerning religious life, there is a Scheutist Catholic church catering to Japanese Catholics. A mass in the Japanese language is held once a month in the house of the Scheutists. Japanese Catholics, however, form a small minority.

Informal Sources of Solidarity

In conjunction with the formal social organizations of the Japanese in the host society of Belgium, numerous services, undertaken by some Japanese at the micro level, are offered to overcome the initial stress of separation from the own country, the own culture and to nurture relationship with fellow Japanese. One example is the non-profit organization, Petit Pois. This organization is the result of a spontaneous initiative of Japanese housewives, who aspired to build out a Japanese community life. One of the most important activities of the organization is the publication of a leaflet. The leaflet contains news on community activities of concern to the Japanese and to Belgians, interested in all things Japanese. This publication of a rather modest nature serves the function of disseminating the news on the different activities, geared towards the Japanese in Belgium and other interested in Japan.

Another publication, 'The Guide on How to Live Conveniently in Belgium' (*Berugii seikatsubenrichoo*) is worth mentioning. The main publisher is the PTA (Parent-Teachers Association) of the Japanese School. The objective is to inform newly arrived Japanese on how to survive and live comfortably in Belgium. Therefore, the advice and information are situated at the practical level. Topics include rules of immigration in Belgium, traffic regulation, list of language schools, health matters, crime and how to deal with it, recreation, local practices such as no showers or bathing after 10 p.m., tipping the garbage man at the end of the year and 'detailed' information on how to live in Belgium according to formal and informal rules. This guide is available on places, where Japanese frequently come such as the Japanese bookstore OCS near the Japanese school, the Tagawa supermarket, the Takanami store, the Japanese beauty parlor Yukiyo.

As the number of Japanese increased from the second half of the 1980s, more small businesses run by and for the Japanese have sprung up. In the above mentioned guide, which can be considered – at least partially – an informal Japanese 'phonebook', consists of a series of services and stores such as Japanese supermarkets, Japanese restaurants, bakeries, taxi companies, (Japanese and non-Japanese) beauty parlors, bookstores, music stores, etc. In contrast to other ethnic restaurants and services, their Japanese counterpart serves in first instance Japanese. Interesting to note is that non-Japanese small businesses are also included in the guide such as an English bookstore W.H. Smith, an Asian supermarket Sun Wah, etc.

Intercultural Exchange

General

Scarce material in all forms or shapes exists on the Japanese in Brussels. Of course, from the Japanese point of view, the community is too small to elicit interest. From the perspective of the host country Belgium, the Japanese together with other small ethnic groups constitute 'invisible' minorities. The general discourse on migrants in Belgium mostly targets labor migrants including Moroccans, Turks, Spaniards and Italians. In addition, apart from the relatively low representation, they belong to a different type of migration, namely high-skilled migration instead of the traditional labor migration. It is certainly true that as guestworkers decide to settle, they pose major challenges for the host society in all aspects of modern life: housing, legislation, labor provisions, crime, education, etc.

Of course, high-skilled migrants, generally educated middle class do not usually need special attention or support from the host society, as they do not come as individuals but as part of a network. They are usually associated with a large-scale organization, either an international company or a governmental institution. Their overseas experience is – so to speak – 'sponsored' (Passin 1983: 25) by formal organizations. They can, in other words, make use of the own social network to live 'conveniently' in Belgium.

It would be premature to conclude that Japanese do not wish to 'integrate' in the host society. Before making a provisional assessment, it seems useful to explore the existing material, if any, on the Japanese in Belgium. A handful of studies has been conducted including a survey by Egawa, a small–scale survey conducted by myself and a documentary 'Little Tokyo in Brussels', made by the program makers of 'Labyrinth' of the BRTN (the National Belgian Television). These few sources provide some insights on the life of the Japanese in Brussels.

Egawa, a fellow at our Department of Social and Cultural Anthropology at the Catholic University of Leuven for three months in 1993, has organized a large-scale survey. I have met her a few times at the Department and also in Japan in 1992. At the Department I attended two meetings with her and Professor Roosens. On these occasions, under the guidance of Professor Roosens, the questions of her survey were being discussed and assessed. She has conducted a survey on the adaptation and intercultural experiences of the Japanese in Brussels. A total of 580 questionnaires was distributed among Japanese expatriates in Brussels. Of this total sample 363 questionnaires were collected, generating a response rate of 63 percent. Among the respondents there was an overwhelmingly number of males or 98 percent of the total. The age group was as follows: 48.6 percent was in his 30s;

35.3 percent in his 40s; 7.6 percent in the 60s and 6.5 percent in his 20s. Of the total respondents, 29.6 percent of the respondents actually chose to move temporarily to Belgium, whereas in the remaining cases, they were told to come. In other words, it was their company, which ordered the transfer to Belgium. Concerning the inconveniences, difficulties and concerns (*fuan*) associated with their overseas life, the respondents were free to indicate as many points of 'distress' as they saw appropriate for their personal case. The language (*kotoba*) problem followed by the weather (*kikoo*) and public safety (*chian*) were cited as the most distressing points. In terms of percentage, this is respectively 72.3 percent, 62.8 percent and 48.2 percent. Concerns about the education of the children (*kodomo no kyooiku*) also ranked relatively high (39.8 percent of the total respondents) among the list of 'difficulties and worries.' Racism or prejudice (*jinrui sabetsu, henken*) was situated almost at the bottom of this list. Only 14 percent thought this to be a matter of concern.

Divergence in adaptation process varied with age, marital status, educational background, overseas experience, and duration of sojourn. Regarding to the age-factor in adaptation, the older generation including those in their 40s and 50s expressed concerns related to family matters such as leaving family members behind in Japan, the education of their children in Belgium, etc. Those in the 50s cited interhuman relationship (*ningenkankei*) as a significant cause of distress (*fuan*). These interhuman relationships referred to the contacts with Belgians, non-Belgian foreigners and neighbors. On the other hand, the younger generation in the 20s encountered other difficulties like discrimination and prejudice. The marital status had also an impact on the divergence in coping with overseas life. Matters such as 'leaving family members behind in Japan'; 'househunting'; and 'traffic' caused more concern among the married than the non-married respondents. In contrast the topic 'feelings of solitude' constitutes the main distress among the non-married ones. Among the married group, differentiation could be found among those, who are accompanied by their family and those, who arrived on their own. The latter group was confronted with items such as 'leaving family members behind', 'eating habits' and 'loneliness', whereas the former group situated distress in matters like 'living facilities', 'interhuman relationship with local Japanese', 'economic responsibility', 'availability of news on Japan', 'interhuman relationship with houseowners and managers' and finally 'racial discrimination and prejudice.'

Concerning the educational background university graduates above the level of high school or vocational school had difficulties dealing with 'life planning after return' and 'different ways of thinking about work and management principles.' Those below that educational level did not experience distress. Important to note here is the level of language (English and French) of the respondents. It sounds obvious that someone with a beginner's level of these two languages will likely experience more stress and distress than their counterparts who master the two languages well. Regarding overseas experiences, those living in Brussels, thought that education of the children to be a priority item of worry. Those, who had been overseas before (40.3 percent) had relatively fewer difficulties in dealing with 'living facilities', 'eating habits', 'availability of news on Japan.' However, their areas of concern revolved around topics like 'family members left behind in Japan', and 'life planning after return.' Those who have had overseas experiences previously as foreign student and researcher did not have difficulties with 'life planning after return' and 'interhuman relationship with non-Belgian foreigners.'

The duration of the sojourn also plays a significant role in adaptation divergence. The newly arrived ones, whose stay was shorter than six months, faced the problem of 'loneliness.' When comparing those, who had been in Belgium for more than three years with those, whose sojourn spanned a period shorter than three years, the former group was more concerned with 'treatment and promotion after return' and 'life planning after return.' The list below gives an exhaustive summary of the areas of distress discussed above and ranked according to the frequency of citation in percentage. The respondents had the freedom to tick as many items as they thought appropriate. Therefore the total sum of the all the percentages is not 100 percent.

Table 11: Difficulties and Distress in (Overseas) Life (*Seikatsujoo no Konnan to Nayami*)

Areas	Percentage
1. Language (*kotoba*)	72.3
2. Weather (*kikoo*)	62.8
3. Public Peace and Order (*chian*)	48.2
4. Family Members Left Behind in Japan (*Nihon ni nokoshite kita kazoku*)	46.3
5. Different Ways of Thinking concerning Work and Management Principles (*shigoto ni taisuru kangaekata, keieihooshin nado no Nihon to no chigai*)	42.8
6. Living Facilities (*juutaku no setsubi*)	41.9
7. Education of the Children (*kodomo no kyooiku*)	39.8
8. Life Planning after Return (*kikokugo no jinsei sekkei*)	37.0
9. Availability of News on Japan (*Nihon ni kansuru joohoo no nyushu*)	31.6
10. Interhuman Relationship at the Workplace (*shokuba de no ningenkankei*)	30.0
11. Treatment and Promotion after Return (*kikokugo no shoguu, shooshin*)	29.7
12. Eating Habits (*shokuseikatsu*)	26.8
13. Health Matters (*kenkoojootai*)	24.1

Areas	Percentage
14. Traffic (*kootsu*)	24.1
15. Beauty Parlors and Barber Shops (*biyooin, rihatsuten*)	23.4
16. Economic Responsibility (*keizaiteki fudan*)	20.8
17. Househunting (*juutaku sagashi*)	20.5
18. Interhuman Relationship with Belgians (*Berugiijin to no ningen kankei*)	20.0
19. Interhuman Relationship with the Landlord and Managers (*oyasan, kanrijin to no ningen kankei*)	19.1
20. Solitude and Loneliness (*kodokukan, sabishisa*)	18.1
21. Interhuman Relationship with Local Japanese (*genchi no Nihonjin to no ningen kankei*)	16.7
22. Racism and Prejudice (*jinruisabetsu, henken*)	14.0
23. Interhuman Relationship with Residents of the Neighborhood (*kinrin no kyojuusha to no ningen kankei*)	11.0
24. Interhuman Relationship with non-Belgian Foreigners (*Berugiijin igai no gaikokujin to no ningen kankei*)	10.2

Source: Egawa 1994: 5

In a more modest way I have distributed questionnaires to a total of 25 Japanese expatriate respondents. I could count on the assistance of former Japanology students, working in Japanese companies. This sample of 25 people was scattered in seven different Japanese companies, all located in the Brussels area. The man/woman ratio was 19 to 6. Like Egawa's survey the main topics are related to how the Japanese live in Brussels in terms of adaptation in the host society, and in particular the difficulties Japanese experience in daily life and the level of intercultural contact between Japanese and non-Japanese in the workplace and in the private realm. Moreover, besides negative experiences in the adaptation process, this survey also looked – if any – for the positive dimensions of sojourn in Belgium. The average age of the respondent is 35.5. In total 80 people worked in the 7 companies, of which 44 people were Japanese, 28 Belgians and the remaining 8 were of other nationalities. More than half of the interviewees have had long-term overseas experiences for professional purposes, prior to the arrival in Belgium. One respondent has even studied in Belgium. The majority came with family.

The duration of sojourn ranged from two to five years, with the exception of a six-month traineeship. The majority (43 percent) socialized among the Japanese colleagues of the company, while only 14 percent mixed with foreigners including Belgians in the own as well as in other companies. Especially females, who worked in small companies, sought Japanese friends from other Japanese companies. In an open question, exploring their views on the less agreeable side or disadvantages of living in Belgium, the following items were collected.

Language barriers:

Language Incompatibility (*Kotoba tairitsu*)

> Concerning language problems, I get often frustrated when I cannot transmit what I think to someone. (*Kotoba no mondai wa aite ni jibun no omotte iru koto o tsutaeru koto ga dekinai koto ga ooku, furasutoreshon ga narimashita.*) There are mainly misunderstandings and sentiments of estrangement due to insufficient mastery of the language. (*Omo ni kotoba no fujiyuu ni yoru gokai/sogaikan.*)

Bad service/unfriendliness:

> Bad Driving Attitude (*unten manaa no warui*); not Respecting Traffic Rules (*kootsu ruuru o mamoranai.*)

When buying something I quarreled (with the shopkeeper) whether I had paid for my purchase (*Kaimono no sai okane o dashita dasanaide mometa koto.*)
At the municipality I complain for about 4 months about the loss of documents.
(*Commune de shorui o funshitsu sare yokkagetsu mo monku o iitsukenakereba naranakatta koto.*)

No sense for punctuality/slowness:

Even when I make an appointment, (people manage to) be not on time. (*Randeebu o totte mo jikan no seikaku de wa nai.*) The install-ment of the telephone line is slow. (*Denwa no tooritsu ga osoi.*)

Lack of logic

Many things are not logical. (*Monogoto ga gooriteki denai.*)

Racism

Racism (*Jinruisabetsu*)
When we asked one Belgian policeman for assistance to a Belgian person, who was clearly sick at the Grand Place, the policeman did not care about the sick person and only shouted: 'I hate the Japanese.'

Similarly, the advantages of living in Belgium were inquired by open questioning. The replies were thus.

Travel, sightseeing, social and cultural outings:

The possibility to travel all over (*Kakuchi ryokoo dekiru.*)
Because there are many nice places with lots of nature, where one can travel. (*Kankoo shi kirei na tokoro shizen no ooi tokoro ga takusan aru node.*)
The past half year I did (a lot) of shopping in Brussels, and I made a trip to Bruges and Ostend. (*Kono hantoshikan de wa Burasserushinai no shoppingu, Buruju, Osutendo e no ryokoo.*)
Traveling with my family inside as well as outside of the country (*Kazoku to no ryokoo, kokunai, gaikoku to mo.*)

I organize parties with friends, go to concerts and take trips. (*Tomo-dachi to patii o hiraitari, konsato, ryokoo ni dekaketari shita koto.*)

Excellent food:

Savoring Belgian cuisine (*Berugii ryoori o taberu koto*)
When eating for the first time sea snails from a food stand (*Yatai no umi tanishi o hajimete tabeta toki*)

Making new friends:

The fact that I have the occasion to acquaint myself with nice friends. (*Tanoshii yuujin ni shiriaeta koto.*)
The fact that I have the chance to meet, understand and talk in different languages with Europeans. (*Yooroppa no hitobito to iroiro hanashi ga deki, rikai shi aeru koto.*)
At the language school I had the chance to meet many friends. (*Gogaku skuuru de ooku no yuujin deaeta koto.*)

Hospitality/public civility:

When I was a student, it was wonderful that I could stay in a (Belgian) friend's house. (*Gakusei jidai Berugii ni ryokoo shita toki, tomodachi no ie ni tomete morai tanoshikatta.*)
The other day when I had a flat tire, a youngster and his father, living in that neighborhood, called out as they were concerned about me. (*Senjitsu kuruma no taiyaa ga pakku shita toki sono fukin no sumai no shoonen to chichioya ga watashi o shinpai shite koe o kakete kureta.*)

In analyzing the two sets of data one can prudently conclude that Japanese expatriates in Belgium on the whole have difficulty reaching beyond the own group. The exchange with the host society is limited. Of course, language explains largely the lack of contact communication and exchange. Nearly all Japanese I talked to during my research period reiterated the language factor as an obstacle. The language barrier has been referred too in many forms: 'language incompatibility' (*kotoba no tairitsu*), 'language problem' (*kotoba no*

201

mondai), 'language non-fluency' (*kotoba no fujiyuu*). It brings about many daily problems such as shopping, going to a hairdresser, and other day-to-day activities. Therefore, special stores and services with Japanese speaking personnel have responded to the needs of the Japanese. Language constraint lies not only in getting one's ideas across but also in expressing one's ideas thoroughly. Since English or French is the second language in Brussels, Japanese are disadvantaged in communication with native speakers of French. Yet deficient language skills cannot account entirely for the lack of contact.

The duration of the stay is relatively short and limited. Moreover, The return becomes an area of distress when the end date is approaching. Those, who have been staying in Belgium for a period longer than three years, are more confronted with the return issue, and everything connected with it such as 'life planning after return', 'treatment and promotion after return', etc. It seems that the duration of stay from two to five years does not encourage insertion and participation and involvement in the local life. Therefore, it allows for temporary isolation, as the necessity to become integrated becomes less urgent for them than ethnic minorities.

Second, willingness lacks on the part of the Belgians to accept the Japanese according to two respondents. The first one was at the receiving end of a racist and discriminatory attitude, while she was just trying to display public civility. The second respondent describes the 'average' Belgian as generally conservative. While asking Japanese housewives about this issue, they always sense a hint of discrimination in the social interaction with locals, without really calling it racism. They feel that locals ignore them, lump them together with other Asians such as the Chinese and Vietnamese. In general, Japanese think that locals know very little about Japan and the Japanese. Furthermore, they show no inclination whatsoever for mending their insufficient knowledge. This process is not only due to the ascribed strong in-group orientation of the Japanese but also due to the attitude of the locals with little interest for the Japanese cohabitants.

Part Three

At the Micro Level

10 A Returnee Family

General

This part is divided into three settings, in which the actual lives and the specific identity formation and management of individual returnees will be dealt with at the micro level. The meat of the three accounts, discussed in chapters 10, 11 and 12, derives from personal interviews, informal chats and participant observation during the period 1990–4 in both Belgium and Japan.

This chapter contains the first ethnographic account. It is the narration of the personal life stories and (overseas) experiences of the different members of a returnee family. I choose to represent this account first, as it would reflect the process of ethnography. It was through the acquaintance with this family that my research and insights were gradually developed. I met S. in Belgium. She played a major role in the development of my research. She was the central figure introducing me into the Japanese community in Brussels, and in Nagoya to the Nanzan International School. Finally, she was also my host during my sojourn in Nagoya. At the time of my visit, the two returnee daughters were absent. One was studying at Keio, Yokohama and the other at the University of Pennsylvania, US. This situation is not at all an exception as for educational purposes the daughters have lived alone for quite some years, away from the parents. The two grandmothers live in their own homes, connected with the center house through a common hallway at both sides of the house. The garden is at first glance a shared and communal domain. There were no physical walls or other separating devices in it. Yet there were implicit boundaries since the plantation of flowers in the own plot, which was roughly the extension of the own house, was a personal matter of the three women. The many meals and conversations I have had with the different members of the family, alongside with the many overheard conversations and non–verbal communication, gave me new insights about the dynamics of Japanese ethnonational identity, and how individuals live, express and cope with it. Particular attention is given to the three generations of women: the grandmother, the mother and the returnee daughter. This approach is adopted because they represent different generations, living in different periods of Japanese recent history, each period marked by a specific internal debate on the own identity and culture. Roughly their personal lives correspond with respectively the early modernization period, the postwar catching-up modernization era and the current times of internationalization/globalization.

The O. Family in Belgium (1989–93)

Acquaintance with the O. Family

I first met Mrs. O. or S. in 1990 at an international symposium in Leuven. At that time she was enrolled as a student in the Master's Program of European Studies. She was one of the few people in the audience, who asked a question to the speaker. Although her English was not perfect, she cared more about getting the message across than expressing herself in a grammatically flawless way. Afterwards, while having a cup of coffee at a nearby café, I talked to her and spoke about my project. She instantly became interested as the many topics I would address, were issues, which mattered to her, although from her perspective as a concerned Japanese mother. Her status was not much different from that of most Japanese females in Belgium, namely a housewife accompanying her husband abroad.

Yet the resemblance stops here. Unlike the majority of Japanese spouses who after household chores seek diversion and company with the in-group members, S. aspired to do something more 'solid' and 'personally rewarding' besides domestic work, shopping and socializing with other Japanese housewives. Not long after our first meeting, I was invited to her house to meet and interview her daughter M., who was at the time studying at the International School of Brussels.

At the azalea apartment

At the time of the first visit, according to the general Japanese practice, she sent me a detailed self-made how-to-get-there map beforehand. At that time the family O. was living in an apartment building. It was a clear mid-February afternoon in 1991. I rang the bell and S. let me in. The living room was filled with boxes, some packed and a few in the process of being packed. S. apologized for the disorder in her living room. She explained to me that they were moving to a larger place, a house with a garden a few streets further. Hence the chaos in the living room. After five minutes, M. came out of her room and we were introduced to each other. We started to make small talk on Saint Valentine

Day, which was the day after, and the specificity of this custom in Japan. Unlike in England and the United States, it was the custom in Japan that on this day female workers in offices offer chocolates to their male colleagues, the so-called *giri choco*, 'duty chocolates.' It is thus called because it was imperative for females, generally of lower rank than their male counterparts to treat their older colleagues to sweets. M. started to talk about her overseas sojourns.

I was in the United States from the age five until ten. I felt great there. I learned English without any problem. I love American food: the 'Whoppers' of Burger King, pizza's, bagel with cream cheese, ice cream...But although I fit in, I remember someone calling me 'Chink', thinking I was Chinese. That was a very humiliating experience. It also made me realize that no matter how much I talk and behave like an American, I was always going to be an outsider. The first year of return was terrible. I felt like a complete outsider. When I returned, I had to study at a local primary school. There was no returnee primary school in the neighborhood we lived. My sister, who was older, could go to a returnee school so she was luckier. I was the only returnee child in school. The other children didn't like me and didn't want to become my friends. I felt very lonely. They bullied me for my odd behavior and for not being like everyone else.

Apart from socialization and identity problems, she still remembered with fear the strong discipline and the rigid application of the rules in school.

Once a boy forgot to bring a book to school. Instead of giving him a warning or another penalty, he was hit until he started to bleed. I can still see the blood dripping from his hands. What is even worse was that we were forced to look at him while he was being punished. So I was all the time afraid for forgetting things. I was always nervous at that time. I was also physically ill. I think that must have been the stress.

Now her mother joined the conversation.

I think the reason why there are so many rules in Japanese schools and why Japanese teachers emphasize 'discipline' is because Japan is a small and overpopulated country and it is necessary to teach Japanese children to follow the rules and to be disciplined in an orderly organized society. That's why Japanese children are taught to conform; why they have no free time for themselves; why they have to study all the time even during vacation.

In 1991 she was a last-year student in the high school of the International School of Brussels. At first in 1989, M. felt a bit out of place at the school. Integration in the larger school environment did not come easily. Although she could talk to other pupils because her English was excellent, she still could not make friends among the English-speaking groups. Participation in extracurricular activities was an integral part of school life. Pupils were expected to participate in all sorts of activities. They were encouraged to join sports clubs, cultural clubs, etc. For M. it was difficult to get accepted at first, especially by American fellow students. She was too timid. In addition, Japanese parents were strict on letting their children going out at night. Other Japanese students had the additional problem of language insufficiency. S. then explained why she herself became active in the school, first joining the PTA as a Japanese parent and afterwards the Board of Directors.

I wanted to set an example for my daughter and also for the other (Japanese) pupils and parents. On the whole Japanese parents do not interfere with the schooling of their children. They don't participate in the school life and therefore many problems facing the Japanese kids are not being discussed in the school. So that's why I volunteered to become a member of the PTA. I volunteered in the library. I've entered the titles of all the Japanese books into the computer. At first I was alone to do this. Later, many Japanese housewives helped me. I also suggested the school to offer the International Baccalaureate Program, which is officially recognized in the Japanese educational system. Otherwise Japanese returnees have to take both a high school graduation test and a university entrance examination. That would be too heavy and also jeopardize the chances to get in the good schools. Through the IB program they have to take one examination less. By my involvement I wanted to show to the other Japanese that they should not isolate themselves from others. I think this non-involvement leads to misunderstanding and even prejudice against the Japanese. The Japanese talk much about internationalization but they don't do much to change the educational system according to the new situation. What's really bothering me is the different time schedule of the school year system. In Japan the academic year starts in April, whereas in almost all other countries, school begins in the month of September. So the returnees, who finish in May lose a whole semester because they can start at the earliest in April of the following year. I think that's a point that needs to be changed. I think universities should allow returnees to enter school in September.

Concerning the educational future of M., a decision has already been made. After considering the two possibilities of the US and Japan, her parents decided that Japan would be the best choice. It was reasoned that in the US, she would be treated as an outsider, as a foreign student. She has applied for Keio University, Tsukuba University, Nanzan University and Aoyama Gakuin University in descending order of preference. The choice of these universities was first based on the existence of a special reception policy for returnees. Second, her outspoken preference for the first two institutions corresponds, as one would expect, with the general sound reputation of Keio, a private university and the State University of Tsukuba. She explained her strategy and the probability chances of entry in the cited universities as follows.

My first choice is Keio University because it is very prestigious. Keio has a special program combining both the Japanese and American system. There is an exchange program with American universities. The teaching method is a combination of the two systems. Because Keio is prestigious, there will be a lot of applicants and it would not be easy to enter. If I fail, I will study at Tsukuba University, where there is a very interesting intercultural program in the International Relations Program. If again I don't pass, I don't think I would have trouble entering Nanzan University, because I had been to the International Section of the Nanzan Middle School (for returnees). Besides there are some links between Toyota, where my dad

211

works and Nanzan University. Aoyama Gakuin University is my last choice for in case everything fails.

The conversation moved on to family related matters. When I inquired on the life course of S., she told me how her life has changed due to overseas experiences.

When I first got married, I devoted the first ten years of my life to housekeeping. As an undergraduate student at Aoyama Gakuin University in Japan, I was not yet conscious how study could change one's life. If I had, I would have persisted in going to Waseda instead of Aoyama Gakuin because Waseda is university with a higher reputation. But my brother decided that the second school was more appropriate for me because I was a woman. I was going to get married anyway and take care of my husband and family. So why bother going to a good school? But when I was married for some time, I became so bored with household work. I didn't want to be just someone's wife but I wanted to be myself. Sometimes I think the trip to the US has helped me make up my mind to do something with my life. I suppose that if I had stayed in Japan, I would perhaps not be able to cope with all the resistance against my decision to study something for myself. It just happened that at the time of my stay in the United States, when my children were older and less dependent. So I had more time for myself. The urge to do something became stronger and stronger. My husband at first did not really understand it but because I didn't give up the idea, he finally agreed and said that I could do so on the condition that I would not neglect my duty as a wife and mother. So I enrolled myself in the MA Program in the Farleigh Dickinson University. I chose the program 'English as a Second Language' because I thought this degree would be useful in Japan. With such a degree I would not have difficulties finding a job in Japan. I still remember what a great experience it was to be in school again. Especially because this time I really wanted to learn something. I have met so many marvelous and inspiring friends. That's also why I want my daughters to be someone besides being someone's wife.

During her stay in Belgium she seized the occasion to get a degree in European Studies. She was determined to do her household and to get a degree. It was difficult to manage her time effectively. In order of priority and urgency, she was first wife of the husband, second, the caring mother of her two children at home and an active mother at school, coordinating the school career of her two daughters and only third a graduate student.

> It's difficult. First I'm first a housewife. I have to cook and entertain people, mostly business relations of my husband. Second I'm a mother of two daughters. Mih. is now studying at Keio and M. at ISB. In 1989 M. didn't feel comfortable in school. I decided to set a good example and I got involved in school as a volunteering parent. And only in the third place I think of myself, what I want to learn for myself. Because it is not easy combining the three jobs I sometimes have to neglect my own studies. I have very little time for study. It's a pity but there is not much I can do about it. I am waiting for the day when I can 'retire' from being a mother. Not until then studying is a luxury for me. I've to wait until my two daughters are settled: good job, financial independence, married, etc.

Changing role of the father: from a 'thin shadow' to a co-parent

K., the husband of S. is the oldest son of the family. He graduated from the engineering Department at Tokyo University in 1964. After graduation he joined Toyota and has been working there ever since. He married his wife S. through an arranged marriage (*omiai*). Like all postwar *sarariiman* (white-collar employee) he worked very hard and devoted most of his time to work-related matters. Asking him what he thought of his wife trying to combine the role of housewife, mother and professional woman, he replied:

> At first I didn't like it. I thought she would not have enough time to do the usual work at home. So I was not really happy with her decision to start studying while we were in New Jersey. But she reassured me that she would manage and do her schoolwork after household duties. I found out a bit to my surprise that she could do both. When I was young I came home very late because I socialized with my colleagues after work. While we were in the States I started

to come home early and I liked that better. I had more time to relax at home and more time to spend with my family. In 1989 I came first with my youngest daughter M. My wife stayed behind because she had to help my older daughter, Mih., who was just entering university. So M., my youngest daughter, took care of me, cooking for me and doing the household. When I saw she had problems with her homework I began to come home right after work to help her. My colleagues understood my situation. Of course I'm quite senior now. In fact sometimes it's convenient that my wife is so active and that she speaks so many languages. For example she has to interpret for my senior's wives on social occasions. Since she knows many people it is also convenient to have her when we are entertaining Japanese clients from Japan in Belgium. Besides dining with them, we have to take them on local trips like a visit to Bruges. I know a lot about Belgium through books but because she goes to college here and because she is curious about so many things, she can organize very interesting trips. And that is very good for my career, too.

As the only man in the family surrounded by females, he at times felt excluded.

Especially when we were still living in New Jersey, S. and the two girls would talk in English and I couldn't always understand them. I must say at that time my English was rather poor. In the meantime I have improved quite a bit. But I still talk English with a Japanese accent. My wife and girls always tease me for my funny accent.

M., the youngest daughter had very fond memories of the first 6 months of their stay in Brussels.

Yes, it was great. I saw my father really changing. I didn't ask him to help me with my schoolwork but he did it spontaneously. I think he changed a lot through my mother, who always insisted on doing new things, solving practical problems. I think he loves her very much. He's very proud of her.

The change from an 'absent father', the *otoosan no kage wa usui* (the father's shadow is thin) phenomenon devoting all his attention to work to an understanding husband and caring father was triggered by the overseas experiences. S. harbored the following feelings.

214

Suppose that we had never left Japan, it would be harder to change the traditional role patterns in the family. I had to convince him very hard in the beginning before he agreed that I could take up my studies. You see we are in fact a very typical *sarariiman* family. My husband is working for Toyota and he will stay there until retirement. The company has been very good to us but I must say I always try to keep a distance. For example I've never wanted to live in the company's apartment because we would lose our autonomy. Now after more than twenty years of marriage I think he understands my aspirations and me.

The older sister and the exigencies of study

Although the family has two daughters, I have never known the oldest, Mih. well simply because in the period of 1990–5, she was not living with her family. When I first met the family she was studying Law at Keio University. Yet during her undergraduate years, she took a year off to come to Brussels to join her parents and to study French. In that one year, I saw her on a few occasions on social events like the International festival at the International School or briefly during the family visits. She took the study of French very seriously. Given her beginners' level of French, she was not accepted at the University of Brussels. She finally enrolled herself at the Alliance Française.

This does not mean that she was completely absent during the fieldwork period. On the contrary the family talked about her on many occasions by making many allusions to her capacities and her drive to obtain her goals. Viewed from the position of the younger sister, the older sister represented her opposite. More clearly M. felt they were two extremes. Whereas her sister was a perfectionist and ambitious in her career, M. took life more easily.

My sister is pretty and smart. I admire her a lot. Since I'm the younger sister, if I go to a place where she had been, people always compare me with her. I didn't like that very much because in many ways

215

she was better than I was. When she turned fifteen she became even more pretty. Her eyes all of a sudden started to become bigger. You see, big eyes are still a rare commodity in Japan and they enhance your chances to find a good husband. Besides, she is tall and skinny and not small and plump like me. In Japan, she has so many admirers. As for me, I'd rather postpone homework if possible. But my sister takes study very seriously. She has always a clear idea of having some sort of a career. I'm different. For a long time I thought I would find a husband, get married and have children like everyone else. We are different not only in character but also in clothing. She dresses herself like a Japanese woman: very classic, no bright colors and always looking sensible. I can't do that. I like things that are a bit extravagant. For example: she would choose (little) pearl earrings whereas I prefer the long silver ones. When I was younger she would always criticize me for not being disciplined and I felt inferior to her. But now after so many years I think we're just different and can't be compared.

Farewell party at a restaurant

In June 1991 I invited M. for a farewell party at a restaurant in Leuven as she was about to return to Japan. I picked her up at the School. Together we drove in the direction of Leuven. In the car we chatted about the traffic. M. remarked:

I think the traffic is very chaotic in Brussels. Of course I don't drive but my sister is now taking driving lessons in Brussels. She's horrified. And my mother   recently got a ticket from the police because she was driving too slowly. The police said that she was hindering other cars. My mother was very surprised. In Japan drivers are different. They are very disciplined.

When we arrived, we had to walk some distance to the restaurant. M. remarked:

I always wonder why there's no one in the streets? What are the young people doing all the time? In Japan the streets are always crowded and filled with people and noise. But here it's completely different. I heard from a friend that they are always inside: in cafés or in a disco.

216

In the restaurant the main topic of the conservation revolved around her return to Japan. As the date of departure was approaching, she was becoming more nervous. Her mother is accompanying her during the trip and during the first period in Japan to make sure that she was properly settled in the boarding house of the university and well–adjusted to life in Tokyo.

> I'm becoming more and more nervous about all the tests. I speak English fluently but I still have difficulties with the grammar of the English language. And I'm really poor in math. So I think I've to study in cram schools when I arrive in Japan. Luckily before going to Japan we are going to spend one week in New Jersey to visit old friends, we had met when we were living there. That's going to be fun. But then afterwards...I don't know how Tokyo will be. I've never lived there, in a big city.

Life at Keio University

In spite of her initial fear for not getting into Keio University, M. was accepted as a September entrant in 1991. She was therefore fortunate on two accounts: she could start school in the university of her first choice and second, she could make use of the special September entrance instead of the usual April entrance. She wrote me a letter after the first semester, trying to come to terms with studying at a Japanese first-rank university and living alone in the metropolitan city of Tokyo. In fact according to a postcard she sent me, the campus of her university was in Yokohama near to Tokyo.

> It's been pretty tough around here; getting used to Tokyo; getting used to school and most of all, getting work done! But now I'm pretty much settled down, and I think I'll be able to survive...though I'm not sure about what my grades will look like! Haha. The campus is very spacious and the equipment very up-to-date. The other students are so smart. Sometimes I have difficulties with reading, especially for the *kanji*. I have to look them up in a *kanji* dictionary and then look them up in a Japanese–English dictionary. Some of my friends wonder whether I am Japanese. Just a joke...I am staying in a

dormitory. I don't go out much because I don't have money. It's all right. I have made quite a few friends in the dormitory.

The Japanese alumni association of the International School of Brussels

Not long after the visit at the Azalea Apartment in 1991, the family moved to a house, where they stayed until their return to Japan. It was a spacious house with a large garden at the back. S. invited me for lunch at the new place. The visit was in the late spring of 1992, some time before my first field trip to Japan. The interior of the house was completely Western. The house was furnished when the family moved in, like most Japanese expatriates' homes in Brussels. Some electronics like a Japanese *waapuro*, Toshiba answering and fax machine and kitchen utensils such as a Japanese rice cooker prove the Japanese presence aside from the neatly arranged slippers at the entrance of the door.

The main objective of the visit was to obtain the list of the ISB alumni, who participated in the first meeting of the ISB Japanese alumni association in Tokyo, held in March 1992 for the first time. The list proved to be very valuable as I did not have to trace down the addresses and telephone number of the ISB alumni, which facilitated significantly my field-work. She served roasted chicken and green salad. She informed me: 'It's very simple food. In fact the chicken is a leftover from yesterday's dinner party. I hope you don't mind. We entertained guests yesterday.' As she and some older alumni organized the meeting, I asked her what she thought of the event.

> It was a very emotional occasion. Of the total 80 ISB alumni, 33 students together with their parents showed up. It was good to see them again. Everyone was very glad to have the chance to meet and share memories. M. did a great job. As the Association consists of ISB

alumni I think the organization should be in the hands of the former students. I was also asked to be the chairman but I declined.

I asked her whether the main objectives have been met. She answered:

> The objective of this association is first to create a forum of ISB alumni to meet and exchange ideas and information. So the primary goal is practical. Second, the meeting, which will be organized every two years, has an emotional value as all members meet each other and feel 'united' by having studied at the same school. As you know in Japan, friendships made in schools last very long. As returnees have studied abroad, without these biannual meetings they will miss out on a very common event of school reunions. The first meeting in March this year has a great emotional value. Of course the organization still needs to grow. We have to wait a few years when the oldest alumni have finished college, worked for some years before the network will start to work.

On this occasion the headmaster of the International School of Brussels accompanied S. to attend the first meeting of the ISB alumni association. In addition, she and the headmaster used the occasion to arrange a meeting with representatives of the Ministry of Education.

> It was unique because the meeting was arranged by a contact at the Japanese Embassy in Brussels. There's also the fact that I was in the company of the president of the school that we got a personal interview with four bureaucrats at the Ministry. Without these two conditions I would not have such a chance. I'm after all just a simple Japanese housewife...Anyway I told them all the problems I've come across as a mother and as an administrator at the International School. One of the main problems is that schools do not have their brochure and registration kit ready for returnees, who plan to enter Japanese universities in September. Japanese universities don't take into account that the academic year in most countries starts in September and not in April like in Japan. Therefore, they should plan the printing of all materials accordingly. Then I asked for a closer cooperation between the Japanese School and the International School of Brussels like dispatching Japanese personnel of the Japanese School to the International School. After all the youngsters didn't choose

themselves to come here. They are here because the company has sent out their father.

Asking her what she thought of the effectiveness of the meeting, she remained realistic.

> Of course, they are bureaucrats. They listened attentively while being very careful in what they said and did. They replied that their task is to follow the rules and not to make them. In last instance it is up to the schools for integrating these youngsters in the larger school environment and society.

Studying at the *Meisjescentrum*

In 1993 the assignment of her husband came to an end. S. contacted me because at the farewell party in the company she was going to a give a speech in different languages, and also in Dutch. As she wanted someone to correct the few sentences and to help her with the pronunciation, she asked me. She also secretly told me that she was staying behind to finish up her degree. A week later or so, I received a telephone call from S.:

> Hello. How are you? I'm alone now. I can do whatever I want for one entire month. My husband left yesterday. I had to drive him to the Charles de Gaulle Airport to take the plane. You see we decided it wouldn't be a good idea to let his colleagues know that we were not going together. They will gossip that I'm not a good housewife and that my husband is a weak man. So in order to avoid this, we had a farewell party in the company. At the party my husband told his colleagues not to bother to see us off in Paris. That would be too troublesome. Do you know where I'm calling from? From the *Meisjescentrum* in Leuven. If you have time, let's have dinner together and I can show you my new room.

Some days later I passed by the *Meisjescentrum*, an all girls'dormitory of the Catholic University of Leuven for a visit. At first I had trouble finding her. I only knew her husband's surname and not her maiden name. Since it was the

policy of the *Meisjescentrum* to use the latter, I left her a note to call me back. When she contacted me, we fixed a date to meet up. I was amazed at her tiny room, in which she had to sleep and study. Books were everywhere, on the bed, on the desk, piled up on the floor. It reminded me of the tiny rooms I had lived in during my own student time. I asked her: 'Don't you think this place is a little too small, even for one person? You don't have problems with that? It is certainly a great change since your previous house in Brussels.'
She replied:

> It's OK. At last I don't need to divide my attention to different things at the same time. I can entirely concentrate on reading and writing papers and getting my degree. Besides it's only temporary. I have waited so long for this moment, to have some peace and do my own things. As I told you over the telephone my husband and I we worked out a plan so that his boss and the other colleagues would not know about this. They certainly would disapprove and think I'm not doing my job as a housewife properly by staying behind. That's why nobody knows I am here. They all think I went home together with my husband.

I inquired on her husband's opinion.

> At first he didn't see the point of it. But I insisted how important it was for me to finish my degree. Then he raised the safety and financial aspect of me staying behind. That's why I decided on the *Meisjeshuis*. I think it's quite safe for a woman to stay in this dorm because there is a curfew at night and the other lodgers are all girls. I also picked out an affordable room. So when I gave him all these points there was not much left against which he could oppose. So here I am.

Visiting the O's in Japan

General

I stayed with the family for about three weeks in their American-style suburban house on the outskirts of the city of

Nagoya in September 1994. I took the bus from Kyoto to Nagoya. After arriving there, I had to take the metro to Shiratori. The first thing I remember while getting off the metro train was a most welcoming cool breeze. Then, I took a general look around me and marveled at the open space and greenery, although the omnipresent signs of fast food chain restaurants – American as well as Japanese – loomed in the background. So this was Shiratori, a residential suburb of Nagoya. More than a year has passed since we last met. As soon as I descended from the station, I noticed her sitting in the car. She had not changed at all. She greeted me and helped me with my luggage.

After the usual greetings, she then explained to me how she would treat me.

> C. L.san, you're very welcome in my house. I am so glad you are continuing your research. I'm also very happy you could come and stay in my house. At the moment, there is plenty of room in the house. Both Mih. and M. are not home. So you can sleep in M.'s bed. If you don't mind, I'm going to treat you in the American way. During daytime because my husband and I've to go out to work, you have to look after yourself. I tell you how to take the public transportation so you will find your way from my house to the school. Of course, you are more than welcome to have supper with us.

After a short ride of ten minutes, we arrived at her house. From the outside, it looked like a standard suburban American house. It was a white-painted wooden house built on a street with a slight slope. A staircase leads to the main entrance of the house, while the garage was situated at the street level. We entered the house, changed our shoes for slippers and through the *genkan* (hallway) went into a spacious room, which was divided in a dining and living room. It was a Sunday afternoon. K., S.'s husband was sitting on the sofa, reading the Sunday newspaper, while a CNN news broadcaster on the large television screen was reading enthusiastically the latest news in the world. He got up and welcomed me.

The next step was to introduce me to the two old ladies, who lived next door to the main house. We went through the garden. There we were stopped by their energetic dog, Choco. We went first to the house of Grandmother N., S.'s mother. She was the older of the two grandmothers. She opened the door and smiled at me while I was being introduced by Sono. Her tall figure, although the back slightly bent forward due to her advanced age made a deep impression on me. Then we walked over to the house of Grandmother O. but she was not at home. S. explained: 'She must have gone to visit her youngest son. You see, he's not married and lives alone.'

After the introduction session, I was showed to the room, where I was going to stay. This *yooshitsu* (Western-style room) was the former bedroom of her two daughters. Although the two daughters were not actually living there, the room was kept intact. There was a desk, a bookcase filled with books, mostly Japanese novels and some English books and a bunk-bed. The window gave out on a balcony, from where I had a view of the roofs of the nearby built houses. While looking down, I could look into the gardens of the neighbors. I was asked to sleep on the lower side of the bunk-bed. That was the bed M. used to sleep.

At the other side of the room was the bedroom of S. and her husband. Although I was not invited into it, I could see from the outside that the room was a *washitsu* (a Japanese-style room): a tatami-covered floor and a rolled up *futon*. After having refreshed myself in the small bathroom on the first floor, I went down and a further guide tour through the house followed. This time I was shown to the study room, a *washitsu*, too. There was a *kotatsu* in the middle of the room, a television, a bookcase and a closet filled with videotapes against the walls. The study room faced a Japanese-style rock garden at the rear of the house (connecting the main house and that of Grandma O.), which matched with the *washitsu* style of the room. This was the place where S. usually worked when preparing her English classes, grading the students' papers, etc. During my stay she taught at two institutes, a private business school and a local university, while applying for a job at yet another educational establishment. Besides her *waapuro* (Japanese language word processor) and her books on the *kotatsu*, there was an extensive collection of videotapes. Asking her why and when she had amassed them, she replied:

> While we were in Belgium, we have taped the films and the programs we liked. I think it's a very playful way to learn and it costs little. While enjoying the film, we also keep up with our languages. Look. This is the French version of *The Sound of Music*. It is one of my favorite films.

Opposite the study room was the bathroom, where a Japanese-style bath (*furo*) was installed. It also served as the laundry room.

From 'empty' commodities to the 'I-have-been-there' goodies

The new middle class in the postwar period displays a drastic change in consumption patterns as well as in consciousness (Horioka 1993). One of the results of the emergence of a mass-consumption consciousness, is the changing interior of Japanese families, the 'rabbit hutches, stuffed with goodies.' What marked the O.'s out, although their consumption pattern may be similar to other families, is the international character of the goods. The 'I-have-been-there' dimension of the commodities refers to the added value of being and acquiring them 'there' on the spot.

As the family O. has lived twice abroad and made many trips while they were abroad, they have sent back numerous items that they purchased abroad. For instance, they have shipped back the wooden desk, made in Mechelen in the bedroom on the first floor besides some chairs purchased at Ikea in Zaventem, Brussels. Moreover, some smaller items on display had been acquired overseas: a terra cotta vase bought in Morocco, a set of crystal Val-Saint-Lambert wine glasses, tiles from Portugal, Holland and Germany, adorning the walls of the living room. On the wall of the hallway connecting the living room with the bathroom hang a detailed hand-drawn street map of Brussels with indications of the landmarks of Brussels including the Grand Place, the Royal Palace, the Munt Theatre, the Palace of Justice, etc.

One night I noticed the map. Both S. and her husband were in the neighborhood. After having pointed to the place where I lived in Brussels, Mr. O. recommended me his favorite Japanese restaurant in Brussels.

It's around this place. (His finger pointed to a street close to the Munt theater.) When you are back in Belgium, you should go and eat at that place and tell the owner that you come with the recommendation of the O's.

Yet of all these 'I-have-been-there' commodities, the 'picture corner' represented the miniaturization of the family's peripatetic life. In fact, these pictures stood on top of the black Yamaha piano, strategically positioned in a corner near the dining table, from where they were highly visible. As one would expect, there were many family pictures, narrating the life cycles of the different family members: black and white pictures capturing family occasions, weddings, birth, graduation parties, awards, etc. Moreover, apart from family photographs, there were also pictures of mostly foreign friends and colleagues. When S. observed my curious look at the pictures, she explained to me:

These are pictures of people, who are all very dear to us...While we're eating, we can look at them. So they remain vivid in our mind. You see I don't have much time to keep in touch with people. Oh yes, we should make a picture of you and add it to the collection.

Meal participation

The original plan was to treat me as a guest in the 'American way', implying a high degree of autonomy of the guest. In my case I had to keep myself busy during the daytime. In other words, S. was not going to take care of me all the time as generally Japanese hosts treat their guests. I was, however, kindly invited to share meals with the family. But she warned me: 'I hope you like Japanese food (*Nihonshoku*) because I will cook as usual.' As a result, my meal participation with the family added to my status as a guest an emic dimension of 'we are of the same group because we *can* eat together, as we share the same rule system' (Ashkenazi 1990: 339). At table, there were usually four people: S., K., Grandma N. and me. In terms of substance, setting and situation, these food events were 'central rice meals' (Ashkenazi 1990: 342), consisting of a bowl of rice and soup (*suimono*) supplemented by a side dish (*okazu*) of fish or meat, vegetables and Japanese pickles (*tsukemono*) all arranged nicely on individual ceramic plates. As I was staying at the end of the summer and the onset of autumn, I had the chance to taste both summer food (*natsu no aji*) and autumn food (*aki no aji*). The *umeshu* (Japanese plum wine) was one of the summer drinks making the exceptional heat more tolerable, especially when the plum wine was made by the woman of the house.

Given my Chinese origin, it was not a problem to eat rice as a staple and use chopsticks (*hashi*) instead of fork and knife to eat my meal. Although the chopsticks were put in a container at the table, everyone has his/her own pair and so did I.

226

I suppose those were the guest's chopsticks. The comportment was very relaxed and informal. As for seating arrangement, often I found myself next to Grandma N. She did not feel uneasy about it. Instead her mind seemed to be uplifted by the idea of having a guest in the house. She was a very elegant old lady. She was neatly dressed in clothes, which were reminiscent of traditional Japan, although she was never kimono-clad. The cut was rather Western: a long-sleeve shirt in combination with a knee-length skirt but the cloth was blue dyed cotton and the print looked very traditional. She was exquisitely well mannered without being mannerist. One night she told me the following story:

> You're very hard working. When I was young, I didn't like to study, at least not for all my classes. I remember in high school, I had a great time with my female friends. We loved tennis. We didn't do any homework. We just played. When you are young, you should enjoy yourself because once you grow up, things will change. I never thought that after my marriage I would go back to school. But it was a good experience to go and study in the capital of Tokyo. The war was the most terrible event in my life. The bombs were dropping off the sky when S. was still a baby of a few months old. It was a miracle that she survived. There was little food, medicine. Everything was destroyed and the situation seemed so hopeless.

S. joined in the conversation and said: 'Yes, it must have been very difficult for my mother. Japan was completely destroyed after the war.' I was very intrigued by Grandma N. mentioning her study period in Tokyo in her twenties.

> No, I did not attend the Tokyo University because at that time (in the 1920s), female students were not allowed there. But I talked to the professor of Chinese medicine (*kanpo*) at the University whether I could audit the class. As the professor agreed, I did this for two years. I was enrolled as a regular student at the Tokyo Women's Pharmacy School (*Tokyo Joshi Yaku Gakkoo*).

I could not help remarking: 'Then, your parents must have been very enlightened to send a girl to school in the 1920s?' She corrected me:

> Well, it was more a necessity than a conscious plan. I was the older of the two daughters in the family and I had to continue the family line. So when I married at the age of nineteen through an *omiai* (arranged marriage) my husband, who was a *yooshi* (an adopted-son-in-law), moved in and took our surname N. But my husband fell seriously ill with tuberculosis. My father then decided to send me to college. In case my husband died I would be in a better position to support the family with a degree. So in 1926, if I remember correctly – I was then twenty-two years old – I went to the capital to study at the Tokyo Women's Pharmacy School. After two years of study, I graduated from that school. I first worked in the laboratory of the Sanitary Material Department of the Ministry of the Army in Tokyo. Then I returned home and had a position in the general hospital in my hometown, Toyohashi for a while. When I came back, I found my husband recovered but I couldn't respect him anymore. Later I remarried, again with a *yooshi*. A bit later I opened my own pharmacy (*yakkyoku*) in my hometown, Toyohashi.

On the third day, I was kindly invited by Grandma O. to have a look at the *higanbana* (Licoris radiata) in her garden. As she is an accomplished *ikebana* teacher, she has an extensive collection of flowers in her garden. At first, I did not know the Japanese term and when I actually looked at it, I recognized it as a sort of amaryllis, except that the stem was not as thick. This was one of the favorite flowers of Grandma O., which she frequently used in her flower arrangements. After having seen the real thing, S. insisted on looking the term up in the dictionary and after some searching we discovered the scientific name for *Licoris radiata*. In Japan, *higan* means the equinox and therefore *higanbana* stands for the autumn equinox flower.

The *nashi-tanka* connection

One night after coming back from my interviews at the Nanzan International School, I saw a full crate of *nashi,* Japanese pears all of the same size and roundness. It looked like a gift. This was proven right since S. explained to me:

> This is what *obachan* ('granny') received from her students. Although she had a pharmacy all her life until a few years ago, she has also composed *tanka* since her teens. When she was thirty-three, she started to teach and compose *tanka* poetry. She soon gathered her own group of students by teaching them on the first floor while on the ground floor, she had a pharmacy. When she turned eighty, she retired and closed her pharmacy but she still continues to teach to her most loyal students. Since she's not asking any money, the students always give her seasonal presents.

In 1991 she received the Toyohashi cultural award for her life-long commitment of composing and teaching *tanka* to the local community. One of the pictures taken on that occasion was standing on top of the piano next to many photographs recording the crucial moments in the life of family and friends. Earlier in 1978, she had been awarded with the order of *Zuihou* from Emperor Hirohito as a mediator in the family court of Toyohashi for thirty years.

Between obligation and self-fulfillment

Although during daytime, I had to rush out to the Nanzan International School for interviews and S. had to go to school to teach, we found many in-between moments to chat. I returned around 6 o'clock in the evening. After I offered several times to help, she finally agreed. When she was alone with me, she very often started to talk about herself and her situation. She sighted:

> It's not simple. When my two children were young, I had to take care of them. Now they are more or less independent, I have to look after

the older generation. I don't mind my mother so much. It is hard to keep my mother-in-law satisfied. She's not really a difficult person and she only eats once a week with us, so I should really not complain, but still...I was very lucky that I could start working in the school after I returned from Belgium. Of course if I didn't leave, I would have become by now the head of the English Department. Instead my younger colleague has that position now. Oh well, it can't be helped.

Yet she stressed that she did not regret going to the United States, where among other things she obtained a Master's Degree in teaching English as a second language (ESL). Asking her why she wanted to continue to work three jobs despite her duties as a housewife and caretaker of two elderly women, she said:

Maybe you're right, doing three jobs is a bit too much. I'm so tired sometimes. I have to cook three meals including breakfast, lunch and dinner for my mother everyday. I have to do the household, cleaning up the place, doing the laundry. Then, I have to prepare my classes. Since Mih. studies at the University of Pennsylvania without a scholarship, we need some extra money. I don't mind working for my daughter because I want the best for her.

Since I was already told that Mih. was a brilliant student at the Law Department of Keio University, I did not understand why she did not work in Japan after graduation. S.'s voice heightened:

She didn't have much luck with the timing. When she came out of school, the 'bubble' economy had burst. It has become difficult for a woman to get a job because male candidates were preferred. Because she couldn't find work immediately, I suggested she go to the United States for another degree. This will make her more competitive on the Japanese job market.

One day in the early evening we had a spare moment together. As she looked extremely concerned I inquired about the cause of her distress.

It's really difficult. My husband was told that he might be transferred to Michigan. I sincerely hope we don't have to go. If I think that our life is going to turn around again...All that packing and unpacking, getting used to the new environment...Then there are also the two grandmothers.

Hopes and dreams

M. went home one week. She looked maturer. First her face has become less round than before. Second she also changed her way of dressing. In the past she used to wear jeans and T-shirt. Now she wore a skirt, pumps with some heels and on her face a small hint of makeup. 'Hello L. I can't believe this. This is really wonderful that you could come and see us.' Like most students, she was glad to be home, where she did not have to worry about household chores like cooking, cleaning, etc. At the dinner table, she rejoiced: 'This does really taste good, home-cooked food. I am really sick of all the fast food. But I can't help eating it because it's so convenient.' As a last year student at Keio, graduation was in sight. Given the negative experiences of her sister, she was somewhat worried.

> If Mih. couldn't get a job, I wonder how I could. But before worrying about that, I'm going to make a trip to Europe with two of my tennis friends. I know, mother, my education costs a lot and I know the family budget cannot afford it but I will earn enough money from my different *arubaito* (student jobs) to cover all the charges. Please mother?!

Her mother replied:

> You see, M., it is tough these days. You know that I have to work more to be able to finance your study and that of your sister. So, we don't have additional money for your vacation plans. But if you can earn your money, I think it's a good idea to show your two friends around in Europe. Father thinks the same way, you know. By the way, did you see the pictures Mih. sent us the other day? She is now more or less settled in Pennsylvania. Look, this is Kimberly. You remember her, Mih.'s classmate in New Jersey?

M. exclaimed:

> 'Waaw, is this Kimberly? I can't believe this. She's gotten so pretty.
> It's great Mih. got in touch with her, again. Gosh, Mih. looked tired
> on the picture.' Grandma N. joined in: 'Is this Mih.*chan*? She has
> grown very pretty.'

One Sunday, the family including S., her husband and M. decided to take me on a trip. Driving the Toyota four-wheel
drive, we departed early in the morning. The destination was
Taisho Mura, a reconstruction of the daily life in the Taisho
period. As I was sitting in the back with M., we had ample
occasion to chat and to gossip about the whereabouts of the
different ISB alumni. Most of them entered university in the
Tokyo area.

> I'm not really in touch with my former ISB friends. I know where
> they are studying. Actually there is D., who is also studying in Keio.
> But I don't have much contact with him. He has become very fash-
> ionable. He hangs out with his group of friends. I have my own
> group of friends. They are members of the campus tennis club. Most
> of them are *kikokushijo* but not all of them. It is OK to be returnee at
> school. On campus, there are many like us. I'm not the only returnee
> so I don't feel out of place. I also have a few non-*kikokushijo* friends
> but still, I feel a difference between them and us. My new boyfriend
> is also a *kikokushijo*. I met him in the tennis club.

When I told her I was very impressed by the presence of
strong women in the family, referring to S. and Grandma N.,
M. replied:

> Oh yes, my grandmother is incredible. When I was young, I was very
> afraid of her. She used to be so strict. She was always so demanding.
> My other Granny O. is much softer (*yasashii*). You see Mih. was al-
> ways the favorite of Grandma N. because she's a bit like her, very
> hard working and ambitious. She also looks like her. But I'm differ-
> ent. I take things not so seriously. I enjoy life. In fact I am not very
> interested in studying. I'd rather play and enjoy myself. But then, my
> mother will tell me that if I don't study, I will meet someone, who
> has not studied and then I will have a hard life. Besides she says that

even when I married a good and rich husband, and I stay at home, I will be bored out of my mind.

Back to Belgium

Brussels revisited: Part One

When January 1995 was drawing to a close, I found M.'s letter in my mailbox. To my amusement, like many Japanese, she misspelled my address and changed singled-handedly 'Avenue Van Volxem' into 'Avenue Van Voleur', probably not realizing the meaning of the revised version. The letter was written on six postcard size sheets, nicely decorated with seven blue tulips on the top, whereas the message 'feeling as if in a beautiful garden of tulip' in 'Japlish' was printed at the bottom of each sheet. This message in 'Japlish', referring to the combined use of English and Japanese, is not easy to understand for English-speaking people because of the Japanese grammatical constructions. A more correct rendition in Standard English would be 'a feeling one would experience while strolling in a beautiful garden of tulips.'

After the usual greetings and references to natural disasters – the Hanshin earthquake in the Kansai region and the floods in the northern part of France, Belgium and the Netherlands – she gave me her exact travel schedule. She and her two friends were planning to travel to Paris, Bruges, Brussels, Heidelberg, Fussen, Venice, Milan and Zurich during the two weeks they were visiting Europe. She rang me from her hotel in Brussels. We fixed an appointment to have dinner together the same evening. The hotel was located in the vicinity of the North Station. When I walked into the lobby, I saw a young Japanese woman tourist checking in. As the telephone line of M.'s room was engaged, I decided to go up myself. The hotel was rather old and shabby. Whereas efforts have been made to keep up the appearance in the lobby, the hallways were shamelessly showing decay and neglect. Moreover, a most disagreeable odor hung in the air. When I knocked at the door, it was M. who opened the door. Her two other girlfriends, resting on the bed seemingly tired by the hectic program, rose. M. introduced us. She had met these two friends at the university's tennis club. Then we discussed what to eat and where to go. The two accompanying friends did not have suggestions because during the trip they entirely depended on M. for advice and suggestions. M. indirectly launched the idea of having mussels and *frites* at *Chez Léon*.

While we were passing the different fish restaurants in the Rue du Boucher, waiters were welcoming us, while uttering Japanese greetings, such as *irasshaimase* (we welcome you), *konnichi wa* (hello). The restaurant *Chez Léon*, although at first one among many is clearly for the Japanese tourists the *primus inter pares* because a long line of Japanese were queuing in front of it. M. seeing these Japanese promptly decided to go elsewhere. She suggested going to another fish restaurant with similar food. While having mussels with *frites*, I asked her why she chose this period to travel to Europe. She said:

> Generally Japanese university students have Spring break in March. University students in the last year mostly make use of the occasion to make overseas travels to Europe, Australia or the US. In fact I'm not going to be graduated until September since I entered school in September and not in April like normal Japanese students.

Given the initial idea of dining at *Chez Léon*, I wondered what they thought of the food in this less-known-to-the-Japanese. M. replied for her friends:

> It's OK. I suggested *Chez Léon* because when we were in Belgium,

we used to eat there with my family. Besides the restaurant is well known among Japanese. It's mentioned in most travel guides.

I asked her friend how she liked the trip so far.

It was very nice, Paris and Bruges. The food is excellent. I like Bruges very much because it's small and in one of the shops where I bought lace, someone even spoke in Japanese to me. I could understand her very well. Yes, it is very nice.

After the meal I took them home as I told them the area of the hotel was not too safe. They eagerly consented. M. added:

Brussels has changed. When I was here everything seemed cleaner and safer. The neighborhood around the hotel seems dangerous and it's dirty. But the hotel is OK. It was a hotel recommended by the travel office of our University. It is affordable, I guess.

As I knew the next day they had to take the train to Heidelberg and they had not yet packed I wished them good luck and enjoyment in their two-week tour of Europe.

Season's greetings *à l'Américaine.*

When 1996 was only a few days old, I found in my mailbox a New Year's card of S. accompanied by a long and warm letter, containing the latest on the family.

Season's greetings!!...

K. was transferred from the engineering Administration Division to the Planning Division of Component and System Development Center (Toyota). He has been very busy lately trying to get used to his new post. He also had been elected and had accepted the position of Chairman for the Shiratori Community. He is busy with meetings of all sorts and he must be present at many of the main events that happen in our district. He is obligated to the duties of his post until next March. After that, hopefully, he'll have more time to himself again. S. has been busy also, (actually, there isn't anything new about that!!) with her teaching career. To add to her hectic schedule, S. had been offered a one-year term based job at the Kawaijuku International Education Center (in Tokyo) which she took up with great enthusiasm since it gave her the chance to visit Tokyo every other week. She enjoyed being able to see M. during these visits, and the same can be said on behalf of M. She will leave this job to take up a new job and position she has been offered by Sugiyama Women's Junior College (in Nagoya) from next April. S. is very excited about her new job and she is looking forward to the new challenge...I guess her schedule will stay the same...FULLY BOOKED!! Mih., who had pursued her studies in law at the University of Pennsylvania, graduated in May, and returned to Yokohoma for a brief time with her shining diploma. She did some job hunting in Japan, and we are happy to inform you that she has been accepted to the legal division of NEC (Nippon Electric Company). She will begin working for NEC from April. In August Mih. returned to New York and was employed for a temporary position as a paralegal at O'Melveny & Myers law firm. In October, Mih. decided to move back to Philadelphia. Mih.'s new place faces a very pretty park and her 14th floor apartment room provides a first-class view of Philadelphia's nightscape. M. was in her senior year at Keio University. M.'s classmates were scheduled to graduate in February, so M. and two of her girlfriends went on a trip to Europe in March. She of course passed by Brussels and dropped in for a quick HI! to the staff of ISB (The International School of Brussels). She was thrilled to have been able to visit Belgium and Europe again. After the trip, M. plunged into the 'GREAT JOB HUNT'. This year was said to be the worst yet for female graduates, but with luck, M. was accepted by the company of her dreams: 'WARNER MUSIC JAPAN.' In September, M. proudly graduated from Keio University with her seven fellow 'September Entrees' classmates. In October, M. went to visit Mih. in New York and moved to Philadelphia with Mih. during her stay. She is now going to Driver's Ed. School and is fretting over getting her license without killing herself!! Well, that's about all for now. As you can see, the O.'s are all doing well and always busy... Our two grandmothers, who are living with us, Grandma N. and Grandma O. are also well and doing fine. Choco, our dog is going to turn twelve this year; getting a bit old but still is very healthy and active. We send our warmest greetings for the holidays this season, and we hope you all have a wonderful new year!! We're sorry that our greetings are a bit late, but we hope to keep in touch with you always!

Brussels revisited: Part Two

At the market-place

It was a cold winter morning in late February 1996. In the previous few days much snow had fallen. S., who is teaching at several universities, decided to make a trip during the spring holidays. In view of her trip abroad she rounded the year up a bit earlier by skipping the *shaonkai* ceremonies organized by students to express their gratitude for the guidance of their teacher. Since she was staying with the Director of the International School of Brussels, who lived in Sint-Pieters-Woluwe, we fixed a meeting at the Stockel station. When I saw her approaching wearing red earflaps, I spontaneously started to apologize for the cold winter, after the greeting session. She did not mind the cold and said:

No, it's cold in Japan too. Last week it has snowed in Nagoya, which is rare. But honestly it's beautiful around here. Everything is covered with snow. I wished I had brought along my gym shoes so that I can make long walks. I don't mind the cold. I just put on many clothes.

As we had limited time – she had to go back to the International School of Brussels in the afternoon – we discussed the planning of our meeting. While walking to the station, she passed the market place. Sights of a precious life emerged in front of her eyes. Therefore, she suggested strolling around the different stands of the market and then getting something to eat. It sounded like a good idea. The reason she wanted to visit the market-place was because she used to shop there every Friday for fresh vegetables, fish and meat during her stay in Belgium. It did not take long until she excitingly exclaimed: 'This used to be the stand where I always buy my vegetables and fruits. I wonder whether they still remember me.' We stopped and she tried to make contact by making a

slight bow with her head. The vegetable vendor, a middle-aged man with red cheeks, smiled in our direction, while
he was serving other customers. One was an elderly
gray-haired Japanese woman, examining and checking the
firmness of the quarter of pumpkin she just bought along
with an enormous *daikon* (Japanese radish). The other cus-
tomer was a younger Japanese woman of middle age, who
thought S. and I were acting strange, busy talking and gestic-
ulating to the vegetable vendor. Then S. wanted to take a picture of his vegetable stand. She wondered whether I could
not ask him for permission. Being a good salesman, he of
course consented and replied immediately, while talking to
S.: 'How are you? I certainly remember you. You certainly
may take a picture of me. Wait, I am going to ask my wife to
stand next to me.' After S. has taken the picture, I asked him
whether he had many Japanese customers. 'Yes, I have many
Japanese clients. They like my very fresh produce. I am the
only one on the market to have big and fresh *daikon*. They
like my *ninzin* (carrots), *hoorensoo* (spinach).'

While he was pointing to the vegetables, he called them by
their Japanese term. Then he turned to S. and inquired: 'So,
are you going to stay here again for some time?' She replied:
'No, no. I am here just for a few days. Thank you very much.
I shall no longer hold you up.' As we were walking, S.'s eyes
wandered from one stand to another, as if she was recapturing and reliving her previous life as a Japanese expatriate's
wife. We passed the fish stand where she used to buy fish. As
many customers were waiting to be served, she decided to
make a picture from a distance.

Enjoying Belgian endives and *frites*

After a while we were a bit hungry and after some negotiations, we decided to have a bite in a small eatery in the shop-

ping center of the Stockel station. Before looking at the menu, she decided to have *frites*. As we were chatting and studying the menu at the same time, taking a long time to order, the waitress started to become impatient and looked at us as if we were complete aliens. Finally, S. decided to order Belgian endives with ham *au gratin*. I ordered something else but made sure to ask for a portion of *frites*. She looked tired. She has hardly slept the last few days. Before departure she had to grade all the exams of her students and make the necessary arrangements for her household. Yet she did not mind the fatigue. She jokingly declared:

> I cannot allow myself to feel tired. I think I have to divert my attention from my physical state to what I want to do. When I was still in Belgium, Mrs. H., who was an extremely energetic woman, said to me, when I felt tired, 'you can do it' (*dekimasu yo*). I must say, these few words really stuck in my mind. They give me much comfort when I feel tired.

As the conversation unfolded, I came to know that although she had hoped to have more time for herself after the graduation of her two daughters, it was not the case. Grandma N., whom I met when I was in Japan and whose mind then despite an emerging deafness, was still extremely alert and lucid, has started to increasingly lose her sense and her autonomy. This was not a surprise since she is slowly turning hundred. Touching upon the subject, she almost broke down in tears. She managed to hold her tears back and told me:

> It's sad but my mother is becoming senile. She becomes more and more dependent. I always have to be at home and keep an eye on her. Now I have a nurse, who comes in during the daytime. But because I have to write down all the tasks she has to do when I am away, it still takes a long time to make sure I have the instructions ready before she comes in. Sometimes I have the feeling that I didn't take enough care of her. We have been away two times for a fairly long period. She stayed behind, alone. Of course she came to see us in New Jersey and in Brussels but those were short visits. It seems I can't do

anything perfect as I don't have enough time and energy. And I can't blame my husband. He is part of the system. He has to follow the rules. I must say that sometimes when things get too hectic, he takes a day off to take up part of the responsibility of the two grandmothers. He's always been very understanding, and especially so in the recent years.

When I remarked that she had accomplished quite a lot in spite of all the obstacles, she smilingly replied:

No, not really. In looking back, my wish was always to study and to develop my own mind and not just be such and such person's wife. I suppose I have done something. Well, let me put it this way. I have always done my best.

When the waitress brought the food, S. was happily surprised by the quantity on her plate: two round Belgian endives wrapped with ham and covered with a brown-colored crust of cheese sauce, accompanied by a plate of mashed potato. I suggested sharing the *frites*. After the meal I insisted on paying the bill. She refused but finally consented. Then she produced two gifts. The first gift, nicely wrapped in rice paper was a box of *ebisenbei* (paper-thin shrimp rice wafers) and a smaller box, containing two hand-made paper dolls, a man and a woman in traditional Japanese costume. She commented: 'Now everywhere in Japan, you can buy these dolls for the *Hinamatsuri* festival. So I thought it would be a good idea to give you a such a gift because this brings luck.' After accepting the two gifts we parted. She had to go to the International School. I offered a ride but she preferred taking the public transportation and looking at the once-so-familiar houses, corners and streets she once passed by on a daily basis. As I saw that her wish was genuine and not purely formal, I did not insist. After wishing each other all the best and the firm promise to keep in touch, I saw her strolling to the bus stop, her mind already gone to distant moments and emotions.

Linking Theory with Ethnographic Findings

The O. family and Japanese ethnonational identity

At first glance the experiential level of returnees at the micro level has very little in common with – or expressed in terms of power and influence – 'irrelevant' and 'negligible' with regard to the discourse on Japanese ethnonational identity. This is mainly a process, which – as can be deduced from the previous discussions – seems largely in the hands of the state and the general public debate at the macro level and of which the basic principles are reflected in institutions such as the educational system at the median level.

First, the process of ethnonational identity formation in Japan diverges from the identity formation of ethnic minorities in multicultural societies. These societies have emerged as a result of the current globalizing tendency. One characteristic of these societies is the possibility of ethnic and other minorities to contest the majority view of the host society. In other words although ethnic minorities both in terms of number and power relationship are less strong in the majority society, they have the right to voice their views in the arena of the public discourse. Their stances often diverge from the majority view. The case of the Japanese differs from the previous pattern. The formulation and development of the Japanese ethnonational identity are situated at the macro level of state policies, allocating rights and impediments according to formal criteria within the own national boundary. As Japanese ethnonational identity is shaped and formulated by a centralizing force, the state and its most prominent and influential actors of the state, it is propagated and promulgated towards all Japanese citizens and therefore universal within the territory of the nation state Japan. This process is not recently 'invented.' On the contrary the formation of the Japanese ethnonational identity is part of the search of Japan for the own national identity. The self-reflection of a nation has become urgent since the Meiji period when Japan joined the ranks of the modern nation states.

Given the scope and the nature of this book most attention has been directed to the postwar development of the Japanese ethnonational identity. However, at the same time the historical continuity of the process is always kept in the background. The ethnographic account of this particular returnee family illustrates clearly how the ethnonational identity affects the personal lives of the individual Japanese. In return these people reflect in the own particularistic/idiosyncratic way the signs of the times they were born and raised in.

In the case of the O. family, the grandmother born in the Meiji period has lived in a period when Japan became a modern and 'Westernized' country, followed by the war period of ultra nationalism. In this period of chaos and war her daughter was born to grow up in the direct aftermath of the conflict, a period that was strongly influenced by American standards and values. She is torn between on the one hand the traditional obligations of a housewife and mother and on the other hand her personal self-fulfillment. Finally, her returnee daughters born in the early seventies face the new challenges of a developed and advanced Japan, trying to cope with modernity and postmodernity such as the dizzyingly fast pace of life and the increased mobility of the workforce not only within Japan but also beyond. While members of different generations face different challenges, there is also the many-layered reality of the different generations living in the present.

The O. family and education

Some might argue that the O. family, how interesting the life history of each member may be, is more an exceptional than a representative case of a returnee family. This is not entirely accurate. In Brussels S. may be more assertive than other Japanese housewives are. Yet it should be noted that she has never transgressed the prescribed cultural norms. Instead of defying the rules, she 'performed' consent and conformity, while in reality she acted according to her will. A manifest example of the dissent-avoidance was her 'false' departure to Japan. Instead of leaving at the Zaventem Airport in Belgium, in which case colleagues and superiors of the company would see them off, they decided to depart in France. After the farewell party at the company, she and her husband officially returned to Japan, at least in the eyes of the Japanese community. In reality she drove him to Charles de Gaulle Airport and saw him off there, while she herself returned to Belgium to finish her MA Degree.

Yet concerning education, she is very representative. She pays lip service to a more universal education, aiming to form and shape the young and impressionable minds into independent, mature and critical ones. This stance corresponds with the *tatemae* principle. Yet in reality her strategy proves to be rather pragmatic and in line with the *honne* principle. The youngest daughter attended the International School of Brussels. In her last year she was busy applying for the better universities in Japan. M. has considered for a moment study in the United States. Very soon she discovered her parents were against the idea. They feared that after graduation she would not be able to find work in the Japanese society. M. was a September entrant at Keio University. Since there was no time gap between her graduation from high school and university entrance, she did not need to attend a *yobikoo*. Although she was not particularly ambitious at school, she was sufficiently warned by her mother that going to a prestigious school would enhance her chances to get a good job and a good husband.

Her sister is more ambitious. When she did not find a job after graduation, her parents decided to send her to the United States to obtain an MA Degree. Since the overseas study was not scheduled beforehand but rather a more desirable alternative for a jobless situation, all deadlines for fellowship applications were past. This did not stop the family from implementing the plan by paying themselves the tuition and living costs of her overseas study. It was reasoned that she would have studied in vain if she stayed in Japan, unemployed desperately seeking work. Second in Japanese society it is entirely acceptable to get a Master's Degree abroad. Such a degree would increase one's opportunities to find a secure position in the job market. To support the additional costs caused by the overseas study of her daughter, S., the mother, had to do more jobs.

Concerning her own studies, S. attempted to improve her own educational background twice. When she went to college, her brother advised her to attend a mediocre university although she was accepted in better ones. Clearly she regretted this choice. Later as she saw a way to obtain a degree in the United States, she seized the chance. Again she was pragmatic about it, since she chose to study 'Teaching English as a Second Language.' This degree, she thought, was highly valued and useful in Japan, which was proven right by reality. During her sojourn in Belgium, she decided to get an additional degree, a European Studies Program. She did this, not only for the sake of intellectual curiosity but also in view of finding a teaching job back in Japan. Unfortunately, she never finished the degree despite major efforts of even staying behind. She was entangled in multiple roles, of which the role of a graduate student was at the bottom of the priority list. Her task as a good housewife and supporting partner to her husband and her responsibility of a good mother, planning carefully the schooling of her children were clearly more urgent.

The O. family and internationalization/globalization

In the literature of international migration most research deals with specific migratory movements and particular groups. Most of the studies have been conducted on the effects of international migration of labor migrants and in particular on the disadvantaged position and issues of integration and insertion into the host society. Yet recently some scholars (Findlay 1990, 1991, 1993) have pointed to the increasing trend of circular moves or the migratory movements of the professionals. As the internationalization and globalization process are unfolding at the moment and even more so in the future, an increasing number of people will be confronted with this kind of multilocal reality.

The differentiation between internationalization and globalization has been discussed in a previous chapter. Internationalization works within a worldview consisting of a collection of allegedly mono-ethnic nation states. Here the *status quo* and the relatively unchanging and durable nature of nation states are central in the internationalization concept. Globalization, on the other hand, takes into account the incessant exchange of material goods, ideas and the migratory movements of people in a group or individually. This process has transformed the world into a complex arena, where issues of authenticity is of less importance than mutual borrowing and even more important the promulgation of such exchange and interchange in the contemporary 'imagined' world community.

This community is made up of contemporary complex societies. The concept of incessant and multiple exchanges and movements of commodities, ideas and people has been dealt with among anthropologists and other social scientists. In the first chapter the most well-known theories have been discussed including the idea of culture as flow (Hannerz 1992, Rosaldo 1993), which creates unprecedented phenomena and categories including 'ethnoscapes' (Appadurai 1991) or the 'footloose' (Hannerz 1992).

In the O. family the two daughters were very young when the family lived in New Jersey. There they have developed the taste for all things American: American food, American sports, American clothing, etc. The house of the family, built in the American suburban style, is a case in point of the globalizing process. In terms of material goods, the 'I-have-been-there' goodies testify the ambulating nature of the family. In terms of daily food a large portion consists of foreign products: scented coffee beans, Belgian chocolates, etc. The former was a gift from a family friend living in Hawaii, whom S. met when she was studying ESL in New Jersey. The latter was a present from a Belgian expatriate and his wife, who just arrived in Japan to work for a major Japanese company. His wife was then teaching S. introductory Dutch.

In addition to material goods, personal relationships, developed in the different places, where the family had lived, are maintained despite spatial and time boundaries. To clarify this point, whenever possible the members of the O. family look up old acquaintances and friends. When M. returned to Japan, she went by way of New Jersey so that she could meet with former friends and acquaintances. On her visit to Belgium after her return, she did not fail to take up contact with her former school, the ISB and other family friends including myself. Her sister, who studied for two years in

Pennsylvania, could count on the emotional support of family friends on the East Coast of the US the family had met more than a decade ago. These are just a few examples of the family's globalized way of life. In the contemporary world traditional barriers and obstacles such as long distance and disrupted and indirect communication have become less relevant, at least for those who have the opportunity and who are willing to take part in this process.

At first sight, these daily habits, tastes and preferences appear particularistic, capricious and idiosyncratic. Yet after a closer inspection one cannot deny the underlying forces that make this rich and dense life possible. Through the overseas sojourns the social network of the family, traditionally confined to the neighborhood and the company has been enlarged to include members, belonging to different networks, different countries, different ethnicity and different culture. Furthermore interhuman contact 'sticks.' This is to say that relationships can alter or give new insights to the involved actors, who without these contacts would never have entertained and developed certain ideas or pursue a certain line of thinking and even a certain way of life. What is interesting to mark in these interhuman contacts beyond all barriers imaginable – borders, culture, gender, etc. – is that they potentially have an explosive character in the positive as well as in the negative sense. In other words, the overseas sojourn can potentially trigger certain ideas and pursuits, which turns one's life in a certain direction. S. would perhaps not have the courage and the persistence to insist – in a gentle way though – her own self-fulfillment.

Grandmother N. has visited her daughter and her family both in New Jersey as well as in Brussels. In spite of her failing senses she still remembered vividly her sojourn in Brussels, where she discovered the course of German she had taken at the University in Tokyo numerous decades ago had proven to be useful. One day standing in front of an 'apotheek' (this is the word for 'pharmacy' in Dutch) in Brussels, she knew immediately what kind of store it was.

The O. family and the debate on multiculturalism in Japanese society

The O. family is very mobile. They have lived twice overseas. There they developed social networks, which they maintain and nurture after return to Japan. In talking about internationalization, their focus is on the United States, Belgium and Japan. Although they have lived in Brussels in the wealthier southeastern part, they have never been in contact with the migrants of Brussels, living in the inner city. Like other Japanese, who are admonished about the relative insecurity of Brussels, they do not go to those parts with high concentration of labor migrants. When M. traveled to Belgium with two classmates, they booked a room in a hotel in the vicinity of the North Station. This was the first time she set foot in this part of Brussels. She thought that in a few years the town of Brussels had changed for the worse very rapidly. In reality, this area has always been run-down. The issue of ethnic minorities is very far from their daily lives. In Japan, they live in a small residential town near Toyota City. They do not live like other Toyota employees in the company houses. Shiratori is a green, quiet and peaceful town. When I was there I did not notice one labor migrant worker.

11 Returnees and their School in Brussels

General Background and Setting

The second setting is located in Brussels, and more specifically in the International School of Brussels (ISB). This school is selected as the field of study on the criterion that the majority of Japanese overseas youngsters continue their studies there beyond the compulsory school age of fifteen. During compulsory age, Japanese children and youngsters, at least since 1979, generally attend the Japanese School (*Nihonjingakkoo*) in Brussels. Most Japanese, after graduation from the Japanese School, continue schooling at ISB. Therefore the ISB was in terms of representativeness the logical choice for selecting, meeting, observing and studying overseas Japanese youngsters. Besides, as already amply discussed in the chapter on the Japanese schooling system, education and in particular socialization in the school environment constitute the focal arena of living and growing up of Japanese youngsters. Of course like most of their counterparts in the rest of the world, they spend long hours in school during a significant part of their formative years. Yet in the case of Japanese school children, the school constitutes the principal area where friendship is fostered and the direction of future life – both personal and professional – determined to high degree.

The age group of the observed body ranged from the age fifteen to eighteen at the first time of meeting. This age group is chosen in function of the six-year time span of the research. Observing this group of teenagers allows me to follow them during the crucial school years both in the host society as well as in Japan. Youngsters I have met for the first time in 1990 have now finished college and entered the job market in Japan. The reasons why Japanese parents opt for the International School of Brussels revolve around the complex situation of Brussels in terms of language, used in social interaction in general and in schools in particular. Besides the many structured and unstructured interviews in the refectory of the school, I also sat in classes. The conversations with the Japanese teacher reveal some underlying tension between the Japanese students and those of other nationalities. This view has been confirmed by Japanese students themselves. The International School of Brussels was established in 1951 as the American School of Brussels to serve the educational needs of the children of American expatriates in business, diplomatic missions and the military. Yet youngsters of other nationalities increasingly enroll in this school as a result of the addition of multinational companies installing the European headquarters in Brussels and the expanding members of the European Union. Consequently, the school adapted to the new situation by accepting other nationalities and by changing the name into the International School of Brussels in 1953. In the same year the school was moved to the current location in the southeastern part of Brussels. It is situated on a hill surrounded by a spacious park. The main administration is housed in the impressive-looking nineteenth century Château de Fougères. There is a large sports field between the main administration building and the high school building, where I visited the Japanese students.

There are three major school buildings housing the Elementary School (nursery-grade 6), Middle School (grades 7–9) and High School (grades 10–12). Each of these three divisions has its own library, cafeteria, and computer room. The American heritage of the school is still visible in the high representation of American students or 43 percent of the total student population, while the remaining 57 percent is drawn from 49 nations. The school with a student population of one thousand youngsters figures as the largest English-speaking international school in Brussels. The ISB qualities propagated by the school include the outstanding academic program, the international outlook (such as the presence of different nationalities and cultures), the basic skills needed in the era of global thinking and finally an atmosphere of a warm community sense. During the research period Japanese represent about 10 percent of the total student population.

At School

Fieldwork, consisting of participant observation, interviews and questionnaires, from 1990 to 1995 at the International School of Brussels, shows that the Japanese are not well integrated in the larger school community. On the whole the Japanese display a rather low profile in comparison with other nationalities. I had the official permission to conduct research on returnees: individual interview, group interview, socializing with them and sitting in classes with the consent of the teacher, of course. I could, in other words, do what I wanted. The school was interested in the findings of the research but was in no instance restrictive on my questions or suspicious of the objectives of the study. On the whole it was rather an ideal place to work in, where I could move freely.

I was offered a conference room, next to the office of the headmaster. It was, in other words, a rather formal location. One had to pass the secretary of the headmaster before entering. When the Japanese pupils were told about the interview location, they sensed uneasiness by the idea of being summoned to a place, so close to that of the headmaster as if they have trespassed the rules of school. Bearing in mind the need to establish a relationship based on trust and empathy rather than fear and formality, I renegotiated with the headmaster, who then suggested the use of either the library or the refectory. I finally chose the refectory as the site of meeting, contact, interviews and participant observation. It was not exactly the most serene place of the school. The noise level was significantly high. Besides the busy chatting and occasional screaming of energy excessive teenagers, there was also the ear-deafening pop music, meant as 'background music.' Fortunately in a later phase of my research due to complaints by fellow students and the surveying teachers, the noise level was cut down to more accepted norms.

At the back of the room there was an open kitchenette, where small snacks such as hamburgers, pizza's and American-style sandwiches were prepared and sold. This was a service, run voluntarily by the students' mothers. Yet students were not obligated to purchase the food of the refectory. They could bring their own lunch packet or they could buy sandwiches. In fact most students brought lunch along and ate it there. The canteen was an interesting place to observe from many perspectives. First, it was the opposite of the teachers' room. Students not only ate their meals there at noon but between classes they came to the refectory to do homework, either in groups or individually, to chat or to take a nap. It was, in other words, the 'natural' environment to study, talk and exchange ideas and above all the most suitable place to observe the socialization process among the in-group members and the others.

It was also the place where Japanese parents – *in casu* mothers – met through the volunteering cooking program. Japanese housewives, often not mastering English, preferred to volunteer in group, with other Japanese women so that they could talk to each other. As for the exchange with mothers of the other groups in school, these contacts were almost non-existent.

One of the major barriers was the language gap. The Japanese teacher informed me that most parents discussed with her the problems of their children instead of contacting the school directly. The Japanese teacher thus played the role of the intermediary between the school and the Japanese, including both parents and youngsters. One parent, S. was first active in the PTA and then in the Board of Directors from 1989–93. As she was integrated in the school structure, many other parents approached her for problems and questions concerning the education of their youngsters in the school.

Minimal involvement in school

Japanese, parents and students alike demonstrated an outspoken aloofness towards the other members of the school. The most cited reason was the language difference. There was simply no way to communicate with each other simply because the Japanese did not speak English and the others exclusively English. Even when Japanese housewives volunteered to cook in the refectory together with others, hardly any communication took place between the Japanese and the non-Japanese housewives. The Japanese housewives were meticulously preparing the food, silent and concentrated, while their Caucasian counterparts were chattering away. When asking them why they volunteered, they replied that they were requested to participate in these school activities by other Japanese. The reason they did not talk to the others was certainly not due to dislike but rather to the insufficient knowledge of English and general unease.

Like their parents, Japanese youngsters studying at the school often felt isolated from the larger English-speaking groups such as the Americans and the Swedes as the result of the language gap and incompatible social life after school. The in-group tendency and exclusion by the out-group members were visible in the refectory. Japanese sat at the same table, often divided along the gender line. They did their homework together. They talked about schoolwork, sports, dieting and other items of interest over an *obento* (lunch box) at lunch or munching chocolate chip cookies during recess periods in the morning and in the afternoon. The language they used among themselves was Japanese.

The minimal involvement in school does not mean that the Japanese did not join sports or cultural activities, organized by the school. On the whole, most Japanese boys liked to do sports and played in different disciplines including soccer, rugby, basketball, etc. Girls, however, were mostly interested in cultural activities such as playing the piano, choir singing, etc. Yet the minimal involvement remained prominent in spite of their participation in social cultural events. They still had difficulties reaching out beyond the own group. When joining sports and cultural events, one of the main concerns was the presence of other Japanese. Yuka, sixteen at the time of the first meeting in 1992, was a case in point. 'I sing in the school choir. I enjoy it very much. I am not the only one Japanese there. There are others.'

Language difficulties as social divide

Before arriving in Belgium and studying at the International School, Sae had never set foot outside Japan. She felt very uncomfortable in school. She explained to me:

> I have many difficulties adjusting because I have had only one year of English in Japan. This is the first time I have been abroad and I'm at a complete loss. I'm very happy that there are fellow Japanese pupils in the school. Otherwise, I would have felt very lonely. So, I have only Japanese friends here...I am going back to Japan soon. I plan to enroll myself in the Nanzan International School for Returnees.

Shizuko displayed a similar attitude of looking for warmth and affection within the Japanese group.

> Belgium is not my first foreign country. Before coming here, I had been in Hamburg for three and a half years. There, I attended one-year Japanese school and two and a half-year International School. There were many Japanese in the International School of Hamburg, much more than here at ISB. Because I'm not good in English, I always speak in Japanese. Here (ISB) I have only Japanese friends.

Yuka, who as previously mentioned sang in the school choir, had a similar experience.

> I think I'm an ordinary Japanese girl. Since there's no Japanese high school in Belgium and as I don't speak French, my mother thought I should do the 'usual' (*futsuu*) thing of studying here (ISB). I've only Japanese friends because it's easier for me to speak in Japanese. I meet them in and outside class.

Yuka had been abroad before coming to Belgium. From the age four to seven she studied in an American school in San Francisco. She remembered that she was one of the few Japanese children in school, where almost everyone else was American. Like Yuka, Yuri has spent a significant part of childhood in San Francisco, to be more precisely from the age of four until eight. During her two years at ISB, where she graduated in July 1992, she had only Japanese friends because she did not speak English well. Hiroshi, too, was in San Francisco from the age of two to four. However, he did not remember that period too clearly. At ISB he was in the ESL program.

Besides difficulties in the spoken language, they had problems with writing English. They did not succeed in producing an essay in Standard English because many of them translated their thoughts from Japanese into English. Some were even aware that this habit did not enhance their writing skills, they nonetheless did it, as in the case of Ryoko. 'I know that speaking a language isn't just a matter of translation. But I think first in Japanese, and translate it into English, and I make mistakes in essays.' Some attribute the writing problems to the lack of the necessary vocabulary. 'Concerning writing an essay in a foreign language, my vocabulary is simply not vast enough' (vocabulary *no fusoku*). 'To express my own thoughts in a foreign language is difficult' (*gaikokugo de jibun no kangae o noberu no ga muzukashii*).

Social exclusion by other nationalities

Not all Japanese were muted due to insufficient English knowledge and lack of intercultural skills. There were students, who had been abroad in an English-speaking country before coming to Belgium and who, moreover, have developed and maintained a profound mastery of English. Minori, a girl with excellent English skills and ample overseas experiences – notably five years in the United States – had the following tale to tell:

> I was used to speaking English, even in Japan. But at ISB, the Japanese cling together and they speak in Japanese among each other. I felt a bit weird. I tried to make friends with Americans but it was difficult. I think there are three groups: 1. the cool group; 2. the moderate group; and 3. the nerds. The cool group excludes Japanese. To

belong, you have to go out and drink. The only non-American members of the group are Swedish girls. They are tall and most of the guys think them to be sexy. Japanese girls, like us, make no chance. We are short, girlish and only think of study. The second group of moderates accepts in principle Japanese but you have to go out on Fridays to eat and drink. Our parents would not allow us to do that. The nerds consider us as competitors. They don't talk to us. So, as I did not fit in any of these three categories, I had to make friends among the Japanese.

Mayumi harbored similar thoughts about the social exclusion by some groups.

I know the Japanese at this school stay among themselves speaking Japanese all the time. I don't like it. In fact ISB was my second choice. When I arrived in Belgium at the age of fourteen, I wanted to go Lycée Français because I have studied one year French in Japan. But I was too old. So I decided to come here. It was no problem because I had already two years of English in Japan. And when I was younger, I was attending an American school in Taipei. But when I first arrived here I was surprised to find many Japanese here, who are always together. At first I tried to make friends with Americans but they didn't accept me. They wouldn't talk to me. Luckily I have some very close South African friends. We get along fine.

Ichiro, a 16-year-old boy at the time of meeting regretted that there was so little interaction between the Japanese and the others. For him and his twin brother, Belgium was not the first overseas experience. From 1976 until 1982, notably from the age of two to eight, their family lived in Chicago, USA. He attended a local American school and supplementary school on Saturdays. He did not have fond memories of the first time he returned to Japan in 1982. He recalled the following:

I think it's a pity that Japanese stick together in this school. Sometimes, I think I should have gone to Saint-John's, where the Japanese group is smaller and where everyone speaks in English. I wish I knew more about the local culture.

Of course there were exceptions to the rule of social exclusion and voluntary isolation like Daisuke and Kondo. Daisuke was very happy about his life at ISB.

> When I first arrived I used to hang out a lot with my Japanese friends. But after I started to play rugby I got to know quite a few people. Then I convinced my parents to let me go out with my sport mates after the game. Somehow they let me because I was arguing that was the only way to learn English and keep up with French. Now I've both Japanese and foreign friends. Some Japanese guys are jealous of me because it's cool to hang out with Americans but I don't care.

Through similar channels some American friends accepted Kondo.

> I play in the baseball team of the school. There's a good team spirit. All the players are nice to me. They treat me like they treat everyone else. I think I'm one of the few Japanese in school, who has American friends.

An illustration of social exclusion: the International Festival

I attended in 1992 the 'International Festival' at ISB. It was in fact a fundraising activity for the school. Parents of the different nationalities were asked to set up a stand to sell the their 'national' food. It was a very festive day, when the gym and the adjacent room were filled with colorful stands. The visitors consisted of mainly students and their parents. First, I made a tour to see how the different nationalities presented themselves. The French had a stand selling Perrier water and mini croissants; the Americans offered chocolate chip cookies; the Chinese sold crisp and spring rolls. On my way to the Japanese stand, I ran into Ichiro and Akira. I asked them why their parents were not here.
Ichiro told me:

> My parents don't really like these activities. Besides I'm old enough to come here alone. They're easy-going. They're not really overprotective or overdemanding when it comes to schoolwork.

258

Then I went to the Japanese stand. To my surprise I found two stands, one selling *yakitori* and another one selling Japanese souvenirs. Some of the Japanese youngsters were even *yukata*-clad. When S. saw me, she stopped me and promptly pushed a plate of *yakitori* into my hands, telling me to taste them. She told me: 'You should taste the *yakitori*. Yesterday, Mrs. I. and I spent the entire afternoon making it.' Indeed, they were very delicious. What was then catching my attention was first the location of the Japanese stands. They were put in a corner. Furthermore, in comparison with other nationalities, the Japanese had managed to have two stands, which of course doubled the fundraising revenues for the school. In the evening of that day, there was a performance by the Japanese band, 'the Joined Kids of Japan' on the program. The band consisted of five people, two female singers, two male guitar players and a male drummer.

They were very proud to perform the songs they had composed themselves. The lyrics were mainly in Japanese, with a few lines of English. On the whole the style was contemporary Japanese pop music. The auditorium was half empty and the audience primarily Japanese. The interest of other nationalities in the school for the Japanese children and their cultural activities was to say the least minimal if not nil. Again, this non-interest reflected the difficulty for the Japanese as a group to integrate them in the larger school environment. Of course, one could argue that Japanese music written in the Japanese popular style did perhaps not cater to the taste of the other teenagers at ISB. In addition, the lyrics did not make sense, as it is often a mixture of Japanese and English. This argument is certainly acceptable up to a certain degree. Yet the complete lack of interest, the absence of key figures of the school administration and the teaching personnel seem to indicate the relative insignificance of the group in the total school environment.

Why in-group tendency and social exclusion?

Several reasons can be given in explaining the isolation – either imposed by the larger community or self-imposed – of the Japanese in school. To start with friendships are fostered at an earlier stage in the Japanese school before entrance in the high school of the International School. Others have met each other in the ESL (English as a Second Language) class, when their English language skills were insufficient for taking the entire program in English. Furthermore, the number of Japanese seemed to play a role in the relatively exclusiveness of the Japanese students. The number of Japanese students has grown steadily. At the moment of the research it constituted 10 percent of the total student population. Yet this has not always been the case. In the beginning when the number of Japanese was low, there was nowhere to hide from the main groups of the school, of which the Americans constituted the majority group. Midori, now a full-time housewife with two children living in a suburb of Yokohama and head of the ISB alumni association, recalled ISB in the late 1970s as a predominant Western school, with very few Japanese students.

> I was the only Japanese in high school. I'm talking about the end of the 1970s. In the beginning, I tried to belong. I joined all the social activities in school. Somehow, I felt I was never accepted. So I gave up and started to concentrate on my studies. Anyhow, I always consider myself Japanese and always thought of returning to Japan.

At school Japanese students were inclined to attend the same classes. During breaks they sought each others company in the refectory. Outside the school they went out, too. They met each other during the weekend to do sports, to exchange *manga*, or have a hamburger at Quick among other things. They did not have the parental approval for going out at night nor did they have enough pocket money. A different lifestyle and a different educational strategy of the involved parents led to the social exclusion of the Japanese from the largest group in school, the Americans.

Apart from the lifestyle difference the return idea played a crucial role for the minimal involvement. Most students were aware that their parents would go back to Japan. Given the almost certain return and the temporary nature of their sojourn, many of them strove to minimize the cultural distance with Japanese society and culture. The return idea became especially tangible in the International Baccalaureate (IB) program. This is a two-year program during the last two years of high school preparing Japanese youngsters to enter Japanese universities in Japan. Youngsters, enrolling in this program knew that they were returning and that the time had come to be serious about one's future. Whereas life had been leisurely before, joining the IB program rendered every other Japanese student into a potential competitor for the better universities in Japan. Even abroad they could not escape from the education 'rat race.' From the last two years onwards students concentrate on getting good marks to the negligence of friendships with Japanese and others, such as the case of Ryoko.

Orchestrated peer and parental pressure: the case of Ryoko

Like most Japanese youngsters in school, she came to Belgium in 1989 because of her father's transfer to Belgium. She chose ISB like all other Japanese youngsters. She said:

> My father's company would only pay for ISB or a Belgian school. As I did not have the courage to study in Belgian schools, I decided to enroll at ISB. I am on the whole happy with my choice. Especially in the beginning I received much help and support from other Japanese in school. Now it's slightly different. I'm 18 and so are my Japanese friends. Recently there has been some tension in the group. In the past we just did our schoolwork and had fun. Now it has changed

because we compete for the same schools and so we have become each other's rivals. Nobody really trusts the other anymore. Besides everyone is working hard to get good grades. I'm a bit worried because when I write an essay I always first think in Japanese. I know that's not the right way. That's why I make mistakes.

One day when I was again in the refectory for more interviews, she approached me spontaneously. She wanted to know whether with a Diploma of the International School she could study in a Belgian university.

I have been thinking of perhaps staying in Europe. Because I think I can learn many languages. If I return to Japan, I will forget everything I have learned: English, French. I already talked to my mother. She is not against the idea except that she cannot advise me on where to study. Could you not give me more information?

It was quite unusual that she would ask me, an outsider in the Japanese community and in the International School environment but I nonetheless promised her to look up the necessary information. In a different conversation, I heard from several of her friends that Ryoko was not doing very well in school. She was especially not satisfied with the poor marks she received for her essays. They all reacted surprised when they heard of her plan. They could not understand why she would like to stay behind, whereas almost all others returned to Japan for university study. It did not take long before I received a telephone call from S. She was very friendly but nonetheless firm. She inquired:

Have you talked to Ryoko recently? Other parents and I are very worried about the plan of Ryoko. She wants to study here in Belgium. I think that would not be a good idea because she will be very lonely (*sabishii*) here. After graduation when she returns to Japan, she will have difficulties. I already advised her mother to dissuade her from this idea.

I realized I was viewed as a possible source of Ryoko's plan. At any rate, this incident was concluded very rapidly, as the language of teaching in Belgian universities is either French or Dutch, which she did not speak.

The Japanese Teacher

General

During the period of 1990-5 I encountered two Japanese teachers. The first teacher, Mrs. H. taught until 1992. She was a middle-aged Japanese woman, who had studied in France. She had the reputation to be strict and distracted at times. She was not liked by all Japanese students. Those, who disliked her, thought her to be too academic, too demanding and otherworldly. In spite of many kind requests and assurance of minimal disruption, I was not allowed to sit and observe in her classes.

The second Japanese teacher is a young woman in her late twenties. She came to Belgium through an 'international marriage' (*kokusaikekkon*). The Japanese term for 'international marriage' refers to mixed marriages between Japanese and non-Japanese. In contrast to the majority of Japanese, she is staying in Belgium on a 'permanent' basis. She met her current husband, S. in Tokyo. He was then a Japanese-language student from Belgium. Half a year after her arrival in Belgium, she found her current position as Japanese teacher at the International School of Brussels in a local paper's advertisement. She was hired because she met all the requirements: native Japanese language skills, necessary documents to stay in Belgium, a university degree.

The role of teachers in Japan has already been discussed. When comparing the subject-teaching approach in Japan, in which the main goal was to prepare youngsters to pass examinations successfully, the Japanese teacher at the International School has more freedom in teaching. First, she is not connected with the *Monbusho*. The Japanese teacher at the International School is recruited locally. She obtained this position not before but after her arrival. Her autonomy was reflected in the way she taught. Although she has escaped the rigid rules Japanese teachers have to abide by, she could not undo the social and moral role of a *sensei*. This implied the responsibility of the teacher *vis-à-vis* the students in- and outside the school environment. Many parents contacted her for all sorts of advice since they did not master the language. Even Japanese youngsters did not have the courage to take up contact with the school administration. Questions, remarks, grievances, etc. were directed to her, which then she had to communicate to the Board of Directors. Her mediating function between the students and the school made her slightly uncomfortable.

> It's difficult. Most parents don't like to contact the administration directly. They tell me their questions and problems and ask me to get the information for them. I feel I have a greater responsibility than just being the Japanese language teacher. I've become the unofficial spokeswoman for all the Japanese in school. The school director, too, needed me as a go-between at the second ISB Alumni meeting (in April 1994) in Nagoya. The school was willing to pay for my travel expenses. But I refused the job because if I consent I'm sure I would have to run around doing errands all the time. What's even worse is that I recently arrived in Belgium. First, I still have difficulties speaking English and French. It's tiring to attend all the meetings in school. It's also frustrating not being able to respond adequately to the complaints about the Japanese students in school.

One night she invited me over to her place to make *sushi*. I picked her up at school. We first went to buy the Japanese ingredients at Tagawa supermarket at the *Chaussée de Vleurgat* and the remaining ingredients at a local supermarket close to her home. She and her husband live in a relatively small apartment. While the rice was cooking in the rice cooker, we had some time to talk. She started to tell me her recent life story. At first when she arrived in Belgium, she felt very lonely. Except for her husband, she did not know anyone in this country.

> I was very excited when S. read in the newspaper that the International School of Brussels was looking for a Japanese language teacher. Of course I was even happier when they accepted my candidacy. I like my job and I like the students. I still have to adjust myself to life here. Besides I feel sometimes lonely because I miss my parents. My mother writes me occasionally but I have not talked to my father since I told him I was going to get married to S. He was very much against my decision to marry S, a foreigner. But I persisted and so did he. He even refused to come to my wedding day.

Attending a Japanese literature class

The class consisted of the second year students of the International Baccalaureate Program. The number of pupils was rather small: seven boys and two girls. The teacher had written on the blackboard a classical poem from the upper left side to the lower right side. The boys were all sitting in the row next to the window whereas the two girls were sitting together at the other side of the classroom. I was seated behind the girls, not directly visible to the pupils, as I did not want to disturb the dynamics of the class. One student read one line of the poem and he had to explain the meaning. Others joined in without raising their hand when they disagreed with the given explanation.

When too many students were talking at the same time, turning the discussion into an inaudible cacophony, the teacher interrupted and appointed one pupil. Important to notice was that some would get up in the middle of the class

265

to throw the wrappings of the sandwich or a finished coke can in the garbage bin without any prior permission.

Being a teacher myself, this sight was rather hair-raising since I was used as a student myself in the past and as a teacher now, that students in class never did anything without the consent of the teacher. During the entire fifty minutes, the girls hardly opened their mouth. They sat there, taking notes and only replied when explicitly asked for. The boys on the other hand did not stop talking. They even were blurting out things, which made no sense. When the fifty minutes were over, the teacher gave the pupils homework. They had to write an essay on the key concepts of the text from their own personal experiences.

Later when we were having a cup of tea in the teacher's room, I asked her whether the pupils were always that lively or only on this occasion with an outsider watching them. She answered:

> Well, this is an international school. Pupils can take food and drinks in the classroom. Sometimes they don't pay attention. They are talking among themselves. They are different from pupils in Japan, where there is much more discipline.

The Japanese teacher and the school administration

In an interview with the then director of the International Baccalaureate Program, he told me the following story:

> The school is very happy to have hired Mrs. W. She is very cooperative, always friendly and very well liked by the students. However, she seems to lack confidence because she hardly has any contact with the other teachers. Moreover, some of the teachers are wondering why none of the Japanese students, who took IB, has ever failed. They think that perhaps she is too lenient for her students.

Some teachers and administrators have been complaining about the 'asocial' behavior of Japanese youngsters. She was very concerned about this negative reputation of the Japanese. She herself acknowledged the difficult situation. As pointed out before, the 'English as a Second Language' (ESL) program plays a significant role in segregating the Japanese from other nationals. Furthermore, some Japanese do have real difficulties with the English language. Even in an adapted program as ESL, they do not completely grasp the meaning of what is taught in class. Although not entirely denying the factual seclusion of the Japanese, she added that the fault did not solely rest on the shoulders of the Japanese pupils but also on the acceptance level of the other pupils. Acting as the unofficial liaison officer between the Japanese – parents as well as pupils – and the school administration, she explained to me:

> I do agree that Japanese stick together but all nationalities do so. Just because Japanese have black hair, they become a target of criticism. I am not saying that there are no problems. Together with my students I try to make the best out if this difficult situation. I'm now teaching the science teacher of the ESL program a crash-course in Japanese so that in case a Japanese student has difficulty in his course, the teacher can communicate the term in Japanese. Concerning the fact that I give everyone good grades, I think all my students are intelligent and make good progress. That's how I give points.

Interaction with the host society

Japanese youngsters have a minimal interaction in the host society. At the institutional level, schools organize activities involving the interaction and involvement in the local culture. Moreover, through cultural and sports events, students came into contact with Belgians. Yae and Mayumi E. both took music lessons from a Belgian teacher. The former learned to play the flute and the latter piano. Mayumi enjoyed these lessons very much.

> I adore my piano teacher. He's very good. He's Belgian from Russian origin. In the conservatory, everyone is very nice and I was immediately accepted. There is a good and warm atmosphere. I like it. When I was taking lessons in Japan, it was completely different. In Japan learning music is very technical. You're not supposed to enjoy it.

Others met locals through sports events. Akira liked to play soccer. Instead of playing in the school team, he became a member of a local (French-speaking) team. He rejoiced:

> I love playing soccer. I learn a lot here. The Belgian players are very serious about the game. That's why I wanted to be in their team and not in that of ISB, where nobody cares about winning. I can't really talk to the other guys in the team because I don't speak French well but we understand each other on the soccer field. I see some of them around in the neighborhood where I live. We say hello but that's all.

Still others came into contact with locals through their family like Minori.

> I don't have many chances to meet Belgians. My family knows a Belgian couple very well. They have a restaurant, where we often go. They're very nice. We mostly talk in English. Sometimes I try to speak French. My mother would also bring home some friends, students of the European Studies Program.

Return strategies during sojourn in Belgium

Past 'return problems'F

or the majority of pupils I observed over the years, the return from Belgium to Japan was not the first time. Learning from previous experiences – mostly negative – they were more prepared for the reverse culture shock. Minori, who has spent three years at ISB recalled thus the first time she returned from the US to Japan, when she experienced an acute culture shock:

> At first, I went to an ordinary Japanese primary school. There were no returnee primary schools in the neighborhood where we live. I was constantly ill. I suppose I had much psychological stress. The other kids in school did not like me. They thought I was strange and I was not behaving like Japanese. What horrified me the most, was the iron discipline at school. I remember a boy was punished with physical violence in front of everyone because he just forgot to bring a book to school. Luckily, when I reached the age of twelve, my mother could send me to Nanzan Middle School, where only returnees study. I really felt at home there.

Yukiko had been in Belgium twice: the first time from the age of five until eight and the second time from the age of eleven until eighteen. In a similar way she experienced difficulties after she had returned from Belgium the first time.

> The first time I was in Belgium, my parents sent me to a local French-speaking school in Watermaal. Then, I spoke fluently French and very little Japanese. Therefore, when I went back to Japan, the other Japanese kids in the (ordinary) school didn't like me. They made fun of me because I could not speak Japanese in the same way as they did. For a long time I did not have any friends in school.

Therefore, when she found herself back in Belgium, she decided to adopt a different strategy. This time, she was determined to socialize exclusively with Japanese pupils. By doing so, she not only kept up with the language but also maintained a group of Japanese friends, who might study in the same university in Japan in the near future. A similar case was that of Yuka.

> When I returned from the United States when I was seven, I was forced to speak in Japanese and to be Japanese. So I lost my knowledge of English.

The return experiences of Kondo's return were not much different.

> I was in Germany from 1977 to 1980. I studied in a local school. When I returned to Japan – I was then nine and half years old – the teacher and the other kids thought I had a 'strong personality', which was not a quality. I was too straightforward. I had too many opinions on my own. I did not fit in. As time went by, I learned to be like the rest.

So remembered a rather unpleasant period, when he returned to Japan at the age of 8 after having spent 6 formative years in the United States.

Yet his reverse culture shock was less severe than the two previous cases:

> In the beginning, I had difficulties with the Japanese language in school. Somehow back in Japan, because I was surrounded by Japanese, I switched back from English to Japanese language. My brother and I started to talk in Japanese. We were not the only 'odd ones' because my family lived in the company's apartment, where everyone returned from abroad. So, we were more or less in the same situation.

Getting organized and emerging involvement in the formal school structure

Given 'past return troubles' predating the experience at ISB, a 'spontaneous' movement to organize and bundle the resources for the advancement of their position both in the International School and in the Japanese society has emerged. One parent had fueled this movement. The International Baccalaureate Program has been established in 1989 as the result of her continuous lobbying. For the improvement of the status of Japanese ISB students in Belgium, she marked out two major areas in need of change.

Point one on the agenda is the structural problems facing returnees, who enter Japanese University in the month of September. This is to say that since the academic year in Japan starts in April, most schools do not have the brochure and the registration kit ready for returnees, who plan to enter school in the Fall. As a result, they are forced to become a *roonin* for at least one semester. This is not the result of simply failing college entrance examinations or not passing the exam of the first-choice university but rather the outcome of the mismatch in timing between the Japanese and overseas educational system.

Point number two is the urge for a closer cooperation between the Japanese school and the International School of Brussels. As already mentioned, the Japanese school is funded by the *Monbusho* and is part of the official overseas education. Youngsters above that age depend on the 'goodwill' of the local schools. One of the foreseeable problems is that an overwhelming majority of Japanese in international schools may result into a potential numerus clausus. After all, how can a school with a majority Japanese student population continue to call itself international?

Therefore S. and a few older alumni in Japan decided to set up an organization to exchange valuable information and experiences for professional and personal purposes and to act as a collective entity in Japanese society. The first reunion of the ISB alumni association took place in Tokyo on April 24–6, 1992. Out of the eighty alumni, thirty-three former students and their parents attended the conference in Tokyo. The second reunion was held on April 8 and 9 in Nagoya and Tokyo. At the reunion in Nagoya seven parents and two alumni shared a traditional Japanese lunch with the honor guests, the director and his spouse of the International School of Brussels. In Tokyo a total of 44 alumni attended the reunion.

Divergence between self- and other-ascription

In order to understand the phenomenon of 'returnees' it seems important to highlight both how returnees define

271

themselves and how others perceive them. First, what is their self- and other-ascription of being an 'overseas returnee' during the sojourn in Belgium? At this point it is crucial to note that the other-reference does not imply the different actors in the host society but the Japanese in the country of origin. The consciousness of difference is situated at the 'imagined' level, as they have not yet returned to Japan. The notion of *kikokushijo* lives only in the minds of the returnees, often influenced by experiences, mostly negative ones, but not proven in Japanese society as a full and adult member of Japanese culture and society. On how others classified returnees and how she viewed herself, Satomi gave the following reply:

> People think returnees are different, they speak foreign languages and they can get in the good universities without taking entrance examinations. As for me, Belgium is my first overseas experience. I speak English better than an ordinary Japanese student. But it's still not perfect. Perhaps I'm different because I've become more confident. I'm very happy I'm here because besides study I can do things people back in Japan cannot. I love sports. So I have been to a Wimbledon tournament, to the Formula 1 Race in Spa. Because my mother likes cultural events I have been to many operas and musicals like *Les Miserables* in London. People think we get the good jobs. I think that's not completely true. For the more technical jobs like engineering, they prefer Japanese students who have studied in Japan. Returnees, especially girls like me, will make a good chance to work in jobs requiring foreign languages and contacts with foreigners.

Mayumi, Ryoko and Yuka had similar ideas.

> People think that returnees are smart because they're bilingual. Some think they're rich because they've been to so many places. They enter the good universities and get the good jobs in big companies and organizations.

Yet concerning the correspondence between the other- and self-ascription, Ryoko added a differentiation between the US returnees and the non-US returnees.

I would like to say that there are two sorts of returnees. Those, who have been to the US and the others. Japanese returnees, who have lived in the States, have more spirit and energy. They speak English so much better than others. You can pick them out very easily: they are always dressed according to the latest fashion and they use make-up. As for me, I'm not like the 'typical' returnee. I'm small, I talk with a soft voice and I don't wear make-up.

Yuka even harbored feelings of dislike for returnees before she herself became one. While thinking aloud, she informed me:

Before I went abroad I didn't like returnees. They were so different from us. They spoke foreign languages, they were so confident of themselves and open. I thought they were so different. Perhaps I didn't like them because I had a kind of inferiority complex. Now I think I have become a little more confident than before I left. But I don't think I'm smarter than others are.

Ichiro did not think himself to be smart.

Other Japanese students are much better in math. They're also much more disciplined. We, returnees, are more relaxed. At least I am. I don't think I'm smart. It's not that I don't like going to school. I'm just an average student.

Return Experiences

The 'us versus them' schism

Apart from interviews, a questionnaire has been distributed to 53 officially listed members of the ISB alumni association as of 1992. Of the total of 55 alumni, two were Americans and one was a Japanese, living in the UK. Of the total 53 contacted respondents of the questionnaire, twenty–two have replied. The male–female ratio of the respondents was 3/19. The age ranged from 19 to 32. Of the total sample, 12 respondents are still studying at college, while the remaining 10 have entered the job market. Among the total ISB alumni, who returned to Japan for university study, there was a marked preference for the Tokyo, Nagoya and Osaka area. The most frequently attended universities were Nanzan, Keio Gijuku and Waseda University, followed by Kyoto, Mie and Osaka Foreign Languages University. Of the two students, who attended college abroad, one had studied at Oberlin, US, and the other was at the time of research studying at Wellesley College, US. The latter went there through a Keio-Wellesley inter-university exchange program. Among the professionals, the so-called *shakaijin*, all worked in Japan except for two cases. One alumnus was at that moment of research employed in England. The other one had worked in the Japanese School in Brunei for three years. Of the college-age alumni, everyone had made use of the special provisions for returnees including a returnee test, special skills test and no test at all in certain cases.

At the university level the special treatment of returnees in university entrance (*tokubetsu waku*) has created tension between Japanese students without overseas experiences and *kikokushijo*. The grudge of 'ordinary' Japanese students (*ippansei*) is rooted in what they think the positive discrimination of returnees in the educational competition. From high school onwards, if not earlier, Japanese students forsake play, personal development and even sleep in order to pass the college entrance exam successfully. The returnees, however, after an overseas sojourn, where often the educational system was deemed to be less rigid, less time- and energy consuming, entered the better universities seemingly without major efforts. Therefore, the image of returnees being 'lazy, loud, irresponsible, negligent' seems very much alive among Japanese people in general and among regular students in particular.

Even among certain returnees some thought it not necessary to insist on the differences. Midori, one of the oldest alumni of the Japanese group, remembered during her university days at Sophia University the following anecdote.

Of course, I am a *kikokushijo* because I have been abroad. But honestly I don't tell anyone that if not necessary. Some people have certain negative images of returnees thinking them to be lazy, spoilt and rude. I must say some of them are really disgusting. While I was still a student, I overheard a group of returnees speak in English among themselves at the lockers of the school. I think it's wrong to speak English in a Japanese environment. But what's even worse was that their English was very lousy, too. That's really snobbish, I think. Of course, my husband knows my background. He is not a *kikokushijo* but we have both visited Belgium. I wanted to show him the places I've been. But for example, all my female friends in this company housing do not know I speak English and that I have been abroad to Europe. It's not just that I think the experience was insignificant, not worth telling anyone but they aren't interested in places they have never been.

Yukiko entertained similar ideas.

When I was still a student at Waseda after my return, I wanted to become friends with other *kikokushijo*. But they were so Westernized and they didn't fit in Japanese society and in the university. I think by watching them I got such an aversion for returnees. So I tried my very best to become more Japanese than the ordinary students.

The negative stereotyping, however, was also contested by some returnees, who themselves became an object of criticism. Kondo, who studied at Kanagawa University, did not agree with the negative image of returnees:

When I tell people that I am *kikokushijo*, I'm automatically stereotyped. They think we're lazy and arrogant, who get in because we are being treated differently. They (non-returnee Japanese students) always think I got in university more easily than them. I think it's rubbish. If what they think is true, then why do I end up in Kanagawa University and not in the better colleges of Waseda, Keio, etc. Like other students, I have failed in some of the entrance exams, too. I flunked the Chiba math test. I got into Kanagawa because I was good in sports. You see, there are four ways of entering Kanagawa: the usual entrance examination, the scholarship test, the special test for

275

people with special (musical, sports) skills and finally a returnee test. Including myself there are only four in our program (International Business Administration). The others are OK excepting for their wrong ideas about us and especially their indifference. During summer camp, for instance, when we have to tell our experiences in high school, no one was interested in my ISB story because they've never been there and don't have any idea what it's like to be abroad and to study in other schools.

Others thought that the system did not take into account the specific situation of returnees. In the case of Junko, who studied foreign literature at Waseda, she thought the English program was extremely poor. She actually requested the program responsible to change her native Japanese teacher of literature for a English lecturer at the same university. Complaints were not only directed towards the level of the language course but also the teaching methods.

Over several cups of coffee in a café near the Shibuya station, she was telling me her personal struggle to get more adequate English lessons in university.

When I returned to Japan in June 1991, I applied for the special returnee exam at Waseda and Gakushuin University. Before going to Belgium, I went to a middle school, affiliated with Gakushuin University. I passed both exams. I chose the first because I thought the facilities were better, the foreign languages department of a higher level and more prestigious. But I'm not happy at all with my choice. First, classes are huge. In some classes, there are five hundred students. The professor talks through a microphone. Half of the students aren't paying any attention at all. The teaching method is not good either. In all foreign language classes, the teacher and students speak in Japanese. The students have to translate all the time leaving no time for conversation and discussion. I tried to switch the English class for a smaller seminar, taught by a native English teacher. That would be more interesting because I would have more chance to talk, to discuss and to develop my ideas in English instead of translating and memorizing an English text. Besides I don't see the point of it. I and a friend of mine, a *kikokushijo*, too, talked to the school administration whether any changes could be made. But it didn't help. They told us to make an effort to adjust.

On the other hand some felt that the level of their native language skills were below that of the 'ordinary' Japanese so that extra effort was needed to do the same task. One law student at Keio recalled that the most difficult part of the entrance exam was the legal jargon in Japanese. Among those, who already entered the labor market, the *shakaijin*, some seemed to have difficulties with the Japanese language. Furthermore, others are still struggling with the (written) Japanese language in correspondence, jotting down notes for superiors. They all seemed to agree that the hierarchical and harmonious model of a Japanese society left little room for airing personal opinions and suggestions. Haruko, a 25-year-old employee explained why she felt different from her other colleagues: 'If I am unsatisfied with something, I cannot express my opinion in public.'

Kikokushijo and self-identity

Identity management is not always consistent and uniform, even not within the relatively small group of ISB alumni, who all share similar overseas experiences. In total 15 respondents did not mind being called returnee; 6 minded and 1 had no opinion. The most cited reason why one agrees being called returnee was that it simply corresponded with the reality of having been overseas.

Apart from the factual reason of having been abroad, there was the added dimension of pride in being a returnee:

Returnee is 'my own identity' (*jibun no aitenditi*); 'the overseas sojourn has greatly influenced my way of living, my way of thinking' (*Kaigaiseikatsu ga watashi no ikikata, kangaekata nado ni ataeta eikyoo ga okii kara*); 'I am glad that I could experience different (things) than (other Japanese) people' (*Hito to cigau keiken ga dekita koto o yokatta to omotte kara*).

Some respondents did not like being called *kikokushijo*. The very fact of calling them 'returnees' meant that they were categorized in a group, which made them different from ordinary Japanese. In other words they contended that coining the specific term of returnee implied a form of 'differentiation' (*kubetsu*) and even 'discrimination' (*sabetsu*) to the disadvantage of the returnees. One respondent, a law student at the University of Kyoto, described his dislike in the following succinct way: 'The term "kikokushijo" symbolized the closed and exclusive character of Japan. I detest it.' A twenty-four-year-old male alumnus, now working in a major trading company had similar problems:

> I don't know. I noticed that my way of thinking, of expressing and general attitude is very different from 'ordinary Japanese' (*futsuu na Nihonjin*). That's why I try to keep quiet about my overseas experiences. I don't want to attract too much attention to my status as *kikokushijo*. In fact I don't like being called *kikokushijo* because I don't want to be seen as someone special or extraordinary. I just want to be like all others, to fit in society.

Apart from linguistic and identity-categorization, some had problems, adjusting to the hierarchical organization of Japanese companies. Although they have studied and socialized in a Japanese cultural environment during their undergraduate years and were thus conscious of what one called 'the up and down relationship' (*ue-shita kankei*) or hierarchy and the corollary of the honorific speech (*keigo*), yet they did not like it. Generally *keigo* is divided in three subcategories: *sonkeigo* (respect language); *kenjoogo* (humble language) and *teineigo* (polite language). The usage of *keigo* is maintained on formal occasions such as at the workplace, especially talking to superiors, or when meeting someone for the first time. As formality has a rather vague meaning, it is argued that *keigo* is used in a situation when one has to be careful.

Hendry (1990: 113) elucidates that

> the Japanese expression translated as 'careful' is *aratamatta* ..., so that a description of an extreme 'aratamatta toki' in English becomes 'a time when you are being most careful in your speech and behaviour.'

Moreover, related to the hierarchical language usage they had to face the *ura-omote* dichotomy, referring to the difference to what one really feels and what one ought to feel. In this respect, it is important to link *keigo*/informal speech with other Japanese classifications such as the *soto/uchi*, the *omote/ura* and the *tatemae/honne* dichotomy universalism. *Keigo* along with *soto* (outsider), *omote* (front) and *tatemae* (public) are associated with *en* (distance) and *ryoo* (consideration for the others), while the dichotomy is related with closeness, familiarity and the lack of inhibition. In relation to the *ura/omote* dichotomy, one should express the *omote*, which is deemed appropriate and proper in the public sphere, whereas the *ura* point of view, or what one really feels should be kept to oneself or to the own group, not to be divulged in the public.

279

Table 12: The Identity Management of Returnees (N=22)

Questions	I agree	I mainly agree	I don't agree	I don't know
	% (abs.#)	% (abs.#)	% (abs.#)	%(abs.#)
Returnees are not Japanese	5% (1)	31% (7)	55% (12)	9% (2)
Returnee has to shed off over-seas experience	0% (0)	0% (0)	95% (21)	5% (1)
Returnees useful for Jap. Interna-tionalization	59% (13)	27% (6)	9% (2)	5% (1)
Returnees are a new type	41% (9)	45% (10)	9% (2)	5% (1)

Source: Own Research Data

Most respondents assessed the overseas sojourn in a positive way. The overseas experience had an added value in their personal and private life. Most of them did not feel the need to discard the experiences and skills they had acquired overseas. At the same time they insist on their status of full-fledged Japanese. A prudent conscientization has taken place among these returnees since the overseas sojourn and experiences might have transformed them into a different sort of Japanese or possibly a new type of Japanese but they were incontestably full members of the Japanese society. In analyzing the figures this process should be properly called prudent since 41 percent of the respondents were positive about the concept of a new type of Japanese and 45 percent of respondents mainly agree. In contrast to previous adjustment problems, there was a marked increase of valorization of the overseas experiences. To put it simply, the overseas sojourn was a good experience and in many cases facilitated the entrance in prestigious schools and in the job market.

Table 13: Returnees (N=22) in the Emerging Japanese Multicultural Society

Questions	I agree	I mainly agree	I don't agree	I don't know
	% (abs.#)	% (abs.#)	% (abs.#)	%(abs.#)
Returnee as social issue looses importance	0% (0)	9% (2)	64% (14)	27% (5*)
Returnee sympathetic to *Nikkeijin* laborers	14% (3)	14% (3)	41% (9)	27% (6*)
Returnee is different from *Nikkeijin*	59% (13)	9% (2)	23% (5)	9% (2)
Japan needs to become a multicultural society	50% (11)	31% (7)	14% (3)	5% (1)

*= one blank reply
Source: Own Research Data

Table 13 is designed in order to find out how the self-ascription of returnee fits into the current large debate on the multicultural/multi-ethnic society. These new developments have been developed in previous chapters. These events are not mere disjointed processes but part of recent changes in Japanese society, affecting the formulation and the stance of the general ethnonational identity and the identity of each individual. They are related in the sense that they represent complementary phenomena of migratory moves from and towards Japan. The group of *kikokushijo* is the result of the outward expansion of Japanese economy and the concomitant phenomenon of the expatriates sent to all corners of the world whereas multiculturalism and globalization reflect the incoming groups of foreign workers in Japanese society.

Respondents themselves thought their situation and the ascribed identity upon return had not fundamentally changed to the extent that all problems and contradictions have been solved and disappeared. They were still conscious of the potential reverse cultural shock in education and the larger society, prioritizing groupism, homogeneity and social conformism.

Concerning the desirability of a multicultural society the majority of the returnees agreed prudently. They consented that the Japanese society needed to become more multicultural in the sense of less exclusive interhuman relationships and more openness in general. Their position to the issue whether and to what extent this openness should apply to other groups including *Nikkeijin* remained ambivalent. At any rate they did not feel connected with the latter given their different linguistic and social background and different sensitivities in spite of a common Japanese descent. Given their limited knowledge of and personal acquaintance with these U-turn migrants, returnees viewed the personal 'marginal' position very differently. In contrast to the *Nikkeijin*, whose locus of socialization is outside Japan, returnees were generally born, nurtured and raised in Japanese society and culture by Japanese parents. Therefore, a majority of returnees constituting 47 percent of the total denied any sympathy for the *Nikkeijin*. And an even greater percentage 59 percent thought returnees to be different from them.

Linking Theory with Ethnographic Findings

Returnees and education

Education is central in Japanese society. While Japanese education aspires to give everyone basic knowledge and sound mathematical skills at the primary and secondary school level, there is much competition at the high school and university level. Compulsory education extends from the age of six until fifteen. Beyond that age students and parents have to plan meticulously the educational future of the youngster since the university one attended influences directly one's professional life after graduation. There is a specific ranking of Japanese universities according to reputation. The rule of the educational 'rat race' is to enter universities with a sound reputation. They include a handful of national and a multitude of private schools. In order to pass a university entrance examination successfully, numerous interviewees have enrolled themselves in a cram school in order to maximize their chances to enter the university of first choice possible. Even in the case when the entrance examination is one specially designed for returnees.

Overseas education and special reception policies in Japan have been set up to minimize cultural shocks after return. It was established to meet the demands of returnee families. Henceforth, one might live abroad but still not severed from the Japanese educational system. Consequently, a unitary school path has been established for returnees in Belgium. Parents send small children to local (mostly French-speaking) kindergartens. From the age of six until fifteen the majority attends the Japanese School in Brussels and youngsters older than fifteen, the International School of Brussels. The reason for establishing one schooling path for overseas returnees reflects the importance of education in Japanese society. In order not to be excluded from the educational career path of an ordinary Japanese, an officially recognized overseas education system was needed. The uniform school track of ISB alumni reflects the centrality of Japanese education. The orchestrated pressure on one returnee, who considered study in Europe, illustrates the rigidity of Japanese educational system. Although exposed to different pedagogical approaches abroad, after return almost all returnees enroll in a *juku*, like 'ordinary' Japanese students. The parents might voice critique towards the Japanese educational system for its subject-centered approach with scarce attention to the personal development of the students, at least at the high school and university level. Yet no one wants to take the risk of falling behind. It is one thing to express disagreement and discontentment, the *tatemae* principle, it is completely another matter to jeopardize one's chances by not doing what others do and therefore miss the boat. This constitutes the *honne* principle of the educational strategy.

Japanese ethnonational identity and the issue of returnees

In assessing Japanese ethnonational identity Aoki's analysis has been adopted in order to have a better understanding of the formulation and the interpretation of this process. To reiterate, the four periods include: 1) negative distinctiveness; 2) historical relativism; 3) positive distinctiveness; and finally 4) from distinctiveness to universalism. The basic principles underlying the formulation of a Japan-specific ethnonational identity until very recently is the dichotomous division between us/them or Japan versus the West. Key concepts or terms are used to demonstrate the characteristic nature of Japanese ethnonational identity.

In the direct aftermath of the war Benedict in her attempt to explain the former US enemy discerned the phenomenon of *on* (social indebtedness) in the cultural pattern of the Japanese, characterized by a strong sense of hierarchy and group-orientation. In the period of negativeness Japan stood for all things negative such as irrationality, feudal thinking, etc. whereas the (non-specified) West was synonymous to all things positive including rationality, democracy, public civility, etc. In the following period of historical relativity Japanese intellectuals attempted to mend the overall negative self-image of Japan by putting forth the duality of Japan, belonging both to the 'West' and the 'East.' Although at first sight, this view of the 'hybrid character of the Japanese culture' shares some common elements with the current ideas of globalization, it should be noted that the two components of Japan and the West are seen as disjointed and separated entities void of mutual borrowing and influences. To be more precise, Japan belongs geographically and racially to the Asian continent but in terms of material culture and technological advancement it belongs to the 'West.'

In the positive period a reversal has taken place. Given the spectacular economic growth of Japan, culminating in the 80s, many actors at the macro level – the state itself – and at median level – such as public opinion leaders in the press or think-tanks, scholars of prestigious universities and others – attempt to explain Japan's peculiar and unique ability to transform from a defeated nation into one of the leading economic powers in the world. The two recurrent themes in *Nihonbunkanron*, namely primordialist holism – including homogeneity and purity – and boundary-defined uniqueness have already been discussed in detail. Last but not least the period starting from the mid-1980s has been marked by a new wave, namely the emerging consciousness of universalism. Japan is no longer seen as the ultimate other in the world. Some Japanese intellectuals, opinion leaders and foreign Japan-scholars started to view and assess Japanese culture and ethnonational identity with 'universal' criteria. This means that theories and ideas invented and reinvented in the 'Western' academic and intellectual world, shared by a large membership of intellectuals in the West are now being applied in the analysis of Japan and the many diverse aspects of Japanese culture and society.

The discourse of the Japanese ethnonational identity is central to the issue of *kikokushijo*. The conscientization of the problems facing 'returnees' after return and the social construction of the returnee 'issue' seem related to the third period of positive distinctiveness. First, the number of returnees became visible in the late 1970s and especially so in the early 1980s. This period marked the height of the *Nihonbunkaron*.

In this period of high self-reflexivity the issue of the returnees became prominent. I suggest situating the debate on the status of returnee as outsiders, marginals or insiders within the larger discourse of Japanese ethnonational identity, the internationalization/globalization process and the process of marginality and belonging. In the period when the outsider status was conferred to returnees, the mode of thinking was primarily based on the us/them dichotomy or the Japanese/Western schism in defining and understanding the issue of returnees. In the *Nihonbunkaron* era Japanese culture seemed in many ways better if not 'superior' to Western culture(s). Therefore in the so-called handicap theory those who have left the cultural realm of Japan become less familiar with it and risk becoming an outsider. The overseas experience is in this perspective interpreted as a discontinuity in the life cycle of a Japanese person. Given the marginal status of returnees, they needed to readapt themselves in Japanese culture and society.

Yet this overall negative other-perception of returnees has been modified in the 1980s when Japanese returnees and other involved actors such as parents and educators were increasingly empowered to negotiate the own identity due to the increasing number of returnees. Some even argue in the singularity theory that the overseas experience has an enhancing if not an outright positive effect on youngsters. Given their exposure to other cultures, society/societies and possibly also other ethnic identities, they develop a more balanced view of the world to such an extent that they could play the role of 'little ambassadors' outside Japan. Of course others think that the overseas experiences have spoiled and changed the youngsters, turning them into Japanese in a 'lesser' way. Seen as half-Japanese, they need to readapt themselves in Japanese society. Finally starting from the second half of the 1980s, returnees were no longer 'oddities' but on the contrary seen as a 'new type of Japanese.'

In juxtaposing my ethnographic findings with the general discourse on Japanese ethnonational identity and the *non-han-shin* flow of the specific identity of returnees, my ethnographic findings contradict the 'outsider status' of returnees. On the whole ethnographic findings of ISB alumni demonstrate that very few perceive themselves as non-Japanese, living at the edge of society with no hope of reinclusion into Japanese mainstream society.

According to the handicap and singularity theories on returnees, the overseas sojourn is seen as the marginalizing agent, rendering returnees different from ordinary Japanese. It is argued that culture shock arises when a returnee maintains two or more sets of cultural values, behavior and thinking. While analyzing the underlying paradigms of this concept, it becomes clear that culture is essentialized to a collection of traits and characteristics, with no interchange between cultures. The relation of one culture *vis-à-vis* another is one of exclusion and radical difference. A second underlying dimension of the culture shock idea implies the total immersion into the local cultures, to such a degree that returnees lose the own 'culture.' Therefore returnees have become a special group of Japanese, different from ordinary Japanese.

While analyzing the ethnographic findings and bearing in mind the flow metaphor of culture, one can raise the question whether the immersion in the local language and culture is a general phenomenon among all returnees at all times and in all countries around the world. Or asked differently is the impact of the local culture and language in certain societies and cultures not more profound than in others? Therefore, the level of integration in the host society is not uniform. The country of sojourn undoubtedly influences the development and personal growth of Japanese youngsters and the degree of immersion. In the literature a distinction is made between returnees, who had stayed in the West versus those who had sojourned in Asia. Those, in the West have a greater chance of integration into the local culture, and those, who had stayed in Asia, would have learned quasi-nothing of the host society as the children and youngsters attend Japanese schools.

Belgium, although a country in Western Europe, has a very complex school system given the bilingual nature of the government. Therefore, most parents choose Japanese schools. The parents, too have minimal interaction in the host society. The observation of the Japanese in the overseas school environment reveals that Japanese students are not easily accepted by other groups. In more concrete terms, Japanese are perceived by others as hard working but boring youngsters. The Japanese language is spoken in- and outside the school environment. Consequently, given the minimal contact with others and limited usage of English to classrooms, returnees do not speak English as fluently as claimed in some studies on returnees and the contact with the native population and culture rather minimal. Another group does not want to stress their 'special' status and the problems facing returnees. Members of this group re-enter in discretion, while thinking that returnees should adapt themselves to Japanese culture.

Concerning the ISB alumni their Japanese identity has been reinforced during their stay in Belgium and especially in school. At the International School of Brussels the Japanese constitute a social group, whose members take similar courses, do similar things in- and outside school and beyond. Even those, who reach out beyond the own group in school, experience non-acceptance by other groups such as the Americans. The exclusion of the Japanese is not solely due to cultural and ethnic reasons but also to a different lifestyle. Japanese parents do not allow their youngsters to go out. For other Japanese the reason of non-communication is due to insufficient linguistic skills and the lack of motivation to socialize as the sojourn in the host society is short. After graduation from ISB the overwhelming majority chooses to return to Japan for university studies. Parental and peer pressure are used, when a member considers study in Europe.

Returnees and emergent multiculturalism in Japanese society

The increasing number of *kikokushijo* and moreover the emergence of foreign laborers in Japanese society have challenged the homogeneity and uniqueness of Japan. At first the outward movement of Japanese expatriates, spouse and children have engendered the debate of internationalization (*kokusaika*) in Japanese society. The semantics notwithstanding some (Befu 1993) argued that this discourse is more triggered by a new form of nationalism rather than international idealism. As an increasing number of Japanese find themselves abroad, they needed a strong Japanese identity, a 'moral support' (*kokoro no sasae*).

The recent emergence of foreign workers in Japan has been explained by a mix of reasons such as the labor shortage in Japan, the large pool of foreign workers in the neighboring Asian countries and the loosening of immigration policies responding to the needs of Japanese industry, especially the SMEs. Evidently Japan remains a very homogeneous society in spite of ethnic minorities (*zainichi gaikokujin*) the so-called oldcomers and the recently arrived migrant workers, the so-called 'newcomers.' Yet because of the increased visibility of foreign workers in society, the phenomenon has been busily discussed and analyzed in the public debate, in which government officials, researchers, journalists and others engage. Whereas before 'internationalization' (*kokusaika*) has been used as the buzzword in the 1980s, recently in the new decade 'multiculturalism' (*tabunkashugi*) is an often-heard term.

The accumulated effect of the two events – increase of returnees and the emergence of a group foreigners in Japan – has rendered the 'foreign' element of returnees less marginal, less threatening and thus more mainstream. After all Japanese returnees are children often born and bred in Japan. From the primordialist view they do not diverge from ordinary Japanese. Yet from the boundary perspective, as they have been abroad and lived outside Japan, they have become different. Migrant workers, of course, constitute from both perspectives the 'other.'

I am very well aware that many would oppose the juxtaposition of returnees with foreign workers, not in the least by the returnees themselves. In a small survey half of the ISB alumni returnees thinks that Japan needs to become a multicultural society, where difference is not seen as a deviance but as variance. In that perspective they think their own situation should receive special attention. The identity formation and possibly the emergence of a 'new type' of Japanese should be tolerated. Most of the returnees still remember vividly the adaptation process into Japanese society after a long sojourn abroad. Numerous returnees have experienced personal bullying from peers, who called them *gaijin* (foreigner). This is a serious insult for returnees, who insist on the full-fledged Japanese identity from a primordial perspective, while their social/cultural belonging is being contested. The majority of returnees have had these experiences the first time they returned to Japan at a relatively young age. As they are themselves recipients of discrimination and exclusion from the mainstream group, they prudently agree that Japanese society should become more receptive and open to those who are different.

Yet this does not mean that they identify themselves – in part or entirely – with other groups, equally or more prone to discrimination and marginalization. A majority of returnees reckons their situation to be very different from *Nikkeijin*. *Nikkeijin* refer to Latin Americans of Japanese descent, who recently entered Japan as semi-skilled workers. I nonetheless think that they both play a role in the process of how Japanese deal with bearers of 'foreign' markers, either from the primordial or from the boundary perspective or both. Of course one could argue that the issue of migrant workers is not a new one. In the past the policy towards ethnic minorities, of which the Koreans constitute the largest group, was basically oppressive. Yet the current debate seems to focus on newcomers. The reason why the silence has been maintained for so long and even in the present is beyond the scope of this book. What can be noted as a reality is that the discourse on the newcomers has already been launched. In contrast to the oldcomers, the foreign workers are discussed in the public discourse, not necessarily by them but represented by many actors in Japanese society. One can speculate that the principal actors and institutions of Japan do not want to open the discussion on the recent war history of Japan. Vehement reactions of the neighboring Asian countries with a collective memory of the Japanese wartime atrocities are thus avoided. On the other hand the strong attention for migrant workers might be caused by a concern of the Japanese government *vis-à-vis* the issue of migrant workers, bearing in mind the situation of 'guest' work migration in Europe and the US.

12 The International Nanzan High and Middle School (*Nanzan Kokusai Kootoo Gakkoo, Kokusai Chuugaku*)

General Setting of the School

The third location is situated in Nagoya, Japan. This private Catholic school was founded by father Josef Reiners in 1932. It was destroyed in the World War II but was rebuilt in 1946. The International Junior and Senior High School section were respectively set up in 1982 and 1983. The two sections only accept returnees and a minority of foreigners, including those of mixed parentage. Through introductions by Belgian professors at the Nanzan University, Nagoya, I first visited the school in 1992, at that time still located in Nagoya City. In 1992 I did not have the occasion to observe or to interview students. Yet I had a conversation with the then director.

> The school caters only to returnees and foreigners. The exclusive membership of returnees and foreigners is quite extraordinary in the educational landscape of Japanese. Normally returnee schools are seen as less prestigious as Japanese institutions. Luckily our reputation is good, I think. Our students can enroll at any time of the year so that they do not fall into a black hole after returning to Japan. Most of the students are from the surrounding area such as Toyota city and the Mie prefecture. There are no students from other regions. Since all returnees, living in the vicinity are accepted without regard to

previous academic record, this system demands a lot from the administration as well from the teaching staff and the involved students. My idea of education is to provide our students a chance to develop their minds and their potentialities. It is a pity though that most Japanese parents choose the 'safety track' for their children. When abroad facing the choice of sending the children home or to keep them there for further study at the Japanese school or the 'local' international school, they will choose the second option. They think their children will improve their English skills so that they have better chances to get into the good universities. But they do not send their children to local schools especially not in developing countries. This trend has led to some problems like an over-representation of Japanese pupils in international schools.

When asking him what the profile was of the average student, he replied thus.

There is an evolution in many ways. Whereas in the 1960s and 70s only a handful elite had the chance to go overseas and so the number of returnees was negligible. In the 1980s the number of returnees has increased rapidly. This has also an effect on the quality of our students here. Now our students, who used to be mostly well-behaved and intelligent, are less motivated and less disciplined.

I revisited the school in 1994. Until 1992 these international sections were located within the complex of the Nanzan secondary school in Nagoya. Due to the pressure of the growing student population, the school was rebuilt on the outskirts of Nagoya. This complex, established with the financial aid of Toyota, consists of twelve units: the Kojima auditorium, junior high classrooms, senior high classrooms, special facilities building, gymnasium, administration building, chapel, clubhouses, athletic field, tennis courts, and a dormitory for the interns. Three lines of school buses, the Issha, Josui and Toyota lines, make the commuting from and to the school possible.

I had the opportunity through the introduction of S. and the chemistry teacher Mr. T., a former teacher of S.'s daughters, to conduct in-depth interviews of some twenty students in conjunction with the questionnaires, distributed to the same group of students. Besides conducting formal interviews, I participated in the school life such as riding the schoolbus to and from the school, eating in the dining room, observing the general school life. Writing about schools is one kind of an activity but it is quite different to actually participate in it. Rohlen's view is the following (1983: 11).

> The tangible stuff of education is classes, recess periods, extracurricular activities, school regulations, homework, teachers, meeting, students socializing, and all the other minutiae of daily events that occur in thousands of schools throughout the school year.

Of the 20 interviewees 11 had been to the US, 5 to Asia and three to Europe (excluding Belgium). The ratio boys and girls is 12 to 8. The age ranges from 14 to 17. Concerning their self-identity, a set of 4 different categories was offered in the questionnaire and during the interview, to choose from – including a. Japanese, like all others (*futsuu na Nihonjin*); b. Japanese, who have to discard the overseas experiences (*kaigai zaijuu keiken no ishiki o suteru beki dearu*); c. Japanese, who value the overseas experiences (*Nihon shakai no kokusaika ni yuukoo dearu to omou*), d. a new type of Japanese (*atarashii taipu no Nihonjin*) and e. other (*sono hoka*). As all categorization is exhaustive, not allowing diversification and deviations in spite of an open question, the oral interview provided the occasion for a more in-depth discussion of their self-perception. Furthermore I selected returnees, who had been in countries other than Belgium.

The results of the questionnaire demonstrate that a great number selected the category 'Japanese, who value the overseas experience' (6 or 30 percent) and 'ordinary Japanese' (6 or 30 percent) followed by that of 'new type of Japanese' (5 or 25 percent) and 'other' (2 or 10 percent). There was one blank answer. Interesting to note is that no one had selected the category of Japanese, who have to discard the overseas experience in order to reimmerse in Japanese society. The average overseas sojourn of the different groups spans respectively 4.5 years; 5.5 years; 6.8 years and 5.5 years. Finally the countries of sojourn of the first category include Thailand, Indonesia, the Philippines, Switzerland, France and England. The second category had been to Singapore, Hong Kong and the US/Hong Kong. The third group of 'new type of Japanese' had stayed in the US, Germany, the United Kingdom and US/Australia. The two 'individualistic' Japanese had both lived in the US. What follows are the most important points, which have been discussed during the oral interview.

Negotiating and Fostering Identities

'International' Japanese

This category is called 'international' Japanese because the overseas experience is perceived as a positive asset in an increasingly international Japanese society. The knowledge of foreign language distinguishes the 'international' Japanese from the ordinary Japanese. Emi, a tomboy-like high school girl, has spent four years in Thailand from the age of ten. She attended a Japanese school there. In spite of the Japanese curriculum, she had to take the Thai language and English. In Thailand, her family lived in a spacious house with a swimming pool, surrounded by lots of greenery. Life was generally pleasant.

> The pace of living was very relaxed. People were friendly. Even strangers on the streets smiled at you. The food was a bit hot but I liked it. Everything was so cheap like fruit, entertainment, etc. Al-

296

though there were many Japanese department stores, such as Isetan, Yaohan, Sogo, I always went with my friends to the Thai stores because they were cheaper.

After her return she enrolled in Nanzan because it was close to home.

I did not experience return problems. I had always lived in Japan before my going to Thailand. There I continued to speak in Japanese and to study in Japanese. But I am glad I had the chance to go overseas. My Thai is not perfect but if I had the chance, I can improve it. Maybe I can specialize in Thai and Japanese and then work as translator or so after graduation. Without my overseas experiences, I would never have had the idea of studying Thai. So I think my overseas experiences were very important.

Ryuma lived in Jakarta for a total period of ten years from the age of 5 until the age of 15, where he attended the Jakarta Japanese School. It was a large school with about 12,000 Japanese students, living on a permanent basis in Indonesia and about 1,030 overseas youngsters (*kaigaishijo*). As in all Japanese schools foreign languages, *in casu* Indonesian and English were taught. He took both languages. He recalled the life in Indonesia thus.

Indonesia is very calm. There's a lot of nature. People are less concerned about money and status symbol like in Japan. Here there's too much stress on money and who can afford what.

When he returned in March 1994, he did not mind attending an ordinary Japanese school. He figured that he has always been studying and socializing in the Japanese educational system, even when he was abroad. Yet his parents and in particular his mother urged him to attend a returnee school. At Nanzan he did not have re-entry problems since his three friends, whom he met in Jakarta, entered school at the same moment. When he was asked how he would describe his identity, he replied:

I don't think I'm a real *kikokushijo* because normally people think that a *kikokushijo* is someone, who has studied in local schools and who speaks foreign languages fluently and especially English. So I don't fit in that image. But I still feel I'm different from other Japanese because I have been abroad and I know something about the Indonesian language and Indonesian life.

Takeo, a 16-year-old boy, has spent 3 years in the Philippines from the age of 12 until 15. During that period, he was enrolled as a student in the International School of Manila. He liked that school.

Everyone was very serious about study. Some graduates went on to Harvard and other prestigious universities. I felt at home there. I had friends from many countries. I had Japanese, Filipino, French and Spanish friends. The main language was English and then Spanish. There was also this 'mood' in the Philippines, which was more relaxed. People were nice and easy-going, not so in Japan.

When he arrived to Japan in April 1994, he experienced a reverse culture shock.

I felt a general unease. I thought there was so much traffic. And then you have these 'crazy guys' in the Sakai area. They look and act as if they belong to the 'Mafia.' I don't have many friends here. My family moved from Chiba to Nagoya and so I don't have any elementary school friend here. I'm not too happy with this school. Students are noisy and they don't work. Sometimes in the middle of a class, a student would pop in to talk to another student in class, neglecting the teacher and disrupting the class.

He clearly felt he was a *kikokushijo*. He discerned a partial difference between him and an ordinary Japanese. He valued the experience in the Philippines, where he was enrolled in a good school with diligent and serious students. Hironori, another 16-year-old boy, spent 4 years in Switzerland. From the age of 12 to 15 he was enrolled in an International Boarding School in the vicinity of Geneva. Strictly speaking his status as '*kikokushijo*' can be questioned as he traveled on his own behalf abroad and not accompanying his parents like most others. Since he was accepted as a regular student in the school, he was included in the research sample. He recalled that there were two sections in school: the American and the European section. The American section, to which he belonged, used English as the standard language and in the European section French was the main tongue. Unlike the other *kikokushijo*, he did not join his parents to go abroad. He convinced his parents to send him to that school given the good experience of his brother, an alumnus of that school, and since he wanted an international education.

> At B.C. (International School in Switzerland) I had mostly American friends. There were very few Japanese. The Europeans spoke French and were less easy-going as the Americans. I was accepted in the American group. I could have stayed in Switzerland. But I didn't like it there too much. It was very boring.

After coming back to Japan, he did not attend Japanese school but Nanzan, an international school. At school he faced problems with the Japanese language but that did not seem to bother him much since he wanted to have a good time.

'Ordinary' Japanese

Some returnees did not like to emphasize the differences, separating the returnee from ordinary Japanese. Despite their overseas sojourn of the average period of 5.5 years, they did not see why they differed from others. Emi, a fifteen-year-old girl, had been abroad twice. She was in Hong Kong from the age three to five and in New York from the age of ten to fourteen. She remembered almost nothing about her stay in Hong Kong. She attended the kindergarten at the Japanese School in Hong Kong. One of her few recollections was going to the Mitsukoshi Department Store. She was in New York from ten to fourteen. She studied in a local elementary and middle school for three and a half years. She recalled the beginning period as follows:

> It was very hard for me to study in English. At the same time, I was attending a *juku* in New York. I was the only girl and the only non-Japanese school student. The other nine boys all attended the Japanese School.

Her parent urged her to enroll in the returnee school of Nanzan. Her impression of the school is on the whole positive.

> I like the school. At the moment, I don't have many friends. That's normal because I just arrived and I hardly know anyone. But I'm sure that as time goes by I will make more friends. So I am not worried.

After school she also attended a *juku*.

> I go to *juku* once a week from 2 p.m. until 9 p.m. The pace is very fast. The subjects I am taking are mathematics, Japanese and English. I have to work on my math because I am in the lowest level now. I also need to improve my English. I feel uncomfortable in English and I have many difficulties with writing.

She preferred to think herself as Japanese like all others: 'Although I have been abroad twice and therefore a *kikokushijo*, I do not want to be different from other Japanese.'

Kei, a 15-year-old boy, had a similar self-definition. He, too thought himself to be an ordinary Japanese. He was in Singapore from the age of twelve until fifteen. There he studied at the Japanese school in Singapore. The school was fairly large. The middle school had fifty-five students when he was there. Although he had to take English in the Japanese school in Singapore, he does not really speak it.

> I don't speak English well. When I was In Singapore, I got by using *tango* (keywords). On the whole, there was a large Japanese community. There were also lots of Japanese stores, such as a Japanese video store, a Yaohan department store, etc.

Asking him what he thought of Singapore, he said:

I think it's an interesting place with many minorities, religions and languages. I know all this from books because I didn't have contact with people from Singapore. On the other hand, it was very strict and rigorous.

When he returned to Japan, he chose Nanzan for the following reasons.

I preferred Nanzan because it's well known. Second Nanzan is less strict than public schools. I have a lot of freedom, here. I can grow my hair the way I like. I can wear whatever I like. There's no school uniform.

He described himself as follows:

I don't mind being called a returnee because I am one. Besides, it helped me getting in the school. But I don't think I am different from other Japanese. Like most Japanese, I want to go to a good Japanese university and then get a good job in a Japanese company.

Yumiko was a fifteen-year-old girl. She wore round glasses, talked in a high-pitch voice and dressed in a uniform-type of outfit. She has been in Hong Kong from 1983 until 1992. She attended for half a year a local kindergarten in Kowloon and switched to the kindergarten, middle and high school sections of the Japanese school in Hong Kong.
She pictured her school and personal life as follows:

Life in Hong Kong is very much like life in Japan. There were many Japanese department stores; Mitsukoshi, Matsukaya, Yaohan, etc. The Japanese school was very large. There were 1,500 pupils in elementary school and 450 in middle school. At school, the only foreign language we had to study was English. Cantonese was not required. Although I have had English in school, I don't speak it well.

After her return, she did not experience any re-entry difficulties because she basically lived as a Japanese in Hong Kong.

I wanted to go to an ordinary Japanese school but my parents wanted me to attend Nanzan because my father and my uncle had studied here before. I don't have any problems with learning nor with socializing in Nanzan. In fact, my two favorite subjects are mathematics and *kokugo* (Japanese language).

Takeyuki was a 14-year-old boy. He was in the United States from the age of 7 until 13. There he attended local schools: two different elementary schools and a high school.

> In school I had mainly American friends because the place where we lived and where I attended the school was a sort of *inaka* (the countryside). I didn't develop any attachment to the place because I knew that we were only staying there temporarily.

After return he wanted to enroll in Nanzan because he thought ordinary Japanese schools would be too strict and too difficult. He did not mind being called a *kikokushijo* since he was one. Yet he defined himself as Japanese.

The 'new type of Japanese' group

This group of 'new type of Japanese' resembles at first sight the 'international group'. Although all interviewees belong in varying degree to the one or the other group, those who define themselves 'new type' felt more connected with the country of sojourn, not only in the past like the first group of 'international Japanese' but also in the future sense. Tatsuyuki is a seventeen-year-old boy with long hair, wearing an earring and casually dressed in a black T-shirt and pants. He liked to be called 'Tats'. He has spent four years in England, where he studied in two local schools.

He recalled his experience in England thus.

> England was great except for the weather and some forms of racism. I was once punched in the face by a homeless person for no good reason. Then, in school, some kids would call me names like *Jap*. Otherwise, I was accepted. My English friends and I used to go to pubs together to drink. My parents didn't really liked that but I did it anyway. I still have contacts with my English friends.

Asking him whether he had re-entry problems, he said:

No, not really. When I came back in July 1994, I could go to an ordinary school. Besides I think in a school environment with returnees, it would be easier for me to make friends, to be accepted. So far, I don't have any problems.

Asking why he found himself a new type of Japanese, he replied:

I am completely at ease when talking and socializing with foreigners. I don't feel the stress some Japanese say they feel when they are together with foreigners. So, that is why I think I am different from ordinary Japanese.

Akira was in Germany from the age of 13 to 15 when his father worked for the Japanese Embassy. His parents decided to send him and his brothers to a local school.

The reason was that my parents wanted us to benefit from the occasion to learn the German language and culture since we were there. Besides sending three children to the Japanese school would also have been too expensive. In the beginning it was hard. I had to take a intensive course of German. Luckily I was there with my older brother, so we could do homework together. Then I was transferred to the NC Gymnasium. I really enjoyed that school. I made a lot of friends. On Saturdays from 2 to 6 p.m. I had to go to the *hoshuuko*. I didn't like that. I have chosen Nanzan because it has the reputation of being less strict (*kibishii*) than ordinary Japanese public schools.

He did not mind being called returnee because he was one. In fact he saw himself as a new kind of Japanese, who is both Japanese and international. After graduation, he planned to study in a German University. Emi, a 15-year-old girl, was born in Los Angeles, USA and lived there until the age of four. Her parents then moved to Australia, where she had stayed for a total of ten years until the age of fourteen. In Australia, she attended a local kindergarten and thereafter KH Public School, where she learned to speak English fluently. While she was attending the Australian school, her parents also made her go to a *juku* to improve her Japanese and mathematics. She had evening classes four times a week.

When she turned nine, her parents sent her to the Sydney Japanese School. She forgot almost all her English. On the whole she had fond memories of Australia:

> I really like the life over there because people always say hello, even when they don't know you. I also like the wide open landscape.

When she returned to Japan, her mother discouraged her from attending an ordinary Japanese school. Her mother's concern was that she would become a target of *ijime* (bullying) by other Japanese children. She did not have problems adjusting herself to the school environment.

> I made a lot of friends here among the foreigners and the returnees. One of my best friend now is half-Italian, half-Spanish and whose stepfather is Japanese. I speak in English to my foreign friends and in Japanese with the *kikokushijo* friends.

After Nanzan, she intended to study at Hokkaido to become a veterinary surgeon partly because Hokkaido reminded her of Australia. Takami is a 17-year-old girl, born in Atlanta, Georgia, where she lived until three. Then her parents moved to Chicago, where they stayed for a total of three years. When the family returned to Japan, she was 5.5 year old, ready to enter elementary school. She recalled the following:

> It was really terrible. Since I had never set foot in Japan until then, I really had a culture shock. What was worse was that everyone treated me as a *gaijin*. In the kindergarten, I was the only person, who was born outside Japan. I think the fact that I have two citizenships really confused them. In elementary school, the teacher called me a *gaijin*.

At the age of 8, her family left Japan once again for Los Angeles. For two years, she attended a local middle school. When she returned to Japan, her parents decided to send her to Nanzan International Middle School, as it was an exclusively returnee school.
She liked the school.

It's easy to make friends here so I'm part of it. I don't worry so much about study. I think it's more important to do what one likes. Some of my friends in the States don't go to college at all because they want to become a secretary, or a translator or an actress. In fact, that's what I really want to do, to become an actress. I'm not really interested in university studies. But my mother wants me to go to college first and then to pursue my dream.

Marie was in the United States from the age of 7 to 12. She attended a local school in the state of Kentucky. She did not have re-entry problems. She chose Nanzan because she already knew some people at Nanzan, whom she had met in Kentucky. These friends introduced her to others. Now she has become integrated in school. She did not mind the label 'returnee.' In asking her why she would call herself a 'new type of Japanese' she replied:

I am a *kikokushijo*. I'm also proud to have the chance to do special things in another country.

'Others'

The two students who defined themselves respectively as 'Asian American' and 'someone who is independent of what others say and do' were not surprisingly the most outspoken of all interviewees. Hitomi, a fourteen-year-old year girl, had lived the greater part of her life in the United States. She was one-year old when her parents moved to Los Angeles. She recalled her sojourn as follows:

I stayed there with my family until the age of eleven. During the week I attended a local American elementary school. I also studied Japanese language, mathematics and social sciences at the Japanese supplementary school on Saturdays. You see, I learned about the Japanese society and history through books. I spoke a mixture of English and Japanese.

The family went back to Japan when she was in sixth grade. She attended a school, which had a special course for returnees. When she heard about Nanzan International School receiving exclusively returnees and foreigners, she was convinced this was her school.

Her current view on the school and the general setting of the school was rather bleak.

> I'm very disappointed with the school. I feel an outsider in so many ways. First, I have problems keeping up with the pace of study. It's too competitive. I've trouble with the language, especially with the *kanji* and mathematics. I also have difficulties making friends because they are all so Japanese. I find the Japanese way of making friends very difficult.

When I asked her what she meant by 'the Japanese way of making friends' she clarified as follows:

> You have to belong to a group and do all the things the members of that group are supposed to do. I think it's ridiculous to always have to do things together with other people. Some girls even go to toilet together! The school is too Japanese: everyone speaks Japanese, the classes are taught in Japanese.

Concerning her identity she did not mind being called a returnee since she was very proud of her overseas experiences. In fact she preferred defining herself as 'Asian American'. At school she was marginalized both for getting bad grades and for refusing to conform. Others called her 'stupid' because she was a bad and asocial student. Feeling out of place, she hoped to leave Japan as soon as possible. She envied her brother, who was born in the States and therefore had dual nationality. Ironically, she told me that her brother did not have the same entry problems as she did. Toda, a 16-year-old youngster, had the most mature look of all the interviewees. He lived in Michigan, USA with his parents from the age of 12 until 15. He studied at a local middle school with a sound reputation. Classes were tough in the beginning. For the first 2, 3 months he had to take ESL in order to be able to attend ordinary education in the States. But since he was a good student, he obtained very good grades. Although he was not completely excluded from social life – he was invited to parties held by American friends – he nonetheless sensed a feeling of non-acceptance. He suspected that this attitude was due to the rivalry between Toyota, one of Japan's leading car manufacturers and General Motors. The father of some of the American co-students in the school worked for GM, whereas some fathers of the Japanese, including himself, were employed at Toyota.

I was not particularly called by names. Because I was 'cool' I didn't experience acts of discrimination but I still felt animosity.

By 'someone cool' he meant a person, who was intelligent and who received good grades. In the first year of his stay in the United States, he attended a supplementary school. As he did not see the point of it, he could – with considerable effort – convince his parents to discontinue supplementary school. When he returned to Japan in March 1994, he intended to go to an ordinary Japanese high school with 'a first-class' (*ichiryuu*) school. Due to the bad timing – he could not meet the deadline of enrollment – he finally chose for Nanzan. He thought the level at Nanzan undemanding but he had nonetheless difficulties with Japanese at first.

I don't worry too much about that. I'm good in math and I want to become even better. That's why I am enrolled in a *juku* to further improve my skills in mathematics.

When he was asked why he attached so much importance to mathematics, he clarified thus.

Later I want to study at a good university, perhaps abroad, in one of those American universities where I can get a solid education. You see, I want to do something in life like building machines or so.

Linking Theory with Ethnographic Findings

It is hard to envisage Nanzan pupils as outsiders while observing and interviewing them in school. When one analyzes the school curriculum, the language of instruction and the overall school environment, one can conclude it is essentially a Japanese private school. The fact that some dissatisfied returnees complain that losing their foreign language skills illustrate how 'Japanese' and 'Japan-oriented' the school is.

Returnees as a 'type' do no exist in spite of persisting essentialized images. The interviews at the International Section of the Nanzan School for Returnees demonstrate clearly that varying degrees of identity strategies abound, even among a small group of twenty students. The adopted categories – of 'international'; 'ordinary Japanese', 'new type of Japanese' and 'others – are not mutually exclusive entities with uniform properties but rather frameworks of tendencies. All categories have in common that each member had chosen to study in a returnee school. Thus, everyone implicitly or explicitly agrees to be returnee.

At first sight there is the paradox of those, who see themselves as 'ordinary Japanese' but at the same time who study in a returnee school instead of an ordinary school. They see the returnee school as an agent of reimmersion. Although they differentiate themselves from 'ordinary students' by their act of studying in a returnee school, at the same time they insist on the self-ascribed identity as 'full-fledged Japanese' at the subjective level. They want to reincorporate themselves into Japanese society and culture in all discretion and smoothness.

Among the different groups the distance between the 'international' and the 'new type' is the shortest. The difference, however, lies in the inclusion of the overseas experience in one's future life. The international person values the overseas experience highly whereas the new type goes a step further by continuing to explore, nurture and incorporate the overseas experiences in the further life planning.

The most striking thing to note is perhaps the overall positive findings of the overseas sojourn. No one thought the overseas experience to be a handicap in the reintegration process in Japanese society after return migration in spite of the wealth of material on return problems. It goes without saying that they study in a returnee school, where overseas experience is the rule rather than the exception.

In looking at the **countries of sojourn**, it is remarkable that those who call themselves 'new type of Japanese' have all lived in 'Western societies' including the US, Australia and Europe. Yet this does not mean that all those, who had been to the 'West', become a 'new type.' In the category of those, who identify themselves as 'ordinary Japanese', some had lived for an extensive period in the US.

The **duration** of the overseas sojourn is also often cited as a possible explanation for adjustment processes or the lack thereof upon return. It is argued, quite logically at first sight, that the longer one lives in a country, the higher the chances for a potential reverse cultural shock after return. Indeed among the group of the 'new type the duration of some interviewees is quite extensive ranging from twelve to eleven years but also from five and three years. In the category of the 'ordinary Japanese' the average sojourn abroad is longer than in the category of the 'new type', notably 5.5 percent versus 4.5 percent. Up to a certain degree the duration might explain why one experiences return problems as illustrated by Takami, and Emi. Exception to this explanation is the case of Akira.

Last but not least even in this small sample of twenty respondents there are still two cases, which – given the own background and aspirations – do not fit in any of the prescribed categories. The case of Hitomi shows that non-adjustment in school is both cause and effect of non-conform-ing with educational expectations – she is doing poorly in school – and with social rules – such as her dislike for the concept of 'friendship' in the Japanese context. The case of Toda reveals a highly individualistic and ambitious person, who prefers to be the architect of his own life rather than choosing one of the 'instant' and 'ready-made' lives.

13 Conclusion

The primary objective of this book is to analyze why return-ees have to negotiate their identity in Japan. As children of Japanese expatriates, they are exposed to different social and cultural settings. In order to understand the changing identity of returnees from the auto- and hetero-ascriptional point of view, different discourses were discussed, too. This is to say that the different discourses at the three interpenetrating macro, median and micro levels needed to be studied to gain a more profound understanding of Japanese ethnonational identity in general and the identity of returnees in particular. These discourses include the historical dimension of Japanese ethnonational identity, culture as flow and post-modernism. Since the Meiji area (1868–1912) Japan has embarked on the road of modernization. After an initial period of a wholesale import of all things, ideas and ideologies Western and the demand for institutional and bureaucratic change and institutions the general mood changed drastically around the 1880s. More and more voices including bureaucrats, scholars and opinion makers urged for the formulation of a specific Japanese ethnonational identity. They argued that in order to fully succeed in this nation building project a strong ethnonational identity shared by all the members of the nation was imperative. This process has been made possible by the formulation of a national ideology, based on certain metaphors and strict rules of membership, disseminated through channels such as the educational system to all members of society. The principal ideological framework of the Japanese nation consists of the 'family state' concept (*kazoku no kokka*) and the 'essence of the nation state' (*kokutai*). In the 'family state' the Emperor fulfills the role of a benevolent father towards his loyal children, the Japanese citizens. This system became increasingly prominent in the 1930s culminating in the mobilization of Japan into World War II. In the decade prior to the outbreak of the war, characterized by the ascending power of the military, the 'national polity' (*kokutai no hongi*) underlined that Japan was a sacred land and ruled by a divine Emperor. In the aftermath of the war, the ultranationalist stance weakened and lost much of its strength. Although the emperor system was not abolished after the war, the role of the Emperor has become symbolic. In the first two decades and more specifically from 1945 until 1963 Japan as a nation witnessed a crisis moment, attempting to recover from the defeat and the war devastation. Yet starting from the mid-1960s the Japanese economy and standard of living recovered steadfastly. The economic success, reaching an apex in the 1980s, gave Japanese leaders and people a sense of pride and self-confidence. The Japanese economy grew at such an unprecedented pace that terms like 'Japan as number one,' 'the Japanese miracle' and other superlative labels have been coined. At the same time Western countries marvel at the economic success of Japan and attempt to unravel the secrets underlying this success. 'The learn-from- Japan' school testifies this trend. In order to understand the keys of Japan's success, many areas have been singled out for emulation including Japanese education, Japanese business management, etc. In this process of digging for the roots of Japanese success, many authors from different walks of life, both Japanese and Westerners, emerged. They engaged in what is in retrospect is called 'the genre of the *Nihonbunkaron*' or the discourse on Japanese culture. The main recurrent themes are homogeneity of the Japanese people, purity of descent and the uniqueness of Japanese culture as exemplified by the 'village' (*mura*) metaphor. The first two characteristics clearly reflect the primordialist side of the discourse, whereas the uniqueness shows the salience of ethnonational boundaries. *Nihonbunkaron* testifies that the different approaches, developed in ethnicity theories, do not need to be mutually exclusive but can in certain cases function in a complementary way. The process of ethnonational identity is not just a concern of political leaders or academic scholars. On the contrary although the ethnonational identity is formulated and shaped at the macro level, it filters down to the Japanese people through certain institutions, of which the school is one of the most potent and important agents at the median level. More than in other societies, the school in Japan is the focal place of instruction and socialization, where young Japanese learn how to become proper Japanese. That is especially the case in primary and middle school. From high school onwards and according to some even at a younger age, school life gains a 'war-like' dimension. At least that is the case for the so-called 'beansprout children' (*moyashikko*) or crammers. These are youngsters, who at all costs, want to overcome the 'college entrance war' (*juken sensoo*) and so enter the universities with a high reputation. This 'ability first' (*nooryokushugi*) system, characterized by an examination-based selection procedure, claims to be meritocratic in that education is open to all endowed with intellectual capacities. In reality, though, the educational landscape is far more complex. The so-called escalator system refers to the need of a meticulous school planning at a very young age, sometimes even at the level of kindergartens since the schools at different levels are linked closely. In or-

313

der not to fall behind, youngsters and increasingly children have to attend *juku*. These are supplementary cram schools. *Juku* instructs youngsters how to pass successfully the tests and examinations. Their pedagogical strategy is a far cry from the humanistic educational tradition, aspiring to mold and nudge young minds into critical and independently thinking adults. The educational 'rat race' has been subject to much critique by the children and their mothers, educational experts and Western observers. Yet no one is willing get behind others by not joining the competition in spite of all the suffering and the sacrifices on the part of the youngsters.

Returnees, after having spent considerable time abroad, experience return difficulties in first instance in the school environment. There, they are often bullied for their difference. From the boundary perspective, they have left Japanese territory and therefore cut off from participation and socialization in Japanese society and culture. Moreover, they have problems with the language, and especially with the written language. For instance, they know less *kanji* (Chinese characters) than ordinary students do. Returnees are generally children of Japanese parents and are thus full-blood citizens of Japan. These primordial traits notwithstanding the overseas experience form a potential handicap in the reimmersion process. According to others, the overseas sojourn is not necessarily a major hindrance, impossible to overcome. The fact remains, though, that the overseas experience usually renders the returnees different, singular, if not peculiar. In the singularity theory there are two possible interpretations. Either one sees the overseas sojourn as a positive asset or as a marginalizing effect after return to Japan. Finally an increasing number of voices supports the idea of a new type of Japanese, who displays a cosmopolitan attitude towards the other. In the first handicap school, returnees are seen as complete outsiders or strangers. In the singularity theory they are 'part-Japanese.' The final analysis of the new type propagates a new generation of Japanese, who are open and self-confident.

The most intriguing challenge is to attempt explaining how this *'non-han-shin'* (non, half and new) flow could have taken place. I suggest connecting certain shifts at the macro and median level with the changing identity of the returnee youngsters at the micro level. At the macro level globalization has reached almost everywhere, including Japan. The idea of homogeneity has always been very strong in Japanese society. Yet from the late 1980s onwards scholars and general opinion makers started to discuss the issue of migrant workers in Japan. These events of increasing mobility in the globalized world have indirectly altered the whole discourse on returnees. Their 'different-ness' or state of marginality pales in comparison with the new group of *Nikkeijin*, Latin Americans of Japanese origin, and even more so with other migrant workers.

At the median level, the social construction of the issue of returnees has been the work of educational experts and the pressure of the parents (Goodman 1990a). Through the high social position of the parents their personal problems have become a social issue. Consequently, special measures like overseas education and special reception schools and policies have been formulated. Some educationalists, writing on the issue of returnees, are in fact returnees' parents. Finally, returnees themselves joined the discussion by researching and studying the issue. The privileged position is certainly true for a majority of returnees. Yet one has to add that in recent years subcontractors migrate abroad in an increasing way, too, together with their children. One might argue whether returnees actually lose a part op their 'Japanese-ness' during their stay abroad. After all, a whole network of Japanese overseas education has been set up. This is to say that children in the age range of compulsory education (6–15) have the possibility to attend full-time Japanese schools abroad. If there are no Japanese schools in the vicinity, then one could at least commute and attend supplementary school in the weekend. Youngsters beyond that age can attend local schools, international schools, and Japanese boarding schools or simply return to Japan.

In reading and analyzing the fieldnotes and the filed notes, returnees in Belgium do not invest much time in the host society. Even those, who attempt to reach out beyond the own group, encounter obstacles to meet and foster enduring friendships. The Japanese community in Brussels, and especially the expatriates, lives in a self-contained and self-sufficient way. Their stay has been 'sponsored' or 'packaged.' Newcomers can count on the assistance of fellow Japanese in daily life. An important detail is perhaps the publication of the *Guide of Living Conveniently in Belgium*, where all practical aspects ranging from legal procedures to health matters to shopping to getting to know the specific products of Belgium and foreign language courses, etc. are included. Concerning the returnee pupils at the Nanzan International School, those, who have spent time in Asian countries, stayed within the own group. Many Japanese accommodations were available so that contact with the host society could be kept at a minimal level. Those, who have lived in Europe or in the United States, occasionally experienced some forms of discrimination. In general, returnees have the firm intention to return to Japan for study and for work.

In terms of self-identity, they felt different from ordinary Japanese. Moreover, the majority of them expressed the willingness to insist on the returnee-specific identity. Whether they did that in order to get good jobs, where knowledge of foreign language and intercultural skills were required or whether they genuinely thought the overseas sojourn is a personal enrichment is difficult to disentangle.

At any rate I do not want to conclude in a deterministic way that the self-identity of returnees, like ethnic minorities, is exclusively used for self-serving purposes. On the other hand I do not share the belief that returnees, while claiming their specific identity, are all cosmopolitans or little ambassadors in a globalizing Japanese society. Perhaps the truth is more complex and balancing somewhere in between.

References

Amino, Yoshihiki (1990) *Nihon no Shiza, Retto no Shakai to Kokka*, Tokyo: Shogakkan.

Anderson, Benedict R. (1991) *Imagined Communities*, New York: The Alpine Press.

Aoki, Tamotsu (1990) *Nihonbunkaron no Hen'yo: Sengo Nihon no Bunka to Aidentitii*, Tokyo: Chuokoronsha.

Aoki, Tamotsu (1994) Anthropology and Japan: Attempts at Writing Culture, *The Japan Foundation Newsletter* 22(3): 1–6.

Appadurai, Arjun (1991) Global Ethnoscapes: Notes and Queries for a Transnational Anthropology, in Richard Fox (ed.), *Recapturing Anthropology: Working in the Present*, pp. 191–210, Santa Fe: School of AmericanResearch Press.

Appleyard, Reginald (1992) Migration and Development: a Global Agenda for the Future, *International Migration* 30: 486–99.

Appleyard, Reginald (1993) International Migration in East-Asia: Situations and Issues, *International Migration* 31(2/3): 266–75.

Arlen, Michael (1975) *Passage to Ararat*, New York: Farrar, Straus and Giroux.

Ashkenazi, Michael (1990) Anthropological Aspects of the Japanese Meal: Tradition, Internationalization and Aesthetics, in Adriana Boscari, Franco Gatti and Massimo Raveri (eds), *Rethinking Japan. Volume II: SocialSciences, Ideology and Thought*, pp. 338–49, Sandgate: Japan Library.

Barth, Frederick (1969) *Ethnic Groups and Boundaries: The Social Organization of Cultural Difference*, London:Allen and Unwin.

Barth, Frederick (1994) Enduring and Emerging Issues in the Analysis of Ethnicity, in Hans Vermeulen and Cora Govers (eds), *The Anthropology of Ethnicity. 'Beyond Ethnic Groups and Boundaries'*, pp. 11–32, Amsterdam: Het Spinhuis Publishers.

Battaglia, Debbora (1995) Problematizing the Self: A Thematic Introduction, in Deborra Battaglia (ed.) *Rhetorics of Self-Making*, pp. 1–15, Berkeley: University of California Press.

Bauman, Zygmunt (1992) *Intimations of Postmodernity*, London: Routledge.

Beauchamp, Edward R. and Vardaman, James M. Jr. (eds) (1994) *Japanese Education since 1945. A DocumentaryStudy*, New York: Sharpe, Armonk.

Beardsley, Richard K., Hall, John W. and Ward, Robert E. (1959) *Village Japan*, Chicago: University of Chicago Press.

Beardsley, Richard K. e.a. (1965) *Twelve Doors to Japan*, New York: MacGraw.

Befu, Harumi (1983) Internationalization of Japan and "Nihonbunkaron", in Hiroshi Mannari and Harumi Befu (eds),*The Challenge of Japan's Internationalization,* pp. 232–66, Tokyo: Kodansha International.

Befu, Harumi (1990) Amerika ni Okeru Nihon Kenkyu no Tokushitsu. In Takeshi Umehara (ed.), *Nihon to wa Nanno Ka*), pp. 44–5, Tokyo: Nihon Hoso Shuppan Kyokai.

Befu, Harumi (1993) Nationalism and "Nihonjinron", in Harumi Befu (ed.) *Cultural Nationalism in East Asia.Representation and Identity*, pp. 107–35, Berkeley: Institute of East Asian Studies.

Befu, Harumi and Kreiner, Joseph (1992) *Othernesses of Japan. Historical and Cultural Influences on Japanese Studies in Ten Countries*, Munich: Iudicum.

Bell, Daniel (1975) Ethnicity and Social Change, in Nathan Glazer and Daniel Moynihan (eds), *Ethnicity: Theoryand Experience,* pp. 141–74, Cambridge Mass.: Harvard University Press.

Bell, Daniel (1979) *The Cultural Contradiction of Capitalism*, London: Heinemann.

Ben-Ari, Eyal (1990) Many Voices, Partial Worlds: On Some Conventions and Innovations in the Ethnographic Portrayal of Japan, in Ayal Ben-Ari, Brian Moeran and James Valentine (eds), *Unwrapping Japan. Societyand Culture in Anthropological Perspective*, pp. 140–62, Honolulu: University of Hawaii Press.

Ben-Ari, Eyal, Moeran, Brian and Valentine, James (eds) (1990) *Unwrapping Japan. Society and Culture in Anthropological Perspective*, Honolulu: University of Hawaii Press.

Benedict, Ruth (1946) *The Chrysanthemum and the Sword*, Boston: Houghton Mifflin.

Berman, Marschall (1983) *All that is Solid Melts into Air*, London: Verso.

Böhning, Roger (1998) *Top-End and Bottom-End Labour Import in the United States and Europe. Historical Evolution and Sustainability*, in van Amersfoort, Hans and Doomernik, Jeroen (eds), pp. 71–85, Amsterdam:IMES.

Boscaro, Adriana, Gatti, Franco and Raveri, Massimo (eds) (1990) *Rethinking Japan. Volume II: Social Sciences, Ideology and Thought*, Sandgate, Folkestone, Kent: Japan Library.

Bourdieu, Pierre and Passeron, Jean-Claude (1977) *Reproduction in Education, Society and Culture* (translated byRichard Nice), London: Sage Publications.

Clifford, James (1988) *The Predicament of Culture*, Cambridge: Harvard University Press.

Clifford, James and Marcus, George (eds) (1986) *Writing Culture: the Poetics and Politics of Ethnography*, Berkeley: University of California Press.

Cohen, Anthony (1994) Boundaries of Consciousness, Consciousness of Boundaries. Critical Questions for Anthropology, in Hans Vermeulen and Cora Govers (eds), *The Anthropology of Ethnicity. 'Beyond Ethnic Groups and Boundaries'*, pp. 59–80, Amsterdam: Het Spinhuis Publishers.

Creighton, Millie (1997) *Soto* Others and *Uchi* Others: Imaging Racial Diversity, Imagining Homogeneous Japan, in Michael Weiner (ed.), *Japan's Minorities. The Illusion of Homogeneity*, pp. 211–38, London and New York:Routledge.

Dacyl, Janina (ed.) (1995) *Management of Cultural Pluralism in Europe*, Stockholm: CEIFO Publications.

Dale, Peter (1988) *The Myth of Japanese Uniqueness*, London: Routledge.

Doi, Takeo (1980) *The Anatomy of Dependence. Exploring an Area of the Japanese Psyche-Feelings of Indulgence*, Tokyo: Kodansha International.

Dore, Ronald (1986) *Flexible Rigidities. Industrial Policy and Structural Adjustment in the Japanese Economy1970–80*, Stanford: Stanford University Press.

Douglas, Mary (1991 reprint) *Purity and Danger. An Analysis of the Concepts of Pollution and Taboo*, London:Routledge.

Duke, Benjamin C. (1986) *The Japanese School. Lessons for Industrial America*, New York: Praeger.

Ebuchi, Kazuhiro (1987) Patterns of cultural adaptation Among the Japanese Overseas: the Case of Japanese Sojourners in Southeast Asia, *Bulletin of Fukuoka University of Education* 34 (4): 1–13.

Ebuchi, Kazuhiro (1994) *Ibunkakan Kyoikugaku Josetsu*, Kyushu: Kyushu University Press.

Eddy, Elizabeth M. and Partridge, William L. (1978) *Applied Anthropology in America*, New York: Columbia University Press.

Egawa, Midori (1994) *Buryusseru Chioku Juzai Nihonjin no Seikatsu Tekio to Ibunka Taiken ni Kansuru Chosa Kenkyu*, Unpublished Paper.

Embree, John F. (1939) *Suye Mura: a Japanese Village*, Chicago: University of Chicago Press.

Eriksen, Thomas H. (1993) *Ethnicity and Nationalism. Anthropological Perspectives*, London: Pluto Press.

Findlay, Allan M. (1990) A Migration Channels Appproach to the Study of High Level Manpower Movements, *International Migration* 28: 15–22.

Findlay, Allan M. (1991) Le début de XXIe siècle sera le temps des émigrants de haut niveaux, in Le Soir, *Les Migrations, un Dossier du 'Soir'*, pp. 107–8.

Findlay, Allan, M. (1993) New Technology, High Level Labour Movements and the Concept of Brain Drain, in OECD, *Changing Course of International Migration*, pp. 149–59.

Fisher, Michael (1986) Ethnicity and Post-modern Arts of Memory, in James Clifford and George Marcus (eds), *Writing Culture: the Poetics and Politics of Ethnography*, pp. 194–233, Berkeley: University of California Press.

Fox, Richard (1991) *Recapturing Anthropology: Working in the Present*, Santa Fe: School of American Research Press.

Fujitani, Takashi (1993) Inventing, Forgetting, Remembering: Toward a Historical Ethnography of the Nation-State, in Harumi Befu (ed.), *Cultural Nationalism in East Asia*, pp. 77–106, Berkeley: Institute for East Asian Studies.

Geertz, Clifford (1973) *The Interpretation of Cultures*, New York: Basic Books.

Geertz, Clifford (1988) *Works and Lives. The Anthropologist as Author*, California: University of Stanford Press.

Gellner, Ernest (1993) *Nations and Nationalism*, Blackwell: Oxford.

Giddens, Anthony (1991) *Modernity and Self-Identity*, Cambridge: Polity Press.

Ginsburg, Faye (1995) Production Values: Indigeneous Media and the Rhetoric of Self-Determination, in Deborah Battaglia (ed.), *Rhetorics of Self-Making*, pp. 121–38, Berkeley: University of California Press.

Glazer, Nathan and Moynihan, Daniel (1975) *Ethnicity. Theory and Experience*, Cambridge Mass.: Harvard University Press.

Gluck, Carol (1985) *Japan's Modern Myths. Ideology in the Late Meiji Period*, New Jersey: Princeton University Press.

Golden, Marita (1983) *Migrations of the Heart*, New York: Doubleday.

Goldstein-Goldini, Ofra (1997) *Packaged Japaneseness: Weddings, Business and Brides*, Honolulu: University of Hawaii Press.

Goodman, Roger (1990a) *Japan's "International" Youth. The Emergence of a New Class of Schoolchildren*, Oxford: Clarendon Press.

Goodman, Roger (1990b) Deconstructing an Anthropological Text: a "Moving" Account of the Returnee Schoolchildren in Contemporary Japan, in Eyal Ben-Ari, Brian Moeran and James Valentine (eds) *Unwrapping Japan. Society and Culture in Anthropological Perspective*, pp. 163–87, Honolulu: University of Hawaii Press.

Goody, Jack (1993) Culture and its Boundaries: a European View, *Social Anthropology* 1: 9–32.

Hamaguchi, Eshun (1994) *A New Paradigm for Japanese Studies: Methodological Relatum-ism*. Paper presented at the EAJS (European Association of Japanese Studies) in Copenhagen, Denmark.

Hamaguchi, Eshun (1998) *Nihonshakai to wa Nani ka? Zasshukei no Shiten Kara*, Tokyo: NHK Books.

Hammersley, Martyn (1992) *What's Wrong with Ethnography? Methodological Explorations*, London: Routledge.

Hannerz, Ulf (1992) *Cultural Complexity. Studies in the Social Organization of Meaning*, New York: Columbia University Press.

Harootunian, H.D. (1970) *Toward Restoration. The Growth of Political Consciousness in Tokugawa Japan*, Berkeley: University of California Press.

Hielscher, Gebhard (ed.) (1980) *Die Frau*, Berlin: E. Schmidt.

Hendry, Joy (1990) The Armour of Honorific Speech: Some Lateral Thinking about "Keigo", in Adriana Boscaro,Franco Gatti and Massimo Raveri, *Rethinking Japan. Volume II: Social Science and Thoughts*, pp. 111–6, Kent: Japan Library.

Hobsbawm, Eric J. (1990) *Nations and Nationalism since 1780. Programme, Myth, Reality*, Cambridge: Cambridge University Press.

Horio, Teruhisa (1993) *L' éducation au Japon* (translated by Jean-François Sabouret), Paris: CNRS Editions.

Horioka, Charles Yuji (1993) 'Consuming and Saving', in Andrew Gordon (ed.), *Postwar Japan as History*, pp. 259–92, Berkeley, Los Angeles, Oxford: University of California Press.

Horoiwa, Naomi (1987) Kaigai Seicho Nihonjin no Tekio ni Okeru Naibu Katto, *Ibunka Kyoiku* 1: 67–80.

Hoshino, Akira (1990) Kikokushijo Shinri Rinsho no Kadai, in Akira Hoshino (ed.) *Kikokushijo no Shinri Rinshoteki Kenkyu*, pp. 110–25, Tokyo: Tokyo Gakugei University.

Hutnik, Nimmi (1991) *Ethnic Minority Identity: A Sociological Psychological Perspective*, Oxford: Clarendon Press.

Iwama, Hiroshi (1992) *Chiisana Daishi no Ibunka Taiken*, Tokyo: Gakuensha.

Iyotani, Toshio (1995) Globalization and Culture, *The Japan Foundation Newsletter* 23(3): 1–5.

Japan Overseas Educational Services (1992) *Statistics of Returnees*, Tokyo: Japan Overseas Educational Services.

Japanese Consulate, Belgium (1994) *Statistical Information Sheet* (Internal Document), Brussels.

Kajita, Takamichi (1993) Tabunkashugi: Sono Genjo to Mondaiten, in NIRA, *Minzoku ni Kansuru Kisokenkyu*, pp.181–95, Tokyo.

Kajita, Takamichi (1994) *Gaikokujin Rodosha to Nihon*, Tokyo: NHK Books.

Kawai, Saburo (1993) Japan and International Migration: Situation and Issues, *International Migration* 31 (2/3):276–84.

Kerr, Clark (1983) *The Future of Industrial Societies: Convergence or Continuing Diversity?*, Cambridge, Mass.:Harvard University Press.

Kerr, Clark, Dunlop, John T., Harbison, Frederick H. and Myers, Charles (1960) *Industrialism and Industrial Man: The Problems of Labor and Management in Economic Growth*, Cambridge, Mass.: Harvard University Press.

Kim, Ok-Pyo Moon (1986) The "ie" in Rural Japan, The Impact of Tourism on a Traditional Japanese Village, in JoyHendry and Jonathan Webber (eds), *Interpreting Japanese Society. Anthropological Approaches*, pp. 185–97, Oxford: JASO.

Kingston, Maxine H. (1976) *The Woman Warrior: Memoirs of a Girlhood among Ghosts*, New York: Alfred A. Knoph.

Kobayashi, Tetsuo (1987) The Influx of Illegal Foreign Workers, *Economic Eye* 18(4): 20–3.

Kobayashi, Tetsuya (1981) *Kaigaishijo Kyoiku, Kikokushijo Kyoiku: Kokusai Jidai no Kyoiku Mondai*, Tokyo:Yuhikaku.

Komai, Hiroshi (1995) *Migrant Workers in Japan*, London: Kegan Paul International.

Kroker, Arthur and Cook, David (1988) *The Postmodern Scene: Excremental Culture and Hyperaesthetics*, London:Macmillan.

Kurimoto, Kazuo (1985) *Kokusai Jidai to Nihonjin*, Tokyo: NHK.

Lebra, Takie Sugiyama (1984) *Japanese Women. Constraint and Fulfillment*, Honolulu: University of Hawaii Press.

Leman, Johan and Byram Michael (1990) *Bilingual and Trilingual Education*, Clevedon: Multilingual Matters.

Linhart, Sepp (1994) Paradigmatic Approaches to Japanese Society and Culture by Western Social Scientists, *The Japan Foundation Newsletter* 22(3): 7–13.

Lynch, James (1983) *The Multicultural Curriculum: Education in a Multicultural Society*. London: Batsford Academic Publishing.

MacDonald, Gaynor (1995) A non-Japanese Japanese: On Being a Returnee, in John C. Maher and Gaynor MacDonald (eds), *Diversity in Japanese Culture and Language*, London: Kegan Paul International.

Marcus, George and Fisher, Michael (1986) *Anthropology as Cultural Critique: an Experimental Moment in the Human Sciences*, Chicago: The University of Chicago Press.

Mason, David (1990) A Rose by Any Other name...? Categorisation, Identity and Social Science, *New Community* 17(1): 123–33.

Miller, Roy A. (1982) *Japan's Modern Myth: the Language and Beyond*, New York and Tokyo: Weatherhill.

Minoura, Yasuko (1984) *Kodomo no Ibunka Taiken*, Tokyo: Shisakusha.

Miyachi, Sooshichi (1990) *Kikokushijo*, Tokyo: Chuokoronsha.

Miyajima, Takashi (1994) *Immigration and the Redefinition of 'Citizenship' in Japan- 'One People-One nation' in Question* (Unpublished Paper).

Miyajima, Takashi (1995) *Kawasakishi Gaikokuseki Shiminishiki Jittai Chosa*, Kawasaki: City of Kawasaki.

Modell, Judith (1989) Ruth Fulton Benedict (1887-1948), in Ute Gacs, Aisha Khan, Jerrie McIntyre and Ruth Weinberg, (eds) *Women Anthropologists. Selected Biographies*, pp. 1–7, Urbana and Illinois: University of Illinois Press.

Moeran, Brian (1990) Introduction: Rapt Discourses: Anthropology, Japanism, and Japan, in Eyal Ben-Ari, Brian Moeran and James Valentine (eds) *Unwrapping Japan. Society and Culture in Anthropological Perspective*, pp. 1–17, Honolulu: University of Hawaii Press.

Mouer, Ross E. and Sugimoto, Yoshio (1990) *Images of Japanese Society*, London: Kegan Paul International.

Mura, David (1991) *Turning Japanese. Memoirs of a Sansei*, New York: Doubleday

Muto, Masatoshi (1993) Japan: the Issue of Migrant Workers, in Daniel Kubat (ed.) *The Politics of Migration Policies Settlement and Integration. The First World War into the 1990s*, pp. 348–52, New York: Centerfor Migration Studies.

Nagayama, Toshikazu (1993) New Developments in Population Movement and the Issue of Foreign Workers in Japan, *International Migration* 21(2/3): 423–33.

Nakabayashi, Katsuo (1981) *Sekai no Nihonjingakkoo*, Tokyo: Sanshusha.

Nakajima, Tomoko (1988) Kokunai Rikai to Kokusai Rikai, *Ibunkakan Kyoiku* 2: 58–67.

Nakane, Chie (1973) *The Japanese Society*, Hamondsworth: Penguin

Neustupny, J. (1980) On Paradigms in the Study of Japan, *Social Analysis* 5/6: 20–8.

Nishimura, Hidetoshi (1985) Educational Reform: Commissioning a Master Plan, *Japan Quarterly* 32(1): 18–22.

Nishio, Kanji (1989) *Rodo Sakoku no Susume: Gaikokujin Rodosha ga Nihon o Horobosu*, Tokyo: Kobunsha

NIRA (1993) *Basic Research on Ethnicity*, NIRA Research Report nr. 930023, Tokyo.

NIS (National Institute for Statistics) Population census 1991. Brussels.

Norbeck, Edward and Parman, Susan (1970) *The Study of Japan in Behavior Sciences*, Houston: Rice University

Ochiai, Emiko (1997) *The Japanese Family System in Transition: A Sociological Analysis of Family Change in Postwar Japan*, Tokyo: LTBC International Library Foundation.

Ohnuki-Tierney, Emiko (1984) *Illness and Culture in Contemporary Japan*, Cambridge: Cambridge UniversityPress.

Oide, Akira (1965) *Nihongo to Ronri: Sono Yuko na Hyogen Ho*, Tokyo: Kodansha.

Okonogi, Keigo (1978) The ajase complex of the Japanese: the Depth Psychology of the Moratorium People, *Japan Echo* 5(4): 88–105.

Pang, Ching Lin (1995) Controlled Internationalization and the Case of "Kikokushijo" from Belgium, in Roosens, Eugeen (guest-editor) Rethinking Culture,"Multicultural Society", and the School', *The International Journal of Educational Research* 23 (1): 45–56.

Parent-Teachers Association of the Japanese School in Brussels (1995) *Berugi Seikatsubenricho*, Brussels: theJapanese School in Brussels.

Passin, Herbert (1983) The Internationalization of Japan – Some Reflections, in Hiroshi Mannari and Harumi Befu(eds) *The Challenge of Japan's Internationalization*, pp. 15–30, Tokyo: Kodansha International.

Patterson, Orlando (1977) *Ethnic Chauvinism: The Reactionary Pulse*, New York: Stein and Day.

Plath, David W. (1990) Fieldnotes, Filed Notes, and the Conferring of Notes, in Roger Sanjek (ed.) *Fieldnotes. The Makings of Anthropology*, pp. 371–84, Ithaca: Cornell University Press.

Portes, Alejandro and Borocz, József (1989) Contemporary Immigration: Theoretical Perspectives on its Determinants and Modes of Incorporation. An Assessment for the 1990s, *International Migration Review* 23(3): 606–30.

Rabinow, Paul (1986) Representations are Social Facts: Modernity and Post-Modernity in Anthropology, in James Clifford and George Marcus (eds) *Writing Culture: the Poetics and Politics of Ethnography*, pp. 234–61, Berkeley: University of California Press.

Rabinow, Paul (1990) For Hire: Resolutely Late-Modern, in Richard Fox (ed.) *Recapturing Anthropology: Workingin the Present*, Santa Fe: School of American Research Press.

Ramakers, Joan (1992) *Asiel en Migratie*, Leuven: Hoger Instituut voor de Arbeid.

Reischauer, Edwin (1976) *The Japanese*, Cambridge, MA: Harvard University Press.

Reischauer, Edwin (1986) Introduction, in Benjamin Duke (ed.) *The Japanese School. Lessons for Industrial America*, pp. ix–xi, New York, Westport, Connecticut and London: Praeger.

Roden, Donald (1980) *Schooldays in Imperial Japan: A Study of the Culture of a Student Elite*, Berkeley: University of California Press.

Rohlen, Thomas P. (1974) *For Harmony and Strength: Japanese White-Collar Organization in Anthropological Perspective*, Berkeley: University of California Press.

Rohlen, Thomas P. (1980) The *Juku* Phenomenon: an Exploratory Essay, in *The Journal of Japanese Studies* 6(2):207–42.

Rohlen, Thomas P. (1983) *Japan's High Schools*. Berkeley: University of California Press.

Roosens, Eugeen (1989) *Creating Ethnicity: The Process of Ethnogenesis*, Newbury Park: Sage Publications.

Roosens, Eugeen (1994) The Primordial Nature of Origins in Migrant Ethnicity, in Hans Vermeulen and Cora Govers(eds), *The Anthropology of Ethnicity. 'Beyond Ethnic Groups and Boundaries'*, pp. 81-104, Amsterdam: Het Spinhuis Publishers.

Roosens, Eugeen (1995) (guest editor) Rethinking Culture, "Multicultural Society", and the School, *The International Journal of Educational Research*, 23(1).

Roosens, Eugeen (1998) *Eigen Grond Eerst? Primordiale Autochtonie. Dilemma van de Multiculturele Samenleving*, Leuven and Amersfoort: Acco.

Rosaldo, Renato (1993) *Culture and Truth. The Remaking of Social Analysis*, Boston: Beacon Press Books.

Rosario do, Louise (1990) Wealth Imports Our Problems, *Far Eastern Economic Review* 21/6/1990, p. 62.

Sabouret, Jean-François (1993) 'Préface', in Teruhisa Horio (translated by Jean-François Sabouret) *L' éducation au Japon*, pp. 7–32, Paris: CNRS Editions.

Said, Edward (1978) *Orientalism*, New York: Pantheon.

Sanjek, Roger (1990) On Ethnographic Validity, in Roger Sanjek (ed.) *Fieldnotes. The Makings of Anthropology*, pp.385–418, Ithaca: Cornell University Press.

Sassen, Saskia (1988) *The Mobility of Labor and Capital. A Study in International Investment and Labor Flow*,Cambridge: Cambridge University Press.

Sato, Hirotake and Nakanishi, Akira (1991) *Kaigaishijo Kyoikushi*, Tokyo: Japan Overseas Educational Services.

Seidensticker, Edward (1983) *Low City, High City. Tokyo from Edo to the Earthquake: How the Shogun's Ancient Capital Became a Great City. 1867-1923*, San Francisco: Donald Ellis.

Shils, Edward (1957) Primordial, Personal, Sacred and Civil Ties, *British Journal of Sociology* 7: 113–45.

Slawik, Alexander and Linhart, Sepp (eds.) (1981) *Die Japanerrin in Vergangenheit und Gegenwart*, Vienna: Institut für Japanologie.

Smart, Barry (1992) *Modern Conditions, Postmodern Controversies*, London: Routledge.

Sonoda, Hidehiro (1990) Sekai no Nihon Kenkyu, in Takeshi Umehara (ed.) *Nihon to wa Nan no Ka?*, pp. 22–34,Tokyo: Nihon Hoso Shuppan Kyokai

Stahl, Charles W. (1991) South-North Migration in the Asia-Pacific Region, *International Migration* 29(2): 163–94.

Stahl, Charles W. (1993) Low-level Manpower Migration to Japan: Trends, Issues and Policy Considerations. Japanand International Migration. *International Migration* 31(2/3): 340–60.

Statistics Bureau Management and Coordination Agency (1989) *Statistical Handbook of Japan*, Tokyo: Japan Statistical Association.

Storry, Richard (1983) *A History of Modern Japan*, Harmondsworth: Penguin.

Taira, Koji (1993) Dialectics of Economic Growth, National Power, and Distributive Struggles, in Andrew Gordon*Postwar Japan as History*, Berkeley: University of California Press.

Takahagi, Yasuji (1982) *Kaigai Kikokushijo ni Okeru Karucha-Shokku no Yoinbunseki to Tekio Puroguramu no Kaihatsu, Shiko*, Tokyo: Education Center for Returnees, Gakugei University.

Tanaka, Hiroshi (1991) *Zainichi Gaikokujin*, Tokyo: Iwanami Shoten.

Tanaka, Hiroshi (1993) Foreigners in Japan, *Japanese Book News* 4: 4–5.

Terasaki, Masao (1994) Japan Foundation Publications. Book Review, *The Japan Foundation Newsletter* 22(3):27–8.

Toyama, Shigehiko (1976) *Nihongo no Kosei*, Tokyo: Chuokoronsha.

Trankell, Britt (1996) *Orientalism and Anthropology in Asian Studies*, Unpublished Paper.

Trouillot, Michel-Rolph (1991) Anthropology and the Savage Slot: the Poetics and Politics of Othernesses, in Richard Fox (ed.) *Recapturing Anthropology: Working in the Present*, pp. 17–44, Santa Fe: School of American Research Press.

Turner, Victor (1977) *The Ritual Process. Structure and Anti-Structure*, Ithaca: Cornell University Press.

Valentine, James (1990) On the Borderlines: the Significance of Marginality in Japanese Society, in Eyal Ben-Ari, Brian Moeran and James Valentine (eds) *Unwrapping Japan: Society and Culture in Anthropological Perspective*, pp. 36–57, Honolulu: University of Hawaii Press.

van Amersfoort, Hans (1998) An Analytical Framework for Migration Processes and Interventions, in Hans van Amersfoort and Jeroen

Doomernik (eds) *International Migration. Processes and Interventions*, pp. 9–21, Amsterdam: IMES.

Van Bremen, Jan (1990) Anthropology and Japanese Studies, in Adriana Boscaro, Franco Gatti and Massimo Raveri (eds) *Rethinking Japan. Volume II: Social Sciences, Ideology and Thought*, pp. 117-123, Sandgate, Folkstone, Kent: Japan Library Limited.

Van der Haegen, Herman et al. (1995) *Multicultureel Brussel*, Brussel: Brussels Gewest.

Van Maanen, John (1988) *Tales of the Field. On Writing Ethnography*, Chicago: University of Chicago Press.

Van Willigen, John (1986) *Applied Anthropology: an Introduction*, Massachusetts: Bergin and Garvey South Hadly.

Varley, Paul H. (1984) *Japanese Culture*, Honolulu: University of Hawaii Press.

Verdery, Katherine (1994) Ethnicity, Nationalism, and State-making. Ethnic Groups and Boundaries: Past and Future, in Hans Vermeulen and Cora Govers (eds) *The Anthropology of Ethnicity. 'Beyond Ethnic groups and Boundaries'*, pp. 33-58, Amsterdam: Het Spinhuis Publishers.

Vermeulen, Hans (1997) *Immigration Policy for a Multicultural Society. A Comparative Study of Integration, Language and Religious Policy in Five Western European Countries*, Amsterdam: IMES.

Vermeulen, Hans and Govers, Cora (1994) *The Anthropology of Ethnicity. Beyond 'Ethnic Groups and Boundaries'*, Amsterdam: Het Spinhuis Publishers.

Weiner, Michael (1997) *Japan's Minorities. The Illusion of Homogeneity*, London and New York: Routledge.

Werbner, Pnina and Modood, Tariq (eds) (1997) *Debating Cultural Hybridity. Multi-Cultural Identities and the Politics of Anti-Racism*, London and New Jersey: Zed Books.

White, Merry (1987) *The Japanese Educational Challenge. A Commitment to Children*, Tokyo: Kodansha.

White, Merry (1988) *The Japanese Overseas. Can They Go Home Again?*, New York: The Free Press.

Wolf, Margery (1992) *A Thrice Told Tale. Feminism, Postmodernism and Ethnographic Responsibility*, California: Stanford University Press.

Wright, Susan (1995) Anthropology: Still the Uncomfortable Discipline, in Akbar Ahmed and Cris Shore (eds) *The Future of Anthropology. Its Relevance to the Contemporary World*, pp. 65–93, London: The Athlone Press.

Yamashita, Hideo (1979) *Nihongo no Kotoba to Kokoro*, Tokyo: Kodansha.

Yasukawa, Jyunosuke (1989) Fukuzawa Yukichi, in Benjamin Duke (ed.) *Ten Great Educators of Modern Japan*, Tokyo: University of Tokyo Press.

Yinger, Milton J. (1994) *Ethnicity. Source of Strength? Source of Conflict?*, Albany: State University of New York Press.

Yoshino, Kosaku (1992) *Cultural Nationalism in Contemporary Japan. A Sociological Enquiry*, London: Routledge.

Zolberg, Aristide R. (1989) The Next Waves: Migration Theory for a Changing World, *International Migration Review* 23(3): 403–30.

Index

For Product Safety Concerns and Information please contact our EU
representative GPSR@taylorandfrancis.com
Taylor & Francis Verlag GmbH, Kaufingerstraße 24, 80331 München, Germany

www.ingramcontent.com/pod-product-compliance
Lightning Source LLC
Chambersburg PA
CBHW070551270326
41926CB00013B/2275